The Search for Domestic Bliss

Ian Dowbiggin

The Search for
Domestic Bliss

MARRIAGE AND FAMILY COUNSELING
IN 20TH-CENTURY AMERICA

UNIVERSITY PRESS OF KANSAS

Published by the University Press of Kansas (Lawrence, Kansas 66045), which was organized by the Kansas Board of Regents and is operated and funded by Emporia State University, Fort Hays State University, Kansas State University, Pittsburg State University, the University of Kansas, and Wichita State University

Library of Congress Cataloging-in-Publication Data

Dowbiggin, Ian Robert, 1952–
The search for domestic bliss : marriage and family counseling in 20th-century America / Ian Dowbiggin.
pages cm
Includes bibliographical references and index.
ISBN 978-0-7006-1947-4 (cloth : alk. paper)
1. Marriage counseling—United States—History—20th century. 2. Family counseling—United States—History—20th century. I. Title.
HQ10.5.U6D69 2014
616.89'1562—dc23
2013035604

British Library Cataloguing-in-Publication Data is available.

Printed in the United States of America

10 9 8 7 6 5 4 3 2 1

The paper used in this publication is recycled and contains 30 percent postconsumer waste. It is acid free and meets the minimum requirements of the American National Standard for Permanence of Paper for Printed Library Materials Z39.48-1992.

To John C. Burnham

Contents

Acknowledgments

This book, the fourth in a series on the history of social reform movements in twentieth-century America, was made possible by generous support from the Social Sciences and Humanities Research Council of Canada, Associated Medical Services, the University of Michigan's Bentley Historical Library, and the University of Prince Edward Island. I also benefited enormously from the assistance of the librarians at the National Library of Medicine and the Universities of Wyoming and Pennsylvania, as well as Catherine Ann Johnson-Roehr at Indiana University's Kinsey Institute, Sarah Hutcheon and Diana Carey of Radcliffe College's Arthur and Elizabeth Schlesinger Library on the History of Women in America, William Wallach of the Bentley Historical Library, and David Klaassen and Linnea Anderson of the Social Welfare History Archives at the University of Minnesota. Special thanks go to William Doherty, William Nichols, and Mary Jo Czaplewski for their willingness to talk about their careers in marriage and family studies, as well as James Reed, who unselfishly shared some of his own historical resources with me. Jason Samuels, director of innovation and technology at the National Council on Family Relations, provided invaluable technical help in exploring the NCFR's online history. I am also grateful to the *Journal of Policy History* for permission to reproduce material from my "Medical Mission to Moscow: Women's Work, Day Care, and Early Cold War Politics in Twentieth-Century America" (23 [2011]: 177–203). Last, but not least, I wish to thank Fred Woodward of the University Press of Kansas for encouraging me along the way during this book project.

Abbreviations

AAMC	American Association of Marriage Counselors
AAMFC	American Association of Marriage and Family Counselors
AAMFT	American Association for Marriage and Family Therapy
AASECT	American Association of Sexuality Educators, Counselors, and Therapists
AFTA	American Family Therapy Association
AIFR	American Institute of Family Relations
AMA	American Medical Association
ASMS	American-Soviet Medical Society
AVS	Association for Voluntary Sterilizations
CAMFC	California Association of Marriage and Family Counselors
CAW	Congress of American Women
CFM	Christian Family Movement
CHAMPUS	Civilian Health and Medical Program of the Uniformed Services
CPUSA	Communist Party of the United States of America
CWHCF	Coalition for the White House Conference on Families
DSM	American Psychiatric Association's *Diagnostic and Statistical Manual of Mental Disorders* (editions designated by roman numerals—e.g., *DSM-IV)*
ERA	Equal Rights Amendment
HEW	U.S. Department of Health, Education, and Welfare
HMO	health maintenance organization
HUAC	House Un-American Activities Committee
JCMIH	Joint Commission on Mental Illness and Health
MCP	Marriage Council of Philadelphia
ME	marriage enrichment
MFL	*Marriage and Family Living*
MSSH	Massachusetts Society for Social Hygiene

NAFL	National Alliance for Family Life
NCASF	National Council of American-Soviet Friendship
NCFR	National Council on Family Relations
NCMH	National Committee on Maternal Health
NIMH	National Institute of Mental Health
NMHA	National Mental Health Act (1946)
NOW	National Organization for Women
NYSCMF	New York State Conference on Marriage and the Family
RBRF	Reproductive Biology Research Foundation
REBT	rational emotive behavior therapy
SIECUS	Sex Information and Education Council of the United States
VOKS	All-Union Society for Cultural Relations with Foreign Countries (USSR)
WAC	Women's Army Corps
WAVES	Women Accepted for Volunteer Emergency Service
WHCF	White House Conference on Families
WIDF	Women's International Democratic Federation
YMCA	Young Men's Christian Association
YWCA	Young Women's Christian Association

Introduction

O n June 1, 2010, political circles in Washington were stunned when former vice president Al Gore and his wife Tipper announced they were separating after forty years of marriage. Much of the shock stemmed from the perception that the Gores' marriage was more solid than that of former president Bill Clinton and Hillary Rodham Clinton. The Gores had carved out their own careers: Tipper as an activist and photographer, and Al as a Nobel Prize–winning environmentalist. In the 1990s the Gores carefully crafted an image of happily married high school sweethearts, highlighted by their passionate onstage kiss at the 2000 Democratic convention when Al was nominated as his party's presidential candidate. Al even claimed that their romance had been the model for Erich Segal's best-selling 1970 novel *Love Story*.[1]

Before their split, the Gores appeared to be "the baby boomer couple who could," in the words of University of Minnesota family therapist William J. Doherty.[2] The Gores looked to be a classic example of how love had conquered marriage in the twentieth century, how matrimony had made the transition from an institution based on patriarchy, deferral of gratification, division of labor, and the selfless raising of children to one based on partnership, mutual affection, and personal fulfillment. The collapse of the Gores' marriage, however, suggests that this triumphalist interpretation of matrimony in twentieth-century America might be inaccurate.[3]

The Gores' marriage is a reminder of both the state of marriage and the reigning viewpoint about the institution in twenty-first-century America. In 2010, as the U.S. population continued to age, about one in two marriages was destined to fail, the percentage of unmarrieds was climbing, and out-of-wedlock births were hitting record highs. The Gores claimed that their own split was "a mutual and mutually supportive decision," but experts preferred to dig more deeply. "The biggest issue," a retired Baltimore divorce attorney observed in 2010, "is that we're living longer, we're healthier, and couples are bored with each other." When married Americans like the Gores reach their sixties, a Mobile, Alabama, clinical social worker concluded, "there's a feeling. If I don't go now, I'm never going to go." A Mt. Lebanon, Pennsylvania, psychotherapist claimed to be "hearing over and over again . . . this malaise, this sense of, 'I'm not satisfied with what I've got.'"[4] Therapists advise Americans "to set aside time to check in with each other, to see if our marriages are on track, and if our needs are being met," in the words of the *Wall Street Journal*.[5] The bottom line is that twenty-first-century Americans crave happiness and self-expression in marriage—a desire that would have mystified their ancestors. As a 2010 *New York Times* headline put it, "The Happy Marriage Is the 'Me' Marriage."[6]

The message that marriage exists for Americans' personal growth, happiness, and overall needs and that it requires plenty of expert opinion and self-examination may strike some people as eminently sensible, but from a historical perspective, this marks a pivotal development in the evolution of matrimony. The "me marriage," as this book documents, is the intended consequence of a century-old struggle on the part of a highly motivated group of reform-minded Americans to transform marriage and family counseling into a bona fide profession with its own clinics, training programs, licensing standards, bodies of expert knowledge, and cultural power.[7] The rise of marriage and family counseling was one of the great professional success stories in twentieth-century America. For centuries, people had been consulting their clergymen, healers, relatives, and neighbors about their family problems, but only in the twentieth century did a profession emerge whose primary purpose was to offer expert advice about family matters, especially relations between spouses. As William C. Nichols, a prominent leader of the field, put it in 1992: after World War I, "the old order in which the family and community were looked to for guidance gave way in favor of seeking help from strangers, whom one paid."[8] The "old order" did not vanish overnight. As late as World War II, there were barely 500 marriage and family counselors in all of the United States, and as late as 1960, Americans with marital problems consulted their clergymen more than they consulted licensed practitioners. In its early stages, wrote two counselors in 1967, marriage and family counseling was often "treated as a ribald joke."[9]

Yet by the early twenty-first century there were roughly 50,000 marriage and family counselors across the country, part of a much larger "caring industry" consisting of 77,000 clinical psychologists, 192,000 clinical social workers, 105,000 mental health counselors, 17,000 nurse psychotherapists, and 30,000 life coaches, to say nothing of the tens of thousands of nonclinical social workers and substance abuse counselors.[10] In the early twenty-first century, while many Americans still sought advice from clergy, 860,000 couples flocked to counselors' offices every year, and over 40 percent of engaged couples underwent some form of premarital counseling or education. These data suggest that in their efforts to fix marital and family problems, therapists have deeply affected the lives of millions of American men, women, and children.[11]

The American search for marital and family bliss through counseling has been a key part of a major revolution in the way Americans think about their inner selves and their relations with friends, family members, neighbors, and coworkers. The outcome of this revolution is a therapeutic viewpoint about marriage and the family shared by countless Americans in the early twenty-first century. "We live in an age consumed by worship of the psyche," wrote historian Eva Moskowitz in 2001, "a belief that feelings are sacred and salvation lies in self-esteem, that happiness is the ultimate goal and psychological healing the means." This therapeutic sensibility—shared by rich and poor, black and white, straight and gay—depicts marriage and the family less as social institutions than as relationships in which individuals first and foremost deserve to achieve emotional self-fulfillment.[12] If they do not, the therapeutic ethos says, the psychological sciences and their adherents can empower individuals to find such fulfillment through counseling by trained professionals—"a new priestly class," in sociologist James L. Nolan Jr.'s words. Thanks to the inroads of "therapism," sex, marriage, and family life—once believed to be private matters—have been redefined as grave matters of public mental health.[13]

The "therapeutic gospel" is heavily indebted to the theories of psychologists such as Carl Rogers, who taught that individuals will never find emotional and mental satisfaction by simply adapting to society and its institutions—notably, marriage and family life.[14] Therapism preaches that when the positive aspects of human nature clash with traditional values and customs, the self must be emancipated from social inhibitions and restraints, such as those of the married state or the family itself. "Where once the self was to be surrendered, denied, sacrificed, and died to, now the self is to esteemed, actualized, affirmed, and unfettered," Nolan writes.[15] As this book contends, it was therapism, not love, that conquered marriage in the twentieth century.[16]

Yet the value ideals of therapism have not led to greater individual freedom overall. The history of marriage counseling reveals that since its origins, its teachings have often contained paternalistic, normative statements buried beneath frequent invocations of nonjudgmentalism and "value-free" science. The counseling profession has succeeded in convincing millions of Americans that their only hope for happiness and personal autonomy is to resort to counseling, enabling the state—in the form of the "priestly class" of experts—to expand "into the private lives of its citizens."[17] As historian Kristin Celello has written, the perception at the turn of the twenty-first century is that "couples with failing relationships who do not seek help were not as committed to marriage as those who did."[18] "Therapy's stress on personal autonomy," argue the authors of *Habits of the Heart*, paradoxically "presupposes institutional conformity" because the workplace and other public settings increasingly require individuals to acknowledge that therapy is the key to teamwork in bureaucratic life, whether in the private sector or the public sector.[19] Submitting to counseling to save one's marriage has become more of a civic duty than a free choice.

How did the values of therapism conquer marriage and the family? First of all, history tells us that no nationality thinks more highly of marriage, nor worries about it more, than Americans do. As French journalist Raoul de Roussey de Sales observed as long ago as 1938, Americans are torn, believing that love and marriage are either "a superhuman ecstasy" or "a psychopathic condition to be treated by specialists." Perplexed when love and marriage fail to live up to their expectations, Americans spend hours and fortunes "trying to make love work." "Husbands and wives and lovers have no patience with their troubles. They want to be cured," as de Sales put it.[20]

Yet this popular predisposition to view matrimony as either an idyllic state or a correctable problem in human relations is not enough to explain Americans' therapeutic perspective in the new millennium. Americans may be the most marrying (and divorcing) people in the world, but their perceptions of marriage have surely been shaped to a profound degree by the enormous volume of expert advice produced by marriage and family counselors over the last hundred years and disseminated through their books, clinical practices, the media, government programs, and the nation's schools.[21] During the second half of the twentieth century, therapism as "a general outlook on life" spread "from a relatively small, educated elite to the middle-class mainstream of American life."[22] Much of this advice can be distilled down to the teaching that marriage and family relations are too important to be left to ordinary Americans. Marriage and family counselors have preached that most Americans cannot find love and marital happiness without the right scientific knowledge, but they have also reinforced the evolving conviction that personal fulfillment and emotional gratification in marriage are not only possibilities but also entitlements. As best-selling author John Gray told his readers in *Men Are from Mars, Women Are from Venus* (1992), with his help, "you will learn how to create the love you deserve."[23] It is not surprising, then, that countless people in committed relationships believe that if they are not "moving forward" as individuals, there must be something wrong with their unions. Taught to perceive every difficulty in marriage as a remedial problem, twenty-first-century Americans are more inclined to flee the marital state than their ancestors were when their expectations fail to match reality.

Marriage and family counselors are not solely responsible for the rise of therapism—the aging of society, the ascendancy of a consumerist culture, the proliferation of media (notably television), and the widening scope of bureaucracy in everyday life have had significant effects—but they have certainly been among the loudest cheerleaders of the trend. Counselors and therapists have insisted all along that they are merely meeting the demands of ordinary Americans, but history shows that they have often been out in front of public opinion. Americans have eagerly consulted advisers about marriage and family matters, but their viewpoints on these topics owe much to the teachings of professionals. Early counselors did their best to stimulate demand by building therapeutic constituencies, first on college campuses and then in the nation's suburbs, churches, workplaces, and entertainment industries. This agenda would never have triumphed if practitioners had not succeeded in popularizing a therapeutic language, a "common moral vocabulary" used by men and women to describe their lives and understand their connections to others, a "mode of moral discourse" that privileges "radical individualism" and devalues obligation, self-sacrifice, and the constraints of social roles.[24] This book's findings confirm what historian Alan Petigny calls "the critical role mental health experts played in persuading Americans to relinquish a more rigid and traditional worldview" in the post–World War II era.[25] Put another way, twentieth-century Americans may have had the therapy urge, but they learned therapism's creed from experts in the field. Marriage and family counselors do not deserve all the credit for the triumph of therapism, but they were certainly in its vanguard.

The rise of marriage and family counseling during the twentieth century may have been a stunning success story, but its triumph was not inevitable; nor was its victory uncontested. Over the years, scholars such as Robert Nisbet, Philip Rieff, and Christopher Lasch have warned that therapism causes Americans to focus on their inner feelings rather than exploring political or social answers to the problems afflicting the country. The field has often been racked by controversy. From time to time there have been serious disagreements over theory and practice among counselors, and the profession has rarely been free of dissent. Yet by the late twentieth century, these conflicts had largely been subsumed under the consensus of therapism, which by then reigned supreme as a "taken-for-granted part of everyday life," in the words of Nolan.[26] Therapism's reach stretches from the "boardroom to the bedroom and back again."[27]

Chapter 1, "A Nucleus of Persons," reveals how a small but cohesive group of self-proclaimed experts connected to the eugenics and birth control movements of the twentieth century laid the foundation for the new profession in the 1930s. In the words of one therapist in 1996, the history of marriage and family counseling shows "how a small group of mavericks from the traditional mental health professions, working in different parts of the United States, independently came to develop a revolutionary paradigm about intimate relationships, emotional disorders, and treatment."[28] The links between the eugenics and the marriage and family counseling movements provide an early example of the field's didactic and paternalistic goals, belying its self-professed "value neutrality" and its claim to be disinterested social science. The initial marriage counseling clinics in the United States tended to copy the private and public marriage advice centers that sprang up in Germany after World War I. They functioned as a public health service designed to improve birthrates among the elite classes and lower the fertility of those deemed hereditarily unfit. In a day and age when the boundaries between eugenics and birth control were consistently blurred, numerous activists believed that the key to the health and happiness of the family was "planned parenthood," or the ability to limit family size by spacing pregnancies—"smaller families of a higher quality," as an official at the U.S. Department of Health, Education, and Welfare put it in 1968.[29] One birth control advocate went so far as to remark in 1968 that marriage counseling was nothing more than "window dressing . . . to make planned parenthood more respectable and acceptable."[30] The message that contraception was the royal road to sexual gratification and personal growth—especially for women—was linked to the notion that people needed to liberate themselves from taboos or impersonal criteria that allegedly stifled biological needs and emotional fulfillment.

Chapter 1 also shows that the establishment of marriage and family counseling as a service-oriented profession addressing the "problems of living" owed a great deal to the efforts of university-based social scientists such as Ernest and Gladys Groves, Ernest Burgess, and Lewis Terman, as well as community-based social workers such as Rabbi Sidney Goldstein and Lester Dearborn. Social scientists created the first undergraduate and graduate courses on marriage, making the college campus the first real power base of the movement. By the late 1940s, colleges were offering hundreds of marriage and family courses. Groves and Burgess also had a hand in launching the National Conference of Family Relations in 1938, renamed the National Council on Family Relations in 1947 and still in existence today. Members of the NCFR, the first such organization in U.S. history, included the leading marriage and family researchers, educators, and practitioners in twentieth-century America. The common belief of these social scientists was that marriage and the home were undergoing fundamental changes and that

Americans needed more research and guidance as they sought to marry and raise families. Echoing the eugenicists, Groves declared that the time for a "laissez-faire" attitude toward parenthood and marriage was over.[31] Parenthood was "the last stand of the amateur," argued NCFR stalwart Evelyn Duvall.[32]

Chapter 2, "The Kinsey Connection," documents how World War II galvanized trailblazing marriage counselors, thrusting the budding field into the national limelight in the 1940s. With millions of men and women mobilized to serve in the armed forces and in wartime industries, experts questioned the accepted status of women as wives, mothers, and citizens. A spate of wartime marriages triggered a national debate over the future of marriage and the family, coinciding with the founding of the American Association of Marriage Counselors in 1942. The AAMC (which changed its name to the American Association of Marriage and Family Counselors in 1970 and the American Association for Marriage and Family Therapy in 1978) quickly emerged as a tightly knit, politically progressive organization that forged close ties to Indiana University sex researcher Alfred C. Kinsey. Leading AAMC members admired Kinsey's research because they—like him—believed that his findings compelled Americans to overthrow their moral conventions regarding sexual norms.

In addition to the AAMC's sympathy with Kinsey's countercultural sexual ethics, a handful of members expressed a fervent admiration for Stalin's Russia—notably, Soviet policies regarding marriage and the family. This is the topic of chapter 3, "Medical Mission to Moscow." In 1946 AAMC pioneer Emily Mudd, representing the American-Soviet Medical Society, visited schools, orphanages, nurseries, and research laboratories in the Soviet Union, and upon her return to the United States, she effusively extolled official Soviet attitudes toward marriage, the family, and the status of women. Long before Betty Friedan claimed to have discovered "the problem that knows no name" in her 1963 best seller *The Feminine Mystique*, Mudd—largely based on her impressions of Soviet society—argued that the key to women's happiness was their ability to work outside the home. Mudd's pro-Soviet opinions, along with the AAMC's close links to Kinsey, underscored the field's eagerness to challenge long-standing values about sexuality and reproduction. This helped pave the way for what Petigny calls the "permissive society" that characterized America in the second half of the twentieth century.[33]

Chapter 4, "Saving People, Not Marriages," describes the turmoil in the field of marriage and family counseling in the 1950s, belying Stephanie Coontz's thesis that counselors exhibited a "myopic" confidence in the stability of marriage and gender roles.[34] On the one hand, the decade was the heyday of Paul Popenoe's Los Angeles–based American Institute of Family Relations, one of the country's few marriage counseling clinics. Popenoe's frequent presence on television, on the radio, and in print signaled the burgeoning postwar media's influence on everyday attitudes and behavior, especially consumerism. On the other hand, after a brief collaboration, the AAMC and NCFR went their separate ways in 1954, chiefly due to different interpretations of sexual norms. Counselors accused the AAMC of being an "elitist" organization that unfairly restricted membership and attendance at its meetings. Other disagreements—sometimes bitter—erupted over the future direction of the field. Practitioners debated whether they actually performed counseling or therapy; whether the field was autonomous, a branch of Freudian psychoanalysis, or a medical specialty; whether counseling should be done with individual clients or "conjointly"; whether clergy needed special training to perform pastoral counseling; whether sex was the most common cause of marital trouble; and whether it was possible for healthy partners to have a sick marriage. Contrary to Celello's thesis that counselors typically viewed divorce as a failure of individuals rather than of the institution of marriage itself, as early as the 1950s, it was evident that many leaders in the field opposed the "let's-keep-people-married bias."[35] Even popular magazines such as *Cosmopolitan*, *McCall's*, and *Ladies' Home Journal* contributed to a "discourse of discontent"; although they encouraged women to accept their domestic roles as housewives and mothers, they also espoused the notion that women had a right to self-fulfillment.[36] As the second half of the twentieth century unfolded, therapism's emphasis on enhancing personal well-being at the expense of preserving marriages spread, but the origins of this trend can be traced back to the ferment within the profession during the supposedly conservative 1950s.

As chapter 4 also documents, therapism conquered pastoral counseling, and religion itself became redefined as "personal therapy" in post–

World War II America.[37] The pervasive religiosity of American family life during the early Cold War made it impossible for therapists to oust clergymen from their roles as counselors to their flocks; however, counselors were highly successful in convincing many clergymen that they needed "the insights of science" to fulfill their pastoral duties. Whereas numerous priests, ministers, and rabbis initially resisted the argument that they lacked the skills to perform their pastoral functions, others welcomed closer ties to secular disciplines. Marriage and family counseling's inroads into pastoral counseling constituted a major victory for the therapeutic ethos in a sphere of human activity that had long been free of formal psychological training and practice.

A major complaint of marriage and family counselors during the early Cold War was that the field lacked power and a clear professional identity based on a common body of research, theory, and clinical training. That situation began to change rapidly in the 1960s and is the topic of chapter 5, "From Counseling to Therapy." In an attempt to align themselves more closely with medical science, many leaders of the movement favored redefining themselves as therapists rather than counselors. Spearheading this transformation were sexologists William Masters and Virginia Johnson. Most accounts of Masters and Johnson emphasize their discoveries about the anatomy and physiology of sexuality, overlooking their close connections to the marriage counseling and therapy movement. "Repairing the conjugal bedroom" was how the media celebrated their work, and Masters and Johnson made it clear that they believed sexual compatibility not only saved marriages but also improved family life. According to Masters, their focus was on the "therapy of the sexually maladjusted family-unit"—a clear signal of their intention to classify human sexuality as a source of family and marital dysfunction.[38] At the same time, they viewed their studies as the basis for a body of empirically tested scientific knowledge that could underpin the growing field of sex therapy in particular and marriage therapy in general. Masters and Johnson's insistence on therapeutic encounters with both marriage partners also represented a break from the early days of marriage counseling, when the wife tended to be the sole client.

Counselors' efforts to professionalize gathered momentum in the 1970s and 1980s, years that witnessed the formal union of marriage and family counseling, as discussed in chapter 6, "A New Value in Psychotherapy." Individuals such as AAMC presidents William Nichols and Donald Williamson led the drive toward professionalization of the field, with the development of its own standards of clinical training and licensing. Over the years the AAMC substantially broadened its membership and eventually renamed itself the American Association for Marriage and Family Therapy (AAMFT). Marriage counseling became subsumed under the wider rubric of family therapy. The organization established its first professional journal in 1974 and in 1982 moved its headquarters to Washington, D.C., intent on lobbying the government in defense of its interests. The U.S. Department of Health, Education, and Welfare recognized the AAMFT's graduate accreditation programs in 1978, and in 1992 marriage and family therapist officially became the fifth "core" mental health profession, alongside psychiatrists, psychologists, social workers, and psychiatric nurses. By 1993 thirty-one states had established licensing or certifying procedures for marriage and family therapists.

Chapter 6 also reveals how, under the influence of family "systems theory," therapists' focus shifted in the 1970s from the individual, as in the old days of counseling, to "the enigmatic processes that lead to family distress."[39] The family emerged as an emotional unit and the source of pathology. As the influence of psychoanalysis waned and the community mental health movement rose, therapists trained their sights on the family unit as well as the community at large.

By the dawn of the twenty-first century, marriage counseling had broadened to encompass sex therapy and couples' therapy, which includes "committed, non-traditional relationships" such as gay and lesbian couples.[40] The field had overcome numerous obstacles to achieve its professionalization, but other challenges lurked on the horizon. The rise of managed care in the last two decades of the twentieth century sparked what some clinicians called "a culture clash" between health insurance companies and therapists, and marriage and family counselors worried about a possible erosion in the quality of care for couples and families, as well as a loss of income for themselves.[41] Health insurance companies and managed care corporations cut back reimbursement for counseling services that did not conform to official diagnoses in *DSM-IV*. Some therapists complained that the use of *DSM* diagnoses would "pathologize" or medicalize common behaviors and attitudes.

The fact that the growth of marriage and family counseling coincided with the highest divorce rates in the nation's history led many to question the field's effectiveness. A 1995 *Consumer Reports* survey found that marriage and family therapists ranked lowest of all groups in the mental health care field in terms of competence. *USA Today* and *Time* ran stories suggesting that it was time for the profession to rethink how therapy worked. One therapist wondered in 1996: "How come Shakespeare . . . knew more about family dynamics than we family professionals?"[42] "Does Couples Therapy Work?" asked the *New York Times* in 2012.[43] The problem of unlicensed therapists without formal training was as formidable as it had been half a century earlier. Time and again, counselors indulged in highly public soul-searching about the future of their profession. Some alleged that counselors' value-neutral approach was tantamount to support for marital breakup. Accusations flew that therapists had helped redefine marriage as just another "lifestyle option."[44]

Those practitioners who advocated a more marriage-friendly approach to counseling were part of a backlash against therapism, which had reached a high point by the turn of the century. One of these was family therapist William Doherty (to whom this book is heavily indebted). Calling himself a "whistle-blower," Doherty lent his passionate voice to the growing chorus of therapists who were alarmed by the long-standing problem of incompetent practitioners doing marital therapy and more recent concerns about therapists "who follow the cultural script that regards marriage as a lifestyle to be abandoned if it is not working for either of its customers."[45]

Thus, while the rise of marriage and family counseling is a resounding success story from a professional standpoint, the field is once again in flux, with therapists openly clashing over different interpretations of marriage and family life. Major questions remain unanswered: What exactly does a happy and healthy marriage look like? Do women care more about their relationships than men do? If women work harder at their marriages, is it because they want to, or because they are told to? Are men really from Mars and women from Venus? The debates of the twenty-first century are a forceful reminder of similar disagreements in the 1950s, a critical turning point in U.S. history and a time when the field was just beginning to gain national notoriety. The fact that the field is no more united today than it was half a century earlier, and the fact that pesky doubts continue to swirl around its claim to provide "hope and healing" for couples and families, suggests that Americans' willingness to invite professionals into their private lives might be living on borrowed time.

Nonetheless, therapism shows few signs of fading any time soon. Most social scientists would agree that, for better or worse, marriage has become a consumer commodity or a lifestyle option. Others argue that twenty-first-century matrimony is merely the newest stage in an evolutionary process that has transformed marriage and the family from patriarchal, social institutions characterized by duty, obedience, and strictly defined gender roles to relationships that are "more joyful, more loving, more satisfying for many couples than ever before in history."[46] By contrast, this book concludes that beneath this series of events lurk disquieting trends that challenge bedrock values. Indeed, the data indicate that these institutions' evolution has raised the bar by which happiness is measured to unrealistic levels. The systemic failure of married and family life to meet these expectations has fostered rampant disenchantment and anxiety among committed couples, which in turn has translated into rising breakup rates among both married and unmarried partners and emotional distress for countless children. Far from making relationships "more joyful, more loving, more satisfying," the "marriage-go-round"—sociologist Andrew Cherlin's phrase to describe Americans' tendency to rush from one marriage to another—has transformed marriage and the family into a battleground of bruised feelings.[47] What the future holds for America's most cherished institutions is unclear. What this book demonstrates, however, is that the current turmoil surrounding marriage and the family has been a long time in the making, and it can be traced to the concerted efforts of a group of clinicians and researchers who sought to launch a social revolution that has overturned the intimate lives of millions of men, women, and children.

CHAPTER ONE *A Nucleus of Persons*

hen Emily Hartshorne Mudd (1898–
1998), arguably America's foremost marriage counselor of the twentieth century,
reminisced about growing up, one vivid
memory stood out. She remembered her
mother, Clementina (Rhodes) Hartshorne (1871–1970), marching in a
"Votes for Women" parade down Philadelphia's Broad Street. Ten-year-
old Emily marched alongside her mother and watched as "the rough
men on the sidewalk" threw tomatoes and eggs at them. "Mother was
never daunted. She went on marching. And I don't remember feeling
afraid because I guess she wasn't afraid," Mudd recounted later in life.[1]

In her writings Emily Mudd never said exactly why this event stood
out in her memory, but it likely convinced her at an early age that reforming the conditions of life for American women was a cause worth
fighting for, would be hotly contested, and would require fierce determination. These conclusions, drawn from watching the opposition her
mother faced when marching to win the vote for women, deeply affected Mudd's involvement in the burgeoning marriage counseling field
and similar reform movements that altered the status of women, the
nature of marriage, and family policy in twentieth-century America. For
Emily Mudd, as for many early practitioners in the field, marriage counseling was chiefly a vehicle for overturning the nation's laws against
contraception, liberalizing attitudes toward sexual behavior, and convincing lawmakers to make it easier for women to work outside the
home, pursue their own careers, and thus enhance their overall emotional satisfaction. The efforts of Emily Mudd and other pathfinders in
the marriage and family counseling movement paved the way for the
triumph of the therapeutic ethos, with its advocacy of reliance on expertise (principally in the psychological sciences) and its condemnation
of traditional values, behaviors, and institutions that seemingly stymie

individual human potential and psychological self-fulfillment. Their success in establishing marriage and family counseling as a bona fide profession testified to the ability of this small phalanx of reformers— what one observer called a "nucleus of persons"—to change the course of twentieth-century history.[2] The emotional lives of Americans have never been the same since.

To most scholars, the pivotal figure in the rise of marriage and family counseling was Paul Popenoe, head of the Los Angeles–based American Institute of Family Relations (AIFR), but not even Popenoe matched Emily Mudd's stature and impact. According to historian James Reed, Mudd's Marriage Council of Philadelphia, one of the first marriage counseling clinics in the nation, "played a role in the development of marriage counselling in the United States analogous to that played by [Margaret] Sanger's Clinical Research Bureau in contraception."[3] Contemporaries agreed. Sex researcher William Masters noted that "more than anyone else Emily Mudd encouraged and helped shape the field of marriage and family-life education, and was one of the first to address the dimension of sexuality as a vital factor in family life."[4] According to William C. Nichols, a later president of the AAMFT, Mudd—not Popenoe—was "the most influential and visible representative of marriage counselling in the 1950s."[5] In 1963 noted psychiatrist William Menninger called Mudd "*the* leading figure in the field of marriage counseling."[6] Popenoe may have been the field's familiar public face during the 1950s, but Mudd was more instrumental in laying the groundwork for virtually every important advance made by the fledgling profession, and she was a key participant in most of the major events that marked the ascendancy of therapism in American family life up to the Watergate era.

Mudd, born in 1898 in Merion, Pennsylvania, was the daughter of Clementina Hartshorne and Edward Yarnall, a prosperous Philadelphia banker and philanthropist. Emily's lifelong interest in women's issues stemmed from two early influences: her mother and her Quakerism. Clementina Hartshorne was a member of the Pennsylvania League of Women Voters and the friend of several pro-suffrage activists, including Mary Winsor, who staged a celebrated hunger strike from prison in

1918. Mudd's interest in women's issues also derived from her Quaker ancestors on her father's side. Historically, and in stark contrast to most Protestant churches, Quaker women spoke during worship, served as ministers, and played what one scholar has called a "disproportionate role" in feminist causes such as women's suffrage.[7] Mudd felt "considerable delight and satisfaction" when she learned that one of her father's Quaker forebears "strongly supported free opportunity for women in medicine on the same basis as men."[8]

After a brief stint in the U.S. Army's nursing corps during World War I, Mudd, a graduate of Vassar, obtained an M.A. at the Lowthorpe School of Landscape Architecture in Groton, Massachusetts. In 1922 she gave up any career plans and married Stuart Mudd, a promising microbiologist attending Harvard University Medical School. Shortly thereafter the Mudds moved to New York City, where Emily met and became good friends with birth control pioneer Margaret Sanger and husband-and-wife physicians Abraham and Hannah Stone, pivotal activists in the budding marriage and family counseling movement. After the birth of the Mudds' first child (a daughter), Hannah Stone fitted Emily with a diaphragm at Margaret Sanger's clinic in Brooklyn, New York (Emily referred to Hannah as "the Madonna of the clinic").[9]

In 1931 Abraham and Hannah Stone opened the Marriage Consultation Center at the New York City Labor Temple, and the next year they moved it to Margaret Sanger's Clinical Research Bureau. The Stones emphasized education about sexuality and birth control in their dealings with clients. As they wrote in 1935: "It has been our experience that an appreciation of the sex factors in marriage and reliable contraception are essential for a well-adjusted and satisfactory marital union."[10] Their friendship with the Mudds underlined the common beliefs uniting many of America's early marriage counselors, especially their faith in the liberating possibilities of birth control. As Sanger had asserted in 1922, contraception freed people from "sexual prejudice and taboo, by demanding the frankest and most unflinching re-examination of sex in its relation to human nature and the bases of human society." In 1923 Sanger insisted that in "back of [female] frigidity is often the fear of pregnancy."[11] As historian Linda Gordon has argued, the Stones' and Sanger's focus on contraception shaped their teachings on the nature of female sexuality. They taught the superiority of the vaginal orgasm and essentially defined any sexual act other than intercourse as perversity.[12] In 1974 Mudd maintained that "Drs. Abraham and Hannah Stone were the first who wrote and emphasized that mutual orgastic response was *the* end-all and the real way, or what-have-you for mutual sexual enjoyment."[13] Mudd, being of a later generation, eventually rejected this viewpoint about women's sexuality, but she remained steadfastly loyal to the notion that contraception freed women to enjoy sex and was the key to women's happiness in marriage. In 1974 she contended that "inevitably," in any marital problem, "the whole question of family planning came in."[14]

In 1925, when Stuart got a job at the University of Pennsylvania's Medical School, the Mudds moved to the Philadelphia area, eventually settling in the same Haverford neighborhood as Emily's sister, Clementine Hartshorne Jenney. The sisters shared child-raising duties, an arrangement that enabled Emily to keep working as an unpaid assistant in Stuart's bacteriology laboratory until the early 1930s. Stuart later became a world-renowned researcher hailed for his work in freeze-drying blood plasma and preventing infections in hospitalized patients. Although their career paths eventually took them in different directions, Emily and Stuart tended to agree on most social and political issues, and over the years they were widely regarded as what a later generation would call a "power couple."

The Mudds' mutual interest in contraception drove them to seek a scientific breakthrough in birth control technology. Together, Emily and Stuart published fourteen papers, including some on the immunological properties of spermatozoa. Their research derived from Stuart's "continuing interest in the quality and quantity of population" and their mutual concerns about "child spacing," in Emily's words. All the while, Emily had in mind her maternal grandmother's thirteen babies (only eight of whom survived). Her grandmother's fertility inspired her, as she put it, to investigate "what could be done about helping women to have children not too close together."[15]

By the onset of the Great Depression, Emily and Stuart Mudd had made their names as prominent crusaders in the struggle to legalize contraception. This battle was highlighted by the 1936 appellate court decision in *United States v. One Package of Japanese Pessaries*, which ruled that antiobscenity laws did not prevent physicians from prescribing

Emily and Stuart Mudd, ca. 1946. (Courtesy of the Arthur and Elizabeth Schlesinger Library on the History of Women in America, Radcliffe Institute for Advanced Study, Harvard University)

contraceptives. Impressed with the example of the Sanger Clinic in New York City, and in the teeth of Roman Catholic opposition—the Church enjoyed considerable political power in the City of Brotherly Love—the Mudds led the campaign to found Pennsylvania's first birth control clinic in West Philadelphia in 1929. It was originally called a maternal health center because, as Emily confessed, she was "afraid" to call it a "birth control clinic. We were trying to straddle between the acceptable health care and the not yet acceptable spacing of children."[16] Even ten years later, as Swedish-born sociologist Gunnar Myrdal noted, "birth control" was still "taboo as a subject for public polite conversation" in the United States.[17]

When the Philadelphia birth control clinic opened, "various women patients were lined up by the liberal social agencies or friends" in the area. Mudd had discovered that, under Pennsylvania law, a pregnant woman could not be jailed, so—pregnant with her second child—she volunteered at the clinic, taking patient histories and dispensing contraceptive information. When the clinic was raided three weeks after opening, neither Mudd nor the clinic's physician was there, so the police only seized the center's records. At that point, the Mudds' social connections came to the rescue. Stuart telephoned the city health commissioner, who socialized with some of the clinic's board members, and he decided, "Oh, well, let's just let things ride." The records were returned, the clinic was never raided again, and five years later, eight other birth control centers had opened in the Philadelphia area. The Mudds had won a major victory for birth control in America.[18]

Meanwhile, Stuart Mudd's involvement in the surging eugenics movement led him to attend the 1932 meeting of the Eugenics Society in London (founded as the Eugenics Education Society in 1908, renamed the Eugenics Society in 1926, and known in the twenty-first century as the Galton Institute), and Emily decided to join him. As a premedical student at Princeton during World War I, Stuart had been heavily influenced by the teachings of biologist Edwin Grant Conklin, an outspoken supporter of the notion that the time had come for human beings to assume control over evolution. Conklin, like many opinion makers of his time, was alarmed about the "menace" to "high civilization" posed by the "great growth of alcoholism, depravity, and insanity" among the "weak" classes of people in society. Among his recommendations was a project to breed "a better race of men," a lesson that impressed the young Stuart Mudd. In the words of historian James Reed, "Conklin left Mudd with an enduring interest in improving human quality," and there is abundant evidence that Emily shared her husband's views on the topic.[19]

Eugenics, a term coined in 1883 by Francis Galton, a cousin of Charles

Darwin, refers to the study of reproductive methods to improve the evolution of the human race. Eugenics was conventionally divided into two types: positive eugenics, to encourage the healthiest people to have big families, and negative eugenics, to prevent people with bad hereditary traits from breeding. An international eugenics movement swept the world in the first half of the twentieth century, reaching from Japan to North and South America. The most notorious example of eugenics was the law enacted in 1933 by Adolf Hitler's Third Reich, which permitted the involuntary sterilization of men and women with a wide variety of physical and mental disabilities. Other political jurisdictions, including Switzerland, the Scandinavian countries, two Canadian provinces, and dozens of American states, passed similar sterilization legislation. Eugenic sterilization statutes were supported by activists, scientists, journalists, liberal clergymen, and elected officials spanning virtually the entire political spectrum. One notable exception was the Roman Catholic Church, which condemned sterilization in 1930. The Mudds were good examples of how countless activists dedicated to ending what Margaret Sanger called women's "biological slavery" viewed eugenics and birth control as highly congruent causes.[20]

By the 1930s the hereditarianism that had initially united the eugenics movement was fading in the face of genetic research that showed "like did not beget like." Biologists argued that characteristics such as low intelligence were not passed down as single hereditary units from parent to offspring, casting doubt on the advisability of mass sterilization as a method of ridding society of undesirable behavioral or mental traits. As the *New York Times* editorialized in 1932: "The evidence is clear that normal persons also carry defective genes which may manifest themselves in an insane progeny. . . . Even if we discovered the carriers of hidden defective genes by applying the methods of the cattle breeder to humanity, the process would take about a thousand years."[21] In the face of these findings, eugenicists began to contend that both nature and nurture accounted for marital and family problems; one stated in 1938 that "parents produce faulty children by bad rearing as well as by bad heredity."[22] By World War II many of those involved in the marriage and family counseling movement had concluded that although "the aims of eugenics are essential to the realization of a better family life," governments did not need to force eugenic policies on their citizens. In the view of many experts, eugenics and democracy were perfectly compatible. "Freedom of parenthood enabled all parents to space births, so that children may have a greater chance for survival, for good health and for proper rearing," one marriage counselor said.[23] In other words, many American opinion makers thought that marriage and family counselors could teach parents how to make the right eugenic decisions.

Emily Mudd wholeheartedly agreed that there was a fundamental kinship between eugenics and marriage counseling. To her, both were examples of sound preventive medicine. After attending the London eugenics conference, she toured a number of marriage counseling centers in Germany and wrote about her travels for Sanger's *Birth Control Review*. By the 1930s, in accordance with Germany's *Bevölkerungspolitik* (population policy), the Weimar Republic had hundreds of marriage counseling centers (Prussia alone had 200) that offered an array of services ranging from venereal disease counseling to referrals for abortion and sterilization.[24] To Mudd, Germany's programs of state health insurance for "anyone belonging to trades below certain income levels" had "excellent eugenic possibilities" because they funded contraceptive services for the social groups whose fertility she and other eugenicists earnestly sought to curtail. She described her journey:

> [I traveled] south through western Germany from Cologne, under the shadow of the great Catholic Cathedral and in the midst of the industrial section where economic depression had been continuous for years, where poverty glared at you from the faces of miserable parents and many children, where prostitution stalked the streets by day and night, and where there was no such thing as a birth control clinic under any auspices, to democratic Frankfurt am Main where the heritage of social progressiveness has been handed down from the Middle Ages, and where the large proportion of intelligent and successful Jews minimizes the power of reactionary groups. There I saw the most poised and adequate handling of the question of Marriage Advice, Birth Control, and Abortion which it has been my privilege to find and hear of, outside of Russia.[25]

At what she called "a model clinic" in Frankfurt, she recounted how a "gaunt, hopeless looking woman, obviously pregnant" and suffering from "deep melancholy," with a "husband in the insane asylum, . . . two feeble-minded children and one epileptic child," was referred to a local hospital for an abortion and sterilization. "All part of the day's routine," she noted admiringly. By contrast, she pointed out that Pennsylvania health authorities would do nothing of the sort for such a patient.[26]

Mudd's account, besides its invidious distinctions between Catholic and Protestant Germany, reveals her fervent admiration for the way German state and city governments, women's organizations, and Protestant churches funded birth control and marital advice bureaus. Her description of the German clinics was clearly intended to be a clarion call to reformers in the fields of contraception and marriage counseling in the United States. Enamored with Germany's policies governing sex, marriage, and the family, Emily Mudd was highly sympathetic to the *Bevölkerungspolitik* notion that women owed a reproductive duty to their respective nations. This paternalist way of thinking and her eagerness to look to Germany and the fledgling Soviet Union for policy guidance remained features of her theories about sex, reproduction, and family life for years to come.

Mudd's impressions of the German marital advice clinics confirmed what she had already concluded as a volunteer at the Philadelphia maternal health center. Most of the women who visited her clinic were in their thirties and already had several children—many "up to ten or twelve." These poor, "very worn out" married women tended to blame their unhappiness on years of successive pregnancies, so Mudd began to conceive of a separate service that would reach "the younger couples before they got into such dire straits." "Is Preventive Work the Next Step?" she asked rhetorically in Sanger's *Birth Control Review* in 1932. If so, "marital advice bureaus" were the answer.[27]

To Mudd, then, one of marriage counseling's primary purposes was to teach young couples how to practice contraception. The impetus for a marriage counseling agency came from a small, elite group of liberal Philadelphians whom Mudd helped assemble; they sought to broaden the scope of birth control services by establishing a clinic where married couples "or those contemplating marriage" could be advised on how to "avoid some of the causes of marital difficulties." To Mudd's pleasant surprise, this group asked her to be the director of the Marriage Council of Philadelphia (MCP) and its first counselor, and she gladly accepted, terminating her post as Stuart's laboratory assistant. Mudd was a canny choice for MCP director. "I came from what in establishment terms would be a reputable family, [a] community family," Mudd admitted. Her social contacts, combined with her husband's high standing at the university and in medical circles, improved the MCP's chances of surviving. According to Mudd, the very name of the MCP conveyed the public image of a pro-family social service, which was a plus when trying to entice affluent Philadelphians or funding organizations to donate to the cause of birth control but not to a birth control clinic per se. As she said: "I think there were . . . perhaps some foundations that felt more free to give to a service called a Marriage Council than they did to birth control." A marriage counseling center might also attract a younger and more educated clientele than the largely poor and older people who typically attended the birth control clinic. Last, but not least, it came in handy for local physicians. Initially, the MCP was housed in two rooms belonging to the Pennsylvania Birth Control Federation, and doctors who feared the social stigma of being associated with the birth control movement could refer patients to the MCP with the knowledge that they would receive covert contraceptive counseling there or at the adjacent birth control office.[28]

The wider context to the founding of the MCP was the worsening economic conditions of the 1930s and their impact on the nation's families and birthrate. The U.S. birthrate for white women fell throughout the nineteenth century, and by the early twentieth century, the average family size for urban, native-born adult women was only two children (the immigrant rate was five to six live births). However, in the 1930s, for the first time in the nation's history, the birthrate dipped below the replacement level, reflecting the severe financial and psychological difficulties facing American couples. The unemployment rate reached 25 percent in 1933, and the incidence of desertion and divorce kept climbing. Many Americans were reluctant to bring children into a world racked by such economic uncertainty. To eugenicists and birth controllers like the Mudds, the most worrisome development of the 1930s was that the poor were continuing to have large families, while the more respectable classes were spacing their pregnancies. Other commentators argued that falling birthrates were just another symptom—alongside easier divorce, juvenile delinquency, and higher employment rates for wives—of the American family's decline. Thus, it was difficult to drum up wide-scale support for birth control when so many Americans were concerned about depopulation. The American birth control movement bent to prevailing attitudes in the late 1930s when it distanced itself from Sanger's message that large numbers of people should have no children at all and stressed instead a "balanced" program of spacing pregnancies that did not necessarily discourage middle-class Americans from having children.[29] With the whole issue of contraception fraught with controversy, a clinic ostensibly dedicated to counseling either couples who had already tied the knot or young people contemplating matrimony was bound to seem a lot less divisive than a service devoted to slashing birthrates on a wide scale.

The veneer of marriage counseling may have reassured many Philadelphians, but at the MCP, Mudd and her staff were actually engaged in subversive activities. In her early writings from the 1930s, Mudd asserted that the MCP supplied clients with information about marriage, but four decades later she admitted that she had also arranged abortions and sterilizations. Mudd's many sympathetic contacts in the medical community contributed by securing hospital facilities and performing the operations. For clients who encountered difficulty getting abortions in Pennsylvania, Mudd sent them out of state to Baltimore.[30]

Clients were normally referred to the MCP by the various social agencies as well as individual physicians, ministers, teachers, and lawyers. In the beginning, the MCP was a modest enterprise; its entire first-year budget was only $500, almost all of it coming from local benefactors. Over time, fees from clients and lecturing, its lending library, and inservice training added to the MCP's budget, but the biggest change came from the influx of government or private foundation funds, which twenty years later made up more than 50 percent of the budget.[31]

The opening of the MCP did not trigger a stampede of clients to the facility, belying the notion that there was popular demand for such a service. In later life, Mudd stated that her objective in marriage counseling had always been to put herself out of business, but a constant theme in the MCP's post-1933 history was an expansion of its activities. It was never clear where responding to public demand for marriage counseling left off and stimulating such demand began. Only fifty clients visited the MCP in its first year, so Mudd moved beyond clinical

Emily Mudd interviewing a woman, ca. 1946. (Courtesy of the Arthur and Elizabeth Schlesinger Library on the History of Women in America, Radcliffe Institute for Advanced Study, Harvard University)

consultative work and undertook a massive public education campaign, including lectures to community organizations (such as the Philadelphia YWCA), University of Pennsylvania medical students, and undergraduates on local college campuses such as Bryn Mawr. Thanks to her contacts in the local press, Mudd's public education program about marriage and the family was covered by the *Philadelphia Inquirer* and the *Evening Bulletin*, as well as by popular magazines such as *Redbook*, *McCall's*, *Modern Bride*, *Reader's Digest*, the *Saturday Evening Post*, and the *American Weekly*, a Sunday newspaper supplement. In her public lectures Mudd tackled a range of topics, including "the use and misuse of birth control." Advocacy of "sex as a vitally important part of the adjustment between two persons" and the notion that married women could pursue their own careers stimulated "tremendous bursts of emotional feeling" in her audiences, according to Mudd. Her later involvement in the debate over women's employment outside the home, a matter of deep personal interest, was kindled by these early encounters with college students from the Philadelphia area.[32] Her efforts paid off; by 1955 the MCP was serving a predominantly white, native-born, Protestant clientele of young married men and women; 66 percent of the men and 42 percent of the women had a year of college or more. But this success meant that during its first two decades of existence, the MCP's clientele became increasingly homogeneous.[33]

Emily Mudd's theories about marriage counseling in the 1930s were striking in their anticipation of the therapeutic approaches to marital advice a generation later, but they also contained elements that were very much a product of her time and place. The ascendancy of psychoanalysis in U.S. psychiatry between the 1930s and the 1960s, plus her friendship with Kenneth Appel, who later chaired the Department of Psychiatry at the University of Pennsylvania Medical School, predisposed Mudd to flirt with Freudian theory when interviewing clients, particularly with regard to the causes of homosexuality.[34] In conformity with the overwhelming consensus at the time that homosexuality was psychologically unhealthy, Mudd advised parents to encourage "healthy personality development" in their sons and daughters that would steer them toward heterosexuality, although she admitted that psychiatry possessed no "cures" for homosexuality and that there were "degrees of homosexuality" in all individuals. Much later, when Freudianism was on the wane in U.S. psychiatry, Mudd stood by Freud, writing that he had "brought the concept of sex as a vital factor in human development and functioning into scientific format and cautious clinical application by 1910. This concept began to make inroads on continental middle class cultures and subsequently gradually invaded the tightness of the calvinistic, Victorian, and puritan standards which in the early 1900s shaped much of the legal, religious, and moral codes of Central and Northeast United States."[35]

Mudd's open fondness for psychoanalytic ideas would fade in the Cold War years, as biological psychiatry began to enjoy a revival. Her own approach to counseling came to focus not on "the reorganization of the personality structure of the individual," as in psychoanalysis, but on the marital relationship itself.[36] Yet her eclectic reliance on psycho-analysis mirrored the broad American viewpoint, up to the 1960s, that in the name of science and enlightenment, Freud had lifted the traditionalist veil covering sexuality and that men, women, and children would benefit immensely as a result. Psychoanalysis justified Americans' sunny optimism that all problems could be licked with the right methods, and it represented a smooth, healthy break from past practices rather than an abrupt revolution in values.[37]

No matter how much she borrowed from Freud's theories, however, Mudd's early utterances on marriage and family counseling revealed aspects of the therapeutic ethos that would reign supreme by the end of the twentieth century. The aim of the new field, in Mudd's eyes, was to "combat the bogies of ignorance, superstition, and fear" with professional expertise.[38] The "philosophy" behind her MCP, as she asserted in 1940, rested on the "definition of the happy family as one which manages to solve its problems, not one which has no problems at all." The fluid boundaries between psychological wellness and dysfunction ensured that almost every person needed counseling. The family that imagined itself to have no problems was simply living a lie, according to Mudd; only psychological counseling of the kind supplied by the MCP could lead to true happiness. A counseling service was "educational," but what mattered "far more" were the client's "attitudes" and "emotions," not "his knowledge or lack of knowledge of facts." What clients *felt* was more important than what they *knew*. Truth in the therapeutic encounter was "grasped through sentiment or feeling, rather than through rational judgement or abstract reasoning"—a curious admission for Mudd, in light of her oft-stated intent to use scientific knowledge to repeal the "ignorance" and "superstition" of earlier historical periods. This awkward tension between science and feelings persisted in marriage counseling for years to come.[39]

Thus, as early as World War II, Mudd was articulating two key aspects of the therapeutic ethos: "the emotivist ethic," which stressed the primacy of feelings over knowledge, and "the pathologization of human behaviour," which was the tendency to define a range of seemingly normal life experiences as the breeding ground for disease—in this case, the superficially happy family and its interpersonal relations.[40] By the time Congress declared war on Japan in December 1941, Mudd had established herself as a pivotal pioneer in the emerging field of marriage and family counseling. The founding of the MCP was a notable accomplishment, and she was in the midst of building a constituency of like-minded reformers who would spread the message that counseling could dramatically ease people's adjustment to marriage. Her advocacy of marriage and family counseling as a means to improve the emotional lives of millions had received attention from various churches. Befitting their history of providing pastoral counseling, churches nationwide convened more than 100 conferences on the problem of marital discord.[41] In addition, schools and colleges, family welfare agencies, legal aid societies, social hygiene associations, and child guidance centers—to say nothing of birth control clinics—were showing mounting interest in marriage and family counseling.[42] According to one estimate, there were more than 150 marriage counseling centers in the United States, and another 100 that provided some kind of marital guidance in concert with other services.[43]

Yet the fate of marriage and family counseling still hung in the balance. As late as World War II, most Americans knew nothing about the profession, had no idea a "marriage problem" existed, and thus had never visited a marriage clinic.[44] Evidence of interest in marriage counseling as a professional service was limited to urban locations such as New York City, Philadelphia, and Los Angeles and to a handful of college campuses, but only a tiny fraction of college students actually took courses in marriage education. In 1948 a committee of marriage counselors lamented that "the vast majority of persons are ignorant of the existence of counselling centers and of marriage counsellors."[45] As late as 1964, one study found that only 10 percent of all marital counseling was done by "professional marriage counselors."[46] A home economics teacher at the Virginia Polytechnic Institute complained in 1953 that much of what passed for marriage counseling "seem[ed] to be oriented to highly urbanized marriage situations which are not typical of the country as a whole." Marriage counselors like Emily Mudd, she contended, based their theories on "the culture of the highly urbanized companionate group which certainly is not typical of the suburban or fringe city, or of the rural family."[47]

Those who *were* aware of the existence of marriage counseling services were often uneasy about activists like Mudd, who appeared to be interfering in intimate family matters. As she noted a quarter century later:

> I did recognize that there was a good deal of hostility and perhaps anxiety obvious in many men and women about marriage counseling. There was a certain amount of resistance to anyone, either a man or a woman—perhaps more especially to a woman— whose work would involve her or him in what was considered to be a private aspect of life and living, the relationship of married partners to each other, which obviously . . . included the sexual relationship.[48]

Moreover, prior to World War II, "there was no money in the practice of marriage counseling. . . . People got extraordinarily small fees and little salaries."[49]

Officialdom was not sold on marriage and family counseling either. Many policy makers suspected that reformers who preached greater frankness about sexuality and birth control would undermine rather than strengthen family values. In the shadow of the Great Depression, the prevailing consensus in Washington and in state capitals was that the traditional family headed by a male breadwinner remained the focus of attempts to construct a welfare state. Government policy rested on the theory that a man's wages should support his wife and children. Talk of making the family more egalitarian and less patriarchal struck some social leaders as subversive. Advocacy of greater freedom for married women, whether it involved employment, sexuality, or fertility, triggered conflicted responses among elected officials. If they believed that dependence on the expertise of professionals like Mudd and the Stones weakened "family responsibility," sympathy for the fledgling profession was likely to be sparse in the corridors of power.

As Emily Mudd struggled to make marriage counseling a success in Pennsylvania, the field took impressive strides on the West Coast. Three years before the opening of the MCP, biologist Paul Popenoe founded the first marriage counseling clinic in American history, the Institute of Family Relations (later the American Institute of Family Relations [AIFR]), located on Sunset Boulevard in Los Angeles. Popenoe claimed that he introduced the term *marriage counseling*, borrowed from the German word *Eheberatungsstellen*.[50] The AIFR was "the first organized attempt in the United States to bring all the resources of science to bear on the promotion of successful family life," and it soon gained a reputation as "the Mayo Clinic of family problems." Its early growth was astonishing. By the mid-1930s, it employed more than forty workers, at a time when Mudd's MCP was little more than a one-person show (even in the early 1940s the MCP's staff ordinarily consisted of only two secretaries and a single counselor). In the pre–World War II period the AIFR counseled more clients than all other U.S. marriage counseling centers combined.[51] By 1962, the AIFR boasted a staff of seventy and had seven branches in the Los Angeles area; it published a monthly magazine, maintained a well-stocked library, and provided degree-based training in marriage counseling.[52] By then, roughly 100,000 people had used its services. With thousands of people visiting the center every year, attending its seminars, subscribing to its correspondence courses, and exchanging letters with its counselors, Popenoe's AIFR was a beehive of activity.

Popenoe's views on marriage and the family were widely disseminated on the nation's airwaves and in its newspapers and magazines. His long-running advice column in *Ladies' Home Journal* was titled "Can This Marriage Be Saved?" Nicknamed "Mr. Marriage," he was a frequent guest on Art Linkletter's popular *House Party* program for fourteen years (it aired on radio and television between 1944 and 1969). Millions of housewives watched the show, accounting for three-quarters of the audience. Popenoe also introduced computer dating, which originated in 1956 on Linkletter's other television program, *People Are Funny*.[53]

Popenoe exuded a sunny, friendly optimism that appealed to countless Californians. He styled himself as a "marriage repairman" and a teacher of "parentcraft." "If your automobile broke down you knew where to go for help," he stated, but where did you go if your marriage was failing? He claimed that the AIFR's counselors were "able to straighten out the difficulties of the marriage" for 80 percent of the couples who sought help, often "by seeing only one partner" (most frequently the wife). The AIFR was flooded with letters from readers and viewers who either asked his advice or lavished praise on him. In 1959, for instance, a woman from Stockton, California, confessed to Popenoe,

Paul Popenoe and wife Betty, ca. 1936. (Courtesy of the American Heritage Center, University of Wyoming)

"I read your column every evening, and think what you advise people to do about their difficulties is human and very sensible."[54] Even by the standards of Hollywood, some of whose female stars became clients, the expansion of the AIFR was spectacular.

Tellingly, Popenoe, like Emily Mudd, came from a background in the eugenics movement. Born in Topeka, Kansas, in 1888, Popenoe moved with his family to California in 1905. He later traveled the world collecting date specimens, but in 1913, as his interests shifted from fruit to genetics, he landed the job of editor of the *Journal of Heredity*. In 1926 he became director of research for the Human Betterment Foundation in Pasadena, California, a eugenics organization that lobbied for the enactment of state laws to allow the sterilization of people with disabilities. In the late 1920s he published three books on eugenics. In 1929 he was awarded an honorary degree by Occidental College and was thereafter known as "Dr. Popenoe," a national expert on heredity, eugenics, marriage, and the family. That same year he founded the AIFR, and he remained its director until 1976.

Like Emily Mudd, Popenoe considered marriage and family counseling an extension of eugenics. The AIFR's funding came from E. S. Gosney, chairman of the Human Betterment Foundation, which Popenoe left in 1931. By then, Popenoe had concluded that "hard-line" schemes to undertake mass, involuntary sterilizations were going out of fashion, and adherents had to scramble to make eugenics more acceptable to the public. As Popenoe and Mudd knew only too well, based on Pope Pius XI's 1930 encyclical *Casti Connubii*, the Roman Catholic Church opposed eugenic sterilization, and over the next three decades it used its formidable political power to thwart the enactment of state sterilization laws.[55] For Popenoe, the battle had already been won in California, whose 1909 law resulted in the sterilization of one-third of all Americans affected by such laws in the twentieth century. Yet sterilization laws applied only to those in institutions, so Popenoe and others in the field sought different means of bringing eugenics to the broad segments of society that needed guidance about marriage and reproduction. By the 1930s, Popenoe's focus had shifted from negative to positive eugenics, from the fertile poor to the broad middle class, whose birthrates, he believed, had to be elevated at a time of overall depopulation. The marriage counselor, he wrote, was "in a particularly favourable position to give advice that will have eugenic value." Americans, he insisted, had to be not "merely family-minded, but discriminatingly family-minded."[56]

Popenoe's stardom within the marriage counseling movement peaked in the 1950s and faded steadily thereafter. Despite building his own formidable branch of the movement, he remained an outsider to the rest of the field, which had its power base on the East Coast. With few academic credentials other than an honorary degree (and, according to Mudd, virtually no interest in hard research), Popenoe was never admitted to the American Association of Marriage Counselors, the field's leading professional organization. Popenoe, in Mudd's words, was "extremely bitter" about his exclusion for the rest of his life.[57] One of the main differences between Popenoe and the East Coast group was his attitude toward birth control and sex education. One study found that of the AIFR's first 1,000 cases, only 7 percent were reportedly caused by "a sex problem," in stark contrast to the judgments of many East Coast counselors.[58] Popenoe, like eugenicists Harry Laughlin and Charles Davenport, was opposed to indiscriminate birth control and believed that marriage counseling could boost family size among the so-called fit classes of society. Popenoe urged marriage counselors to try to increase birthrates among the "best" types of people by preventing divorce, while East Coast counselors tended to be less interested in saving marriages. To Popenoe, "the public has so long refused to face the facts of divorce. It doesn't want to think about what these broken homes really mean but insists on trying to sugarcoat the whole thing with 'getting her [the wife's] freedom' and that sort of talk. . . . That is exactly what's the matter with these people. They are meeting their matrimonial problems on a completely childish level."[59] Popenoe was convinced that in the vast majority of cases, divorce was a disaster for the nation and for the individuals involved.

Popenoe's reaction to Betty Friedan's best-selling book *The Feminine Mystique* (1963) revealed the divergence between his brand of marriage counseling advice and the emerging values of the women's movement of the 1960s. Popenoe called *The Feminine Mystique* "shrill" and claimed it provided "little supporting evidence." He objected to Friedan's attacks on the domestic ideal of a breadwinner father and a nurturing, homemaker mother. "It is obvious," Popenoe wrote, "that, in general, the home must be given first place in the life of both men and women—otherwise the survival of a nation is endangered. Beyond that, it is imperative that the ablest women, who can create the best homes, also bear and rear a fair proportion of the nation's children—otherwise leadership will gradually die out."[60]

Popenoe's conviction that college-educated women like Friedan were most useful as homemakers, wives, and mothers demonstrated his faith in positive eugenics, but by the 1960s, his theory about women's destiny was rapidly falling out of favor in a field dominated by individuals such as Emily Mudd, who thought the institution of marriage should be reformed to enable women to achieve fulfillment outside the home. His condemnation of homosexuality as a "definite evil" differed from the comparatively less judgmental interpretations of Mudd and other counselors.[61] Popenoe soon became a target for radicals: in 1970 a group of women staged a sit-in at the offices of *Ladies' Home Journal*, and among their demands was that the magazine discontinue Popenoe's column "Can This Marriage Be Saved?" As the 1970s wore on, Popenoe attacked the women's liberation and gay rights movements for being "enemies of family life," which he believed was the linchpin of civilization.[62] After his death in 1979, the AIFR did not survive for long, closing in the 1980s with little fanfare.

Nonetheless, it would be a mistake to define Popenoe as a hidebound traditionalist. As historians Molly Ladd-Taylor and Eva Moskowitz have argued, Popenoe taught husbands to pay attention to their wives' sexual needs. He also acknowledged "the dissatisfaction many women felt with full-time wife and motherhood [and] asserted their right (and the right of their husbands) to be happy in marriage, in the process contributing to a 'discourse of discontent'" that bridged the gap between the Depression and the women's movement of the 1960s.[63] In his monthly column, Popenoe candidly addressed the troubling emotional effects of bad marriages and taught housewives how to overcome the psychological tensions they often experienced when trying to conform to the domestic ideal. His advice invariably stressed adjustment to rather than rejection of women's marital roles, but at the same time, he insisted that counseling was intended to encourage couples to bring their dissatisfactions out into the open so that both husband and wife could confront them. Popenoe may not have encouraged married women to protest, but he recognized that they were sometimes angry, unhappy, or depressed in their roles as housewives. He certainly agreed with most others in the marriage counseling field that American couples needed advice from scientifically enlightened experts who dealt on a daily basis with the myriad pressures exerted on the mid-twentieth-century American family. In 1965 an AIFR brochure read: "How long since you checked up systematically and scientifically on your marriage? It deserves regular attention, just as much as any other aspect of your health. . . . Even a very successful marriage needs to be reinvigorated from time to time; provided with new interests, given new directions, furnished with new techniques for meeting changed conditions and avoiding dull routine and boredom."[64] Popenoe's advice to American couples to define their relationships as health matters that "deserve[d] regular attention" from experts could have been reprinted forty years later, and no one would have blinked an eye.

Popenoe's AIFR and Mudd's MCP proved to be footholds for marriage and family counseling in American society, but it was on college campuses where interest in marriage as a subject for study truly flourished in the 1930s. By 1937, more than 200 colleges and universities (out of a total of 672 across the country) offered courses in marriage preparation.[65] University social scientists endeavored to convince Americans that without scientific research, their marriages would likely fail and their families would become dysfunctional, and college students appeared to be receptive to their professors' teachings. Because they tended to be "the more promising graduates of the high schools," college students were naturally more intellectually curious about new topics of study than were their peers.[66] Young men and women, often anticipating their own marriages, flocked to these college courses looking for practical information on how to choose a compatible spouse and what to expect once they tied the knot. Having postponed marriage to pursue an education, many students sought advice on dating issues, especially the ethics of premarital sex.[67] Since sex education was virtually nonexistent in high schools at the time, they were excited to learn about normally taboo topics. Additionally, young women were flattered when their professors described their future roles as wives and mothers as worthy of scientific study. In the words of Ernest Groves, an early advocate of college and university marriage preparation courses, "it takes intelligence to be a modern wife."[68] Although interest among male students was robust, these courses were largely designed to encourage female students to choose marriage rather than careers after graduation.

Two outspoken leaders of this current were Stanford University psychologist Lewis Terman (1877–1956) and University of Chicago sociologist Ernest Burgess (1886–1966). Both believed that the family was undergoing a transition from what Burgess called "an institutional to a companionship form."[69] In the process, the family ceased to be constrained by "traditional rules and regulations, specified duties and obligations, and other social pressures" exerted by conventional "mores, public opinion, and law." Thus, "the task of adjusting to marriage is a vastly more complicated and precarious business today than it used to be," stated an expert in 1932.[70] This transformation of the family had various causes, including the shift from a rural to an urban society, "from stability of residence to mobility, [and] from familism to individualism." Affection, equality, sympathetic understanding, and comradeship were the chief characteristics of the modern family, according to Burgess. Patriarchy and its "authoritarianism" had been overthrown by "the democratic family based on equality of husband and wife, with consensus in making decisions and with increasing participation by children as they grow older."[71] To Burgess and others in the field, the family was morphing from an institution into a relationship.

Terman, who collaborated with Popenoe, had designed and administered intelligence tests during World War I (he introduced the idea of the intelligence quotient, or IQ), but he switched to the study of personality assessment in the 1930s. Likewise, Burgess had made his name in the study of urban ecology but changed fields in the early 1930s, when he designed his first study of marital compatibility. Believing that the social and cultural differences between the sexes could be quantified, Terman argued that individual personalities determined a marriage's chance of success. Thus he, like Burgess, was convinced that research could predict marital happiness. In 1938 Burgess told *Time* magazine that matrimonial success "now depends more than ever before upon the findings of research in the psychological and social sciences."[72]

The studies of Terman and Burgess buttressed the perception that extensive research in the social sciences was necessary to save American marriages, but their findings did not always dovetail with those of Mudd and the Stones, especially with regard to sexuality. In an attempt to measure which factors showed a marked correlation with "adjustment in marriage," Burgess found that sexual factors were outweighed by others. For example, agreement over "desiring children," "close attachment of husband and wife to their respective parents," happy marriages for both spouses' parents, and similar family backgrounds,

Tenth annual meeting of the National Council on Family Relations, New York City, 1947. (Courtesy of the National Council on Family Relations)

including "nationality, religious preference, church activity," and levels of education, were more important than sexual factors in predicting a happy marriage. Getting along with the in-laws also scored high on surveys.[73]

The growing conviction among social scientists that research on marriage and the family was urgently needed paved the way for the formation of the National Conference of Family Relations in 1938 (renamed the National Council on Family Relations in 1947). From its inception, the NCFR was dedicated to family research, policy, and practice, with the goal of improving the quality of family interactions. The NCFR was a response to the mounting interest in the welfare of the family, but it was also viewed as an organization that could help reconstruct the family into a democratic institution. NCFR members came from all over the country and from a wide variety of disciplines and specialties, including psychiatry, psychology, medicine, sociology, home economics, and the churches. Prominent Americans such as anthropologist Margaret Mead and psychiatrists William Menninger and Adolf Meyer were NCFR members. Pulitzer Prize–winning author Pearl Buck was a speaker at the NCFR's annual meeting in 1941. Emily Mudd chaired the local arrangements committee for the NCFR conference "The Role and Functions of the Family in a Democracy," held at Philadelphia's Sylvania

Hotel on December 26–27, 1939. Mudd also served as a conference chair when the NCFR met again in Philadelphia on April 4–6, 1946.

An early major influence on the NCFR was sociologist Ernest Groves (1877–1946). Indeed, Groves rivaled Mudd as a torchbearer for the broad acceptance of marriage counseling as more than a specialty linked to the eugenics and birth control movements. In 1940 he wrote approvingly that "the interest of college young people in preparation for marriage has removed the idea that domestic counselling is merely for the handicapped or the incapable."[74] Groves's main claim to prominence was his advocacy of marriage courses on college campuses. His research output was slim: among marriage and family counselors, Groves was known as the man who wrote the same book twelve different times.[75] Born in Framingham, Massachusetts, Groves became a vocal proponent of "frank education for marriage" when his first wife died during pregnancy in 1916. At Boston University he developed the first credit course in marriage and the family in 1920, and after moving to the University of North Carolina in 1927, he continued to offer credit courses in marriage preparation. In 1934 Groves launched the annual Conference on the Conservation of Marriage and the Family, begun by his second wife, Gladys, at the North Carolina College for Negroes (later North Carolina College–Durham).

Groves, known popularly as the "professor of marriage" or the "doctor of troubles," served as the NCFR's third president. Like Popenoe and other marriage and family counseling trailblazers, Groves struggled in the early years to position the field in the mainstream of American life, cover up its links to the eugenic sterilization movement, and expand its potential clientele to include the country's respectable classes, not just low-income groups or people with mental and physical disabilities. "Among the thousands of fine young men and women" graduating every year from college, Groves found a huge new pool of "highly selected" clients. According to Groves, however, these college students were headed for matrimonial "lives of unhappiness," thanks to "squeamish" educators who imposed a "prudish conspiracy of silence regarding marriage problems" and "neglect[ed] . . . the emotional life of their students." Colleges and universities should be in the business of "mental hygiene," he stated—that is, "preparing the student for life."[76] Groves assured his students that he was nonjudgmental and "cast no stones," but he encouraged them to keep "digging back" into their lives for the events that led to their emotional difficulties. "It will be hard. It will hurt," he admitted, but it would ease their minds in the long run.[77] Groves shared with Mudd and Popenoe a faith in science for dealing with problems of personality; he saw marriage and family counseling as a form of mental hygiene that enabled experts to intervene and prevent psychological disorders from occurring later in life. Groves was one of the first to promote counseling as a service and a resource on which a growing number of Americans of all walks of life would come to depend.

Sidney E. Goldstein (1879–1955), one of the three founders of the NCFR and its fifth president (1945–1946), was another who believed that the family was at a historical crossroads. Goldstein, of mixed Jewish and Irish ancestry, was an associate rabbi under Rabbi Stephen Wise at the Free Synagogue in New York City; both were avid supporters of eugenics.[78] Goldstein, chairman of the Jewish Institute on Marriage and Family and the New York State Conference on Marriage and the Family (NYSCMF), was arguably the most vocal U.S. clergyman in favor of a scientifically grounded approach to preparing people for marriage. By the outbreak of World War II, he was tirelessly advocating that the NYSCMF organize a program of public education and counseling services in New York City to provide information and guidance about what men and women should expect both before and after marriage. As Goldstein told the NCFR in 1938, the institution of marriage was in crisis due to "a deepening rebellion on the part of children and on the part of women and corresponding restlessness toward the routine and regimentation of married life." Since "the home, the school and the church" had failed to solve the crisis, the time had come for "the Government of the State" to take the lead and "assist in establishing consulting centers throughout the State and across the country." Knowledge about marriage had to be "democratize[d]," Goldstein averred; by that, he meant that "normal men and women, married or unmarried, are just as much in need" of marriage and family counseling "as abnormal groups." "We cannot rear the right kind of family in the wrong kind of home," he stated. "No couple should be permitted to enter the state of matrimony without instruction and guidance in at least the elementary matters of marriage and family organization." Goldstein elevated marriage and the family to the level of a vital national policy and declared society's institutions—notably, the family—incapable of understanding and solving the problem. The family had to be reconstituted on the new foundations of biology, psychology, economics, and ethics. Only professional expertise, to his mind, could save the country.[79]

More successful—but also more controversial—than Goldstein's efforts to launch marriage counseling in New York City were those of Lester Dearborn in Boston. Dearborn, described in 1934 by *Time* magazine as a "stocky, soft-spoken . . . happily married but childless" forty-year-old, was similar to Popenoe, in that he had no formal education in psychiatry, psychology, pastoral counseling, or social work. Yet his lack of credentials did not stop him from becoming one of the first in the marriage counseling field to openly argue that the gulf between the nation's ideals about sex and marriage and the behavioral reality of Americans' intimate lives was gaping, predating Alfred Kinsey's similar but more ballyhooed claims by a decade. Early in his career, Dearborn worked as a high school teacher, and in the late 1920s he started lecturing on "sex hygiene" in the Boston area. In 1932, as an employee of the YMCA, he shifted into marriage counseling at the Massachusetts Society for Social Hygiene (MSSH). Since its inception in 1911, the MSSH had been advocating medical measures in the fight against venereal disease and prostitution, but in 1928 it reorganized to emphasize "family life education" as the best way to combat these social problems. By the 1930s, the MSSH had hired Dearborn to lecture on sexual topics to groups such as the Camp Fire Girls, the Harvard Church Young People's Society, the YMCA Young Men's Club, and Boston's Nursery Training School. He quickly gained a reputation for his candor, and his lectures covered subjects that polite society considered "abnormalities and perversions." For example, nervous MSSH officials wondered why Dearborn had to spend a full thirty minutes on masturbation.[80]

Dearborn was an early contributor to a professional discourse that helped redefine normal sexuality at a time when popular tolerance for sexual deviation in the form of homosexuality, masturbation, premarital "petting," and oral and anal sex was almost nonexistent. Dearborn believed that many if not all homosexuals could be taught to adjust to heterosexual marriage, but his other views about homosexuality were far less conventional. He objected to "the popular clamor for drastic legislation dealing with the so-called sex perverts," referring to the drive for stiffer sentencing of homosexuals and other nonconformists. One historian has argued that the word *psychopath*, used so freely both before and after World War II by criminologists and mental health experts, "served in part as a code for homosexual."[81] In a day and age when many Americans did not distinguish between homosexuals and "sex offenders," Dearborn contended that "a great many" gay men and women were "highly intellectual and very useful citizens."[82] Given the permissible language used to describe homosexuality in the pre–World War II United States, Dearborn's remarks were decidedly unorthodox, and he was among the first and most authoritative commentators to argue that healthy sexuality could include nonprocreative acts outside marriage. Dearborn hardly convinced his audience to accept all his views on sexuality, but his listeners were apparently sufficiently impressed with his earnestness and forthrightness that they began to request that he provide individual counseling. According to Dearborn, he and the MSSH did "nothing more than let it be known through our lectures that such a [counseling] service existed, and this has generally been done in answering the question 'Where can we go for help?'" By 1932, he had performed about 110 such consultations at the YMCA.[83]

Working for the MSSH—a respectable public health organization—helped shield Dearborn from accusations of obscenity when he dispensed sexual and contraceptive advice to young clients, whether in his lectures or during private consultations. His MSSH patrons tended to dismiss moral objections to the sexual content of his teachings as the "outbursts" of "hysterical" women. Like other marriage counseling pioneers, Dearborn insisted that he was merely responding to public demands for more information about sex, but his relatively few clients, who were largely white, Protestant, heterosexual, and middle class, suggested that his impressions were based on a limited sample of American society. Other matters, including finances, child rearing, and how to get along with in-laws, also preoccupied his clients. Nonetheless, Dearborn maintained that the "chief basis of marital discontent" was "incompatibility on the subject of sex," and in many cases, he stated, this could be remedied by premarital sex.[84] This conviction plunged him into a nationwide controversy in 1934.

The setting for the imbroglio was a conference titled "Education for

Marriage and Family Social Relations" held at Columbia University's Teachers College on June 3, 1934. There, a group of marriage and family experts tackled the question: "What shall we tell young people who have premarital relations?" The question was timely, given that countless young people across the country were postponing marriage due to the grim economic conditions. No transcript exists of the meeting, but according to Dearborn, who was there, the first speakers maintained that premarital sex often caused discord in marriage. Unable to remain quiet, Dearborn rose to state that a marriage counselor "would be placed in an awkward position if he believed that intercourse prior to marriage invariably led to unhappiness in marriage." This statement was disquieting enough; what he had to say next sparked a firestorm of protest. Dearborn insisted that roughly 50 percent of his more than 300 unmarried clients had admitted to having premarital sexual relations. *Time* magazine, in its coverage of the meeting, reported that "all over the room conferees were on their feet, shaking fists, pointing fingers, shouting and shrilling Mr. Chairman, Mr. Chairman." One attendee exclaimed, "Petting is cruelty to man."[85]

In addition to *Time*'s coverage of the incident, the *Atlanta Constitution* took issue with Dearborn's remarks, and several southern newspapers ran the story. Dearborn tried to clarify: he had not been urging the country's youth to have intercourse before marriage. But he quickly discovered that he had few defenders at Teachers College or among other counselors, including Paul Popenoe, who had chaired the conference. Dearborn was relieved, however, when Emily Mudd rushed up to him after the meeting to "comment favorably on my statement." Maurice Bigelow, the main organizer of the conference at Columbia University, desperately tried to do damage control; in letters to the nation's press, he disassociated the conference from Dearborn's views, which, he insisted, had not been met with "general approval." Yet Dearborn himself was convinced that Mudd was not the only one who shared his opinions about premarital sex. This would become evident twenty years later when leading members of the AAMC would challenge the condemnation of sexual relations before marriage.

The 1934 controversy over premarital sex blew over quickly enough, but its significance lay in the fact that although many Americans believed they needed more information about the nature of married life as a way to prevent divorce, they resisted some of the teachings of early marriage counselors, notably those related to sexual issues. The nation's heartland tended to respect science and the power of education to make life better, but there were firm moral boundaries beyond which most Americans were unwilling to go. Fearful of sending the wrong message to the nation's young people, Americans did not want to hear that large numbers of them were engaging in sex before marriage, and they especially did not want educators like Dearborn saying that such conduct was normal and did not harm one's prospects for a happy marriage. The 1934 controversy revealed the large cleavage between the values of most Americans and those of leading marriage counselors. Twenty years later, the press took a much gentler attitude toward Dearborn, calling him the "favorite Dutch uncle of prospective newly-weds" and saying that his advice on "the sex factor in human life" had made him "Boston's expert repairer of shaky marriages."[86] Yet in the midst of the Depression, it appeared that most Americans were not prepared to accept the therapeutic vision of the nation's leading marriage counselors, who realized, to their chagrin, that they were out in front of public opinion.

Thus, as the war clouds began to gather in the late 1930s, it was unclear exactly what the public at large thought about the status of marriage and the family in America. In contrast, there was little doubt about how the handful of individuals behind the new profession of marriage and family counseling felt. Mudd, Popenoe, Dearborn, Burgess, Goldstein, and Groves were united in thinking that the family was in the midst of a disorienting period of transition, moving from a patriarchal institution with firmly assigned gender roles to an institution that owed its members much more freedom. The coming years would test but ultimately vindicate their resolve to alter the nation's attitudes toward matters that had once been consigned to the realm of family privacy. By then, the country would be in the midst of a revolution that would redefine Americans' intimate relations with their spouses and their family members.

*I*f the future of marriage and family counseling was uncertain by the end of the 1930s, the Japanese attack on Pearl Harbor on December 7, 1941, helped change that. America's entry into World War II unleashed a series of events that deeply affected the lives of countless men, women, and children and altered the history of marriage and family counseling. As millions of women (many of whom were mothers) entered the wartime workforce and millions of armed forces personnel were shipped overseas, the marriage rate rose sharply, causing experts to insist that in this time of emergency, the country required unprecedented research, counseling, training, and public education about the challenges facing married couples and families. Fierce debates raged at the national, state, and local levels over precisely what kind of marriage and family policies the nation required.

Against this backdrop of flux in Americans' lives, the field of marriage and family counseling took its first shaky steps toward professionalization. Spearheading the process was a small group of like-minded activists from the fields of birth control and eugenics. Calling themselves the American Association of Marriage Counselors (AAMC), these opinion makers were united in their quest to convince Americans that they should turn to mental health experts for guidance and relinquish their adherence to long-standing, conventional codes of conduct. No one cast a bigger shadow over this group than sexologist Alfred Kinsey, who preached that there was a wide gap between accepted cultural mores and private sexual behavior and that a vast overhaul of society's attitudes toward a range of sexual practices was long overdue. The central role played by Kinsey during the AAMC's early years is a neglected story that illustrates a core tenet of therapism: liberation from customary forms of authority, notably in sexual matters, that clash with individuals' search for self-fulfillment. By the 1970s, the therapeutic viewpoint, with its emphasis on self-emancipation through the intervention of experts who relentlessly challenged traditional norms, was well on its way to cultural ascendancy.

According to historian Ellen Herman, World War II was a "watershed in the history of psychology."[1] In a sign of the times, a new edition of *The Basic Writings of Sigmund Freud* sold a quarter of a million copies in 1947. *Life* magazine noted in 1957 that the war had sparked the "greatest upsurge" of interest in psychology in U.S. history.[2] The perception in the media and in educated circles was that the war had taught valuable lessons about mental health. The tremendous emotional toll borne by enlisted men in combat led the U.S. military to employ hundreds of psychiatrists and more than 1,500 psychologists to study the enemy, test troops for their mental battle readiness, treat men's emotional wounds, and advise military leaders on the importance of psychological factors in military strategy. Fully 12 percent of all U.S. recruits were rejected by psychological screening. So many combat personnel became psychiatric casualties that Allied Supreme Headquarters lamented the "lost divisions" due to mental breakdown. Once World War II was over and the Cold War ensued, the standoff between the United States and communist Russia was known as a "sykewar," code for psychological warfare.[3]

Others argued that World War II revolutionized the study and practice of psychiatry and psychology. In the latter stages of the war, the armed forces adopted new methods of psychiatric treatment that normally took place only a few miles from the front and provided battle-fatigued personnel with a shower, a shave, a warm meal, and a chance to catch up on their sleep. Military psychiatrists discovered that such methods enabled more than half of psychologically disabled servicemen to return to their units.[4] The experience of rehabilitating battle-weary servicemen unleashed a wave of therapeutic optimism that swept through the ranks of U.S. psychiatry as the war came to a close. An article in *Collier's* magazine announced that "any doubts about the efficacy of psychiatric treatment have been dissipated in the heat of war. Thousands of men have been returned to normal life and even to combat life by uses of the new therapy."[5]

World War II also appeared to prove that psychiatrists' insights into human nature could be used during the postwar era to construct an entirely new definition of citizenship that stressed emancipation from long-standing values and loyalties. One exponent of this viewpoint was Kenneth Appel, chairman of psychiatry at the University of Pennsylvania and president of the American Psychiatric Association in 1953. Appel, who also served on the MCP's board of directors, echoed the remarks of Canadian psychiatrist Brock Chisholm, the first director general of the World Health Organization, when he argued that "isolationism," "the idea of national sovereignty," and family loyalties were "out-moded" and "psychologically unsound" viewpoints in the postwar world. Other mental health experts, such as the Menningers from Topeka, Kansas, maintained that mental health problems were a lot more common than previously thought and could benefit from early detection and treatment. In 1956 William Menninger warned that "there isn't a person [in America] who does not experience frequently a mental or emotional disturbance severe enough to disrupt his functioning as a well-adjusted, happy and efficiently performing individual."[6] On that score, Menninger and the country's marriage and family counselors were in accord.

When journalists reported the neglect and abuse of patients in state mental hospitals around the country, Congress passed the National Mental Health Act (NMHA) in 1946. It called for the federal government to assume responsibility for "improv[ing] the mental health of the people of the United States" by funding training programs for psychiatrists, psychologists, and social workers. In 1949, as a follow-up to the NMHA, Congress ordered the creation of the National Institute of Mental Health (NIMH), with a price tag of $7.5 million—the first time in U.S. history that Washington took the lead in mental health care policy making. The NIMH's budget jumped from $8.7 million in 1949 to $100 million in 1960. The national interest in mental health, fanned by government and the media, prompted the *New York Times* to report in 1949 that the United States would need 27,000 more psychiatrists to adjust to the postwar global environment. As if on cue, membership in the American Psychiatric Association grew by 57 percent between 1950 and 1956. Convinced that a mental health crisis was sweeping the country, Americans appeared to be mobilizing to prevent an outbreak of psychological disorders that might disrupt society's cherished institutions.[7]

No institution was thought to be in more jeopardy than the family. According to Emily Mudd, "following World War II government as well as private interests were vastly disturbed by the question of mental breakdown. There was general conviction on the part of psychiatrists and social workers that pathological conditions in a family and the relationships of family members to each other were correlated with mental illness."[8] To the NCFR's Evelyn Millis Duvall, "the disruption of family life" due to war included "the separation of family members, bereavement and soul-shaking anxieties, working mothers, shifts in discipline, hurried romances and hasty marriages, war babies, [and] new moral codes."[9] To these problems Ernest Burgess added "juvenile delinquency," which he claimed had been on the rise since Pearl Harbor, and in 1944 he declared the need for "a great increase in marriage counseling."[10]

The debate over marriage and the family often focused on the influx of women into the economy, notably in war-related industries. At the beginning of the war, women made up a quarter of the workforce. At the end of the war, 18 million women—accounting for a third of the workforce—were employed outside the home. Although most women worked in traditionally female industries, such as the service sector, about 3 million were employed in war plants. Government propaganda celebrated the trend toward female employment by popularizing the fictional character "Rosie the Riveter," a patriotic and efficient factory laborer.

The unsettled conditions on the home front and the atmosphere of patriotic emergency led to a spike in the number of marriages, as young men and women of all classes found themselves working side by side on the factory floor or socializing in urban areas with large military installations. Wartime population disruptions challenged conventional mores regarding sexual behavior. One U.S. soldier, after exchanging wisecracks with a young woman behind the counter at a YMCA, turned to his buddy and said in surprise, "I've never flirted before in my life. I've only been in the army five days, and now look at what I'm doing."[11] When gay men and women left their families and hometowns, they frequently encountered new opportunities to meet fellow homosexuals. Against the backdrop of war, gay men and women began to establish their own bars, social clubs, and political organizations—forerunners of the gay liberation movement of the 1960s.[12]

For heterosexuals, the marriage rate jumped in 1940 to the highest in the country's history, but in 1941 it climbed by another 15 percent. City officials on the West and East Coasts reported a sharp increase in the issuance of marriage licences in December 1941, drawing the attention of First Lady Eleanor Roosevelt, who, on February 1, 1942, cautioned young college women not to marry in a "patriotic fervor." The data showed that many of these newlyweds were not childhood sweethearts but young people who had been relative strangers when they exchanged their vows. Such statistics alarmed many officials, who predicted a rash of postwar divorces, which duly occurred between 1945 and 1947. Yet warnings about "marrying in haste, repenting at leisure" seemed to have little effect. Sociologist Henry Bowman complained, "Everybody seems to be doing his best to hasten the soldier and his girl to church."[13]

Meanwhile, counselors were quick to conclude that, with the country at war, the time was right for the field to organize. In the 1930s a group had formed to discuss maternal health and marital relations under the auspices of the National Committee on Maternal Health, an organization dedicated to clinical studies of contraceptive methods. The group was disbanded in 1937, but a new one formed in 1940 that included NCFR founders Emily Mudd and Ernest Groves, Lester Dearborn, Abraham Stone, Brooklyn gynecologist Robert Latou Dickinson, and New York City psychiatrist Robert Laidlaw. The group's intention was to meet and present marriage counseling cases so that the participants might learn from one another's clinical methods. Yet these conferences also reflected a nascent professional consciousness, an awareness that, as practitioners, they shared a strong interest in establishing counseling as a respected specialty within the wider field of mental health. On June 20, 1942, many of the same researchers and clinicians assembled at Laidlaw's New York City office to form the American Association of Marriage Counselors (AAMC), which formally organized three years later.[14]

In launching the AAMC, Mudd, Dickinson, Laidlaw, Dearborn, and Groves were joined by physician Valeria Parker from New York and Lovett Dewees, an obstetrician and consulting physician at the Bryn Mawr hospital near Philadelphia. Lester Dearborn was chairman of the group between 1942 and 1945. From its inception, the AAMC, headquartered in Manhattan, intended to restrict its membership to a small

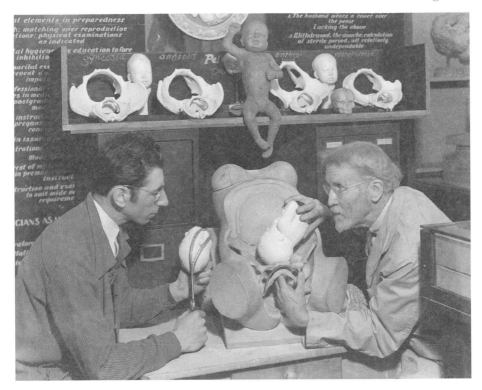

Robert Latou Dickinson (right) with plastic models of female anatomy. (Courtesy of the Kinsey Institute for Research in Sex, Gender, and Reproduction)

group, in contrast to the more inclusive NCFR; indeed, the AAMC had only thirty-one dues-paying members in 1944. The AAMC leadership wanted to avoid the problems of the earlier discussion group, whose meetings had proved so popular and attracted so many participants that, in Dickinson's words, "the frankness of speech was lost." Thus, the AAMC limited itself to like-minded "persons who could talk frankly and openly about the various aspects of the social and sexual relations between men and women."[15]

The AAMC also insisted on stringent professional qualifications for admission, typically a medical degree or a Ph.D. Half the original group were physicians, with the rest coming from the fields of sociology, psychology, and social work. As late as 1950, more than one-quarter of AAMC members were gynecologists. In later years, therapists accused the original AAMC of "elitism," due as much to its New York City headquarters as to its admission requirements. Yet in the 1940s, the association clearly believed that it could convince the public of the need for counseling only if its members possessed the highest expert credentials. At its inception, the AAMC was anything but a populist, inclusive organization.

Officially, the AAMC was founded with "the purpose of establishing standards, exchanging information, and helping in the development of interest in marriage counselling." Its founding members all believed that "marriage counselling was important to the healthy development of our society," in Mudd's words.[16] Yet the roster of AAMC founders also suggested that they were firmly united along specific ideological lines. Its early leadership was liberally represented by vocal spokespeople in favor of rolling back long-standing attitudes toward sex and reproduction while advocating eugenics and birth control. Abraham Stone admitted that his "interest in marriage counseling came primarily through work in planned parenthood."[17] Emily Mudd and Abraham and Hannah Stone bridged the gap between marriage counseling and Margaret Sanger's Clinical Research Bureau in Manhattan, as did physician and AAMC member Lena Levine (1903–1965), who ran the Sanger clinic with Abraham Stone after Hannah's death in 1941.

No one exerted more influence over the early AAMC than Robert Latou Dickinson. An AAMC member remarked in 1950 that the "Association should be named the Dickinson Society."[18] As Robert Laidlaw disclosed in 1977, "the AAMC was conceived because of RLD's [Dickinson's] feeling of a need for a group that could 'talk straight talk' about the clinical aspects of sexual problems. To us now this seems old hat, but . . . this was rather a daring move in the early 40s."[19] When Emily Mudd's history of the organization's first twenty-five years was published in 1968, it featured a photo of a bust of Dickinson. Most early AAMC members agreed with Dickinson that the key to a happy marriage was overthrowing conventional moral codes about sex and reproduction, a major aspect of the emerging therapeutic ethos.

Dickinson, born in 1861 in Brooklyn, New York, never met a progressive cause he did not like, from eugenics to sex education to euthanasia. Dickinson ranks with Alfred Kinsey, William Masters and Virginia Johnson, and Shere Hite as one of the most influential sexologists in twentieth-century America. His book *A Thousand Marriages*, published

YBP Library Services

DOWBIGGIN, IAN ROBERT, 1952-

SEARCH FOR DOMESTIC BLISS: MARRIAGE AND FAMILY
COUNSELING IN 20TH-CENTURY AMERICA.
                                    Cloth   250 P.
LAWRENCE: UNIV PR OF KANSAS, 2014

AUTH: UNIV. OF PRINCE EDWARD ISLAND. TRACES THE
IMPACT OF COUNSELING PROFESSIONALS ON MARRIAGE.
LCCN 2013035604
  ISBN 070061947X   **Library PO#** AP-SLIPS

		List	29.95	USD
9395 NATIONAL UNIVERSITY LIBRAR		Disc	14.0%	
App. Date 4/09/14 SOC-SCI 8214-09		**Net**	25.76	USD

SUBJ: MARRIAGE COUNSELING--U.S.--HIST.--20TH
CENT.

CLASS HQ10.5   DEWEY# 616.891562   LEVEL GEN-AC

YBP Library Services

DOWBIGGIN, IAN ROBERT, 1952-

SEARCH FOR DOMESTIC BLISS: MARRIAGE AND FAMILY
COUNSELING IN 20TH CENTURY AMERICA.
                                    Cloth   250 P.
LAWRENCE: UNIV PR OF KANSAS, 2014

AUTH: UNIV. OF PRINCE EDWARD ISLAND. TRACES THE
IMPACT OF COUNSELING PROFESSIONALS ON MARRIAGE.
  LCCN 2013035604
  ISBN 070061947X   **Library PO#** AP-SLIPS

		List	29.95	USD
9395 NATIONAL UNIVERSITY LIBRAR		Disc	14.0%	
App. Date 4/09/14 SOC-SCI 8214-09		**Net**	25.76	USD

SUBJ: MARRIAGE COUNSELING--U.S.--HIST.--20TH
CENT.

CLASS HQ10.5   DEWEY# 616.891562   LEVEL GEN-AC

in 1932, was based on 1,200 detailed sexual histories and was the first to closely examine the role of sex in marital relations.[20] To compile this information, Dickinson had used his considerable skills to win the trust of patients, particularly women; persuade them to answer deeply personal questions about their sex lives; and convince them to submit to intimate clinical procedures that would later be condemned as unethical. By the 1940s, Dickinson—known as "Bobby" or "Dr. Bobby" to his friends, and recognizable by his neatly trimmed Vandyke beard—was legendary as a sex educator who pioneered the use of rubber and plastic pelvic models for medical teaching purposes.[21] He was also renowned for his "straight talk" about sex.[22] His studies of sexuality led to his close collaboration with Indiana University zoologist Alfred Kinsey, author of the best selling *Sexual Behavior in the Human Male* (1948) and *Sexual Behavior in the Human Female* (1953). Dickinson introduced Kinsey to "Mr. X," the polymorphously erotic man on whom Kinsey based many of his theories about human sexuality.[23]

Yet Dickinson's interests extended well beyond sex education and research. From 1946 to his death in 1950, Dickinson was president of the Euthanasia Society of America, a Manhattan-based organization that advocated the legalization of voluntary mercy killing. He was a member of the American Eugenics Society and urged the public to "pursue a sound eugenic program" to counter what he perceived as an overall decline in national intelligence due to uncontrolled breeding.[24] His advocacy of eugenics accounts for his membership in the nonprofit group known as Birthright Inc., founded in 1943 and dedicated to popularizing vasectomy for men and tubal ligation for women as birth control methods to serve eugenic purposes. In 1950 (shortly before his death) Birthright's headquarters moved from Princeton, New Jersey, to Dickinson's own Manhattan studio at the New York Academy of Medicine.

Throughout the 1940s there was a noticeable and telling overlap in membership between AAMC and Birthright (which changed its name to the Human Betterment Association of America in 1950 and the Association for Voluntary Sterilization in 1964 and is now a nongovernmental organization known as Engender Health). Initially, Birthright advocated the enactment of state sterilization laws. However, as public and official support for involuntary sterilization faded rapidly in the 1940s, Birthright shifted its efforts to making obstetricians "more sterilization minded," in the hope that they would convince their poor female patients to undergo tubal ligations, particularly right after giving birth. In 1948 a spokesman for Birthright declared that too many "half wits and morons" were being born in the United States and that the best way to cut their birthrate was to "educate the doctors," who could then subtly pressure their patients, especially low-income and minority women with large families, to have surgery to end their fertility. Birthright hoped to achieve negative eugenic ends—reduced birthrates for the underprivileged classes—through this type of "voluntary" sterilization.[25]

Dickinson was certainly not the only marriage counselor who belonged to Birthright, another reminder of the field's indebtedness to illiberal, eugenic thinking. Laidlaw was Birthright's president from 1953 to 1964. Mudd, Abraham Stone, Lovett Dewees, and Washington, D.C., psychiatrist Walter R. Stokes were other prominent members of the group. Paul Popenoe also joined Birthright in its formative years. The American Civil Liberties Union's Harriet Pilpel was legal counsel for Birthright and for the Planned Parenthood Federation of America, as well as the AAMC's lawyer (and she worked for the law firm that handled Kinsey's legal affairs). Pilpel's law office on Park Avenue in Manhattan served as the AAMC's address in its early years. Social worker Frances Dow was AAMC secretary until 1951, when Birthright (by then renamed the Human Betterment Association of America) hired her as a field administrative assistant to survey physicians, community agencies, social workers, and laypeople to learn what would convince them to endorse voluntary sterilization.[26]

Millionaire Clarence Gamble (1894–1966), heir to the Ivory soap fortune, was Birthright's key benefactor in the 1940s. Gamble had befriended the Mudds back in the 1920s, and together they played a pivotal role in founding the Pennsylvania Birth Control Federation, one of the most activist groups of its kind in the nation. Like the Mudds, Gamble was a fervent advocate of eugenics, and in 1935 he attended the International Congress for Population Science in Berlin. Gamble's German hosts appreciated the warm praise he heaped on Adolf Hitler, whose government had passed a law in 1933 permitting the involuntary sterilization of people with a range of physical and mental disabilities.

Gamble devoted much of his fortune, time, and energy to searching for a foolproof contraceptive device for women, but it was clear that his focus was on those women who lacked the desire, education, privacy, or sanitary conditions to practice consistently reliable birth control. In Emily Mudd's words, "Dr. Gamble was deeply committed to explore the relationship between what was then called the differential birth rate— the fact that the less privileged group in the United States was outnumbering in births the more privileged group."[27] To Gamble and Birthright, sterilization was the best method for those "tired out mothers from low-income groups" who lacked the "motivation" to use contraception.[28] In 1957, disappointed by the obstacles he encountered in trying to put his eugenic ideas into practice, Gamble founded the Pathfinder Fund, a Boston-based nonprofit organization dedicated to funding population control programs in Asia, Africa, and Latin America.[29] Mudd served on Pathfinder's board until 1974, and in the early 1960s she secured a desperately needed three-year Pathfinder grant for the AAMC totaling $24,000. Mudd assured Gamble that, for those people trained to do marriage counseling in the United States, "the whole question of family planning [inevitably] came in." As Mudd recounted, "The marriage counsellor had the opportunity of working with the client so that they could understand their prerogatives in connection with family planning."[30] In other words, before he would donate funds to the AAMC, Gamble had to be convinced that marriage counseling would serve the contraceptive purposes that he believed were vital to constructing a eugenic nation. Mudd's powers of persuasion did the trick.

Next to Dickinson and Mudd in stature among AAMC pioneers was Robert Laidlaw (1901–1978). Born in Englewood, New Jersey, Laidlaw never let polio, which left him confined to a wheelchair, constrain his activities. His eclectic interests included clinical psychiatry, family planning, population control, marriage counseling, parapsychology, eugenics, abortion, sex education, and psychedelic drug research. Chief of psychiatry at New York City's Roosevelt Hospital and consultant in psychiatry at Union Theological Seminary, Laidlaw urged "a much more realistic program of sex education," the end of guilt over masturbation, the acceptance of premarital sex, and "a far more tolerant and understanding, and cooperative attitude on the part of society towards the homosexual."[31] Laidlaw worked with Dr. Harry Benjamin, the so-called father of transsexualism, who coined the term to refer to people who wished to live and be accepted as members of the opposite sex. When a New Jersey music teacher changed his gender and was suspended in 1974, the case went to the New Jersey Supreme Court, where Laidlaw testified that the teacher's sex change would have "no significant effect" on her students (the court refused to reinstate the teacher but awarded her back pay).[32] In his own words, Laidlaw was a tireless supporter of "a freer, more permissive attitude" on the part of society as a whole toward a wide range of sexual behaviors that were once considered perversions.[33]

Laidlaw's stature within marriage counseling, like Mudd's and Dickinson's, highlights the strong historical links between Alfred Kinsey and the field, a topic that Kinsey scholars have tended to overlook.[34] Indeed, Kinsey viewed marriage counseling as an indispensable ally in his efforts to alter the accepted definitions of sexual deviance. Robert Dickinson was instrumental in introducing Kinsey to the AAMC membership, and Robert Laidlaw, Lester Dearborn, and Emily Mudd became close friends with Kinsey in the 1940s. Other active "Kinseyite" AAMC members were Walter Stokes, a 1924 Olympic gold medalist and birth control crusader, and psychotherapist Robert A. Harper of the Merrill-Palmer School in Detroit, Michigan (Harper served as AAMC president from 1960 to 1962). Though notoriously wary of any formal association with official organizations, Kinsey was an AAMC affiliate member and attended at least a dozen of the group's meetings, often as a keynote speaker. While he kept other groups, such as the Planned Parenthood Federation of America, at arm's length, he seemed to have no such reservations about the AAMC, likely because marriage counseling had a comparatively uncontroversial reputation as a nonpartisan branch of public health. After his death, the AAMC donated a $1,000 memorial gift to the Kinsey Institute at Indiana University. In the words of a Kinsey coworker, there had always been "special emotional ties" between Kinsey and the AAMC.[35]

Born in Hoboken, New Jersey, in 1894, Kinsey was the second most polarizing figure in 1950s America (after Senator Joseph McCarthy). Since high school, Kinsey had imagined himself as "the second Darwin," but in the late 1930s he was at a crossroads in his life. He was an Indiana

University scientist with a modest reputation as an expert on the gall wasp (a tiny insect found in oak trees) when, on June 28, 1938, he launched a noncredit "marriage course" at the university. At the time, approximately 250 colleges and universities were offering sex education courses, most of them under the guise of "hygiene" or "marriage education" courses. In 1923 Vassar College had introduced the first "preparation for parenthood" course at the college level.[36] Content varied greatly from one college course to another, but one unifying theme was an emphasis on the findings of scientific research. According to the University of Chicago's Ernest Burgess, even clergymen looked to science for the answers to sensitive moral questions regarding sexual behavior. Another common theme was the practical nature of these courses: students repeatedly demanded that their instructors "get down to 'brass tacks,'" that is, teach useful information. Michigan State's Judson Landis noted in 1948 that "if the students do not feel that their needs are being met, they will show little interest in the course."[37] One college girl wanted "more discussion on the ways to get a husband . . . in other words, how to attract men so they will want to marry you," and *Mademoiselle* magazine recommended in 1955 that personal appearance courses be offered for credit in U.S. universities.[38] A handful of marriage educators, such as Vassar's Joseph Folsom, resisted the urge to simply teach conventional values. To critics, these courses were short on candor and long on moral platitudes. Mary Steichen Calderone, Vassar class of 1925 and the so-called grandmother of sex education, enrolled in her college's "hygiene" course and recalled that the physician teaching the class told them, "Now, girls, keep your affections wrapped in cotton wool until Mr. Right comes along."[39]

Initially, 98 undergraduates (70 women and 28 men) enrolled in Kinsey's course, and when it was offered again in the fall of 1938, 200 students (110 women) signed up, "an unprecedented expression of student interest," according to Kinsey's biographer James Jones.[40] Kinsey's marriage course changed not just his life and his career; it set in motion a series of events that shaped the history of twentieth-century America.

What the students were exposed to in Kinsey's marriage course was anything but impartial, disinterested information. Kinsey's studies of the gall wasp had convinced him of "individual variation" in everything from taxonomy to sex, so he taught his students to tolerate a wide range of sexual needs and behaviors—in the process, challenging concepts of moral right and wrong that had been ingrained since childhood. The main part of his instruction was an exceedingly graphic description of birth control methods and sexual techniques, which he believed was necessary if young marrieds wanted mutually satisfying sex lives. The course was Kinsey's opportunity to "preach . . . a new sexual morality, with respect for diversity at its center and himself as its prophet," in Jones's words. As one of Kinsey's friends teased him upon learning of the marriage course, "By golly, I believe they will be having copulating schools at Indiana before long."[41]

Kinsey resigned from teaching the marriage course in 1940, due to a backlash over its content from the public, other Indiana University faculty, and the local medical community. But in the meantime, he had decided to devote his career to the formal study of human sexuality, convinced that there was a huge difference between accepted theories about sexual behavior and actual practices. In his studies he was aided by a team of capable, highly motivated research assistants, all of whom were white, male, heterosexual Protestants of Anglo-Saxon descent: Clyde Martin, a onetime student of Kinsey's; Paul Gebhard, who became director of Indiana University's Kinsey Institute for Sex Research (opened in 1947) upon Kinsey's death in 1956; and Wardell Pomeroy (1913–2001), a prison psychologist who joined Kinsey's team in 1941, left the Kinsey Institute in 1963 for private practice in sex therapy, and played a prominent role in the marriage and family counseling movement in the 1960s and 1970s.

Crucial to the research conducted by Kinsey and his team of investigators were interviews from which they compiled individuals' sexual histories stretching back to childhood. In private meetings, Kinsey had begun gathering sexual histories from his students in the marriage course, refining his interviewing techniques over time. The data gathered from these interviews were the basis for Kinsey's two major publications, *Sexual Behavior in the Human Male* and *Sexual Behavior in the Human Female*. His findings, documented in these two volumes, shocked countless Americans. Kinsey claimed that there was a tremendous gulf between the nation's moral standards of sexual behavior and actual sexual practices inside and outside America's bedrooms. For instance, he reported that 50 percent of women and 67 to 98 percent of men were not virgins when they married, and most had no regrets. His studies also found that more than a third of men and more than a quarter of women had had at least one homosexual experience between adolescence and old age. To his admirers, Kinsey's studies were frontal assaults on the hypocrisy surrounding sex in America.

When it came to finding people who were willing to share their sexual histories with Kinsey, Emily Mudd proved invaluable. In 1944–1945 Kinsey made three visits to the Philadelphia area, where Mudd arranged approximately 1,200 interviews, largely with college students at Temple, Swarthmore, Bryn Mawr, Haverford, and the College for Women at the University of Pennsylvania, as well as Philadelphia public school children, parents and teachers from Germantown schools, and children from the Salvation Army Home for Children.[42] Kinsey gratefully told Mudd in 1944 that "in all of the six years of research, no one has lined up more histories for us than you, unless it be Dr. Dickinson."[43] In 1974 Mudd admitted that she had been "devoted" to Kinsey: "I considered myself extremely fortunate to have had the opportunity of being associated with him and his work, and have him associate himself with the work we were doing in Philadelphia."[44] Kinsey's trust in Mudd was reflected in the fact that he invited both her and Laidlaw to serve as editorial consultants on *Sexual Behavior in the Human Female*.

Mudd first met Kinsey in late 1943. Dickinson had pleaded with her to attend a meeting at the New York Academy of Medicine on December 18. "A Dr. Alfred Kinsey will present his pioneering work to a small group. We want a woman present. You must come," Dickinson implored. Even though it meant missing her first child's birthday, Mudd relented. At the meeting she found herself in a small room with only ten people. Seated next to her was Allan Gregg, director of the Division of Medical Sciences at the Rockefeller Foundation since 1931. (Three years later, Gregg would convince the Rockefeller trustees to approve a $120,000 three-year grant for Kinsey—funding that would continue until 1954.) Kinsey struck Mudd as "very tense and earnest" as he spoke to the audience about his data on the sex lives of the men he had interviewed. "We all got fascinated," Mudd remembered, "not only with the material—but with the potential of what this man was doing and proposing to do. We sat spellbound and then asked many questions." By this point, Dickinson had told Kinsey about Mudd's MCP, and when the meeting broke up, Kinsey asked Mudd to join him for lunch the next day at New York City's Stouffer's restaurant. There, they talked intently about Mudd's clinic and how its work fit in with Kinsey's own research. Both Mudd and Kinsey were so interested in their conversation that they got up, left the restaurant, and hailed a taxi, only to discover sheepishly (in Kinsey's words), "My God, Emily, we walked out of there and didn't pay our bill." The bill was subsequently paid, but the oversight revealed that, to their mutual delight, Kinsey and Mudd had much in common when it came to their theories about the overall role of sex in marriage.

In 1944 Kinsey spelled out what he and Mudd had in common. To Kinsey, they were each working in their respective fields to advance the same cause, and marriage counseling was the most powerful means for shaping the "motivating patterns which are deep-seated in social custom, and ingrained in the individual's own experience."[45] As he informed Mudd:

> This work we are doing on Human Sex Behavior, of both married and unmarried people, the tremendous development in the field of contraception and sterility, and all of the work which Sociologists have done on problems of marital adjustment, are in the last analysis made available to people through such things as marriage manuals, Marriage Counsels, and the abundance of less formal advice which is being given from a variety of quarters. There will undoubtedly be a great development of Marriage Counseling within the next few years. All of this development may very well miss the mark unless someone takes time to evaluate the extent to which this advice actually affects the lives of the individuals who are advised. *This is your job.* You are in a better position than any of us to test this particular aspect of the thing. Your experience in your own Counsel, and your splendid contacts through the Philadelphia area, should make it possible to do this better than anyone else I know now. . . . As your program is now set up, I anticipate a most profitable outcome.[46]

At the December 28, 1949, meeting of the AAMC, Kinsey spoke about the need to revise the laws on sex offenders—including the laws against sodomy—and urged the "marriage counselors and sex educators" in his audience to help "bring legislation into line with known facts."[47] For her part, Mudd basically agreed that she and her colleagues in the AAMC could—and should—help Kinsey spread his ideas. As she modestly told Kinsey in 1947: "As the weeks pass and I am in contact with various kinds of professional people I believe that I may be of some small help in explaining the broad scope and sound scientific basis of your study to those who know less than I do about it. I expect you know that ever since you and your staff first came to Philadelphia we have held ourselves in readiness to be of any assistance possible in connection with the promotion of your work."[48]

Mudd was one of the few people who were not overawed by Kinsey, which impressed him.[49] Upon her return to Philadelphia after the 1943 meeting in New York, she arranged for Kinsey to visit her clinic in March 1944 and examine its record-keeping methods, especially the MCP's recording of clients' sexual histories. During the same visit, Kinsey spoke at Philadelphia's Wistar Institute to a small group of medical people from the MCP's board and the city's five medical schools. Each attendee had been personally invited by Mudd, who, like Kinsey, wanted to keep the press away for fear of adverse publicity. Just as Kinsey began speaking, however, Mudd's friend Lawrence Saunders, president of the W. B. Saunders Company of Philadelphia and a nonmedical member of the MCP's board, arrived dramatically, announced to the audience that "Emily Mudd told me about this meeting," and promptly sat down in the front row. Saunders, a publisher of scientific textbooks, eventually published Kinsey's first major book on sex, another example of Mudd's pivotal contributions to Kinsey's career.

Before long, Mudd and Kinsey were referring to each other by their first names and visiting each other's homes. Mudd addressed Kinsey as "Prok" (short for Professor Kinsey), the affectionate nickname given to him by his wife, Clara, and his students. On a 1944 visit to Philadelphia, Kinsey, Wardell Pomeroy, and Clyde Martin spent Easter Sunday at the Mudds' home, where Kinsey "cornered" Emily Mudd and each member of her family for a sexual history. Kinsey sat on the floor with Mudd's three-year-old son, "who was running around with his toys. Dr. Kinsey drew pictures for him to see whether he knew the difference between a male and female," Mudd remembered.[50] She seemed unaware of the sexual antics occurring behind the scenes in Kinsey's own home, including his homoerotic activities, the filming of group sex, and the wife swapping among Kinsey's team, including his own wife Clara. After a 1947 visit to Kinsey's home, Mudd wrote, "I enjoyed in particular meeting Mrs. Kinsey and the other fine and attractive wives of the staff as well as the children." Mudd, sounding relieved, told Kinsey that the perception that Kinsey's home life was conventional "will help in interpreting to those who ask many questions. . . . I expect you will know what I mean by this remark."[51] Like virtually everyone outside the Kinsey Institute, Mudd remained ignorant of the disparities between Kinsey's personal life behind closed doors and his public image as a typical husband and father.

Mudd's influence, like Dickinson's, fostered close relations between Kinsey and the marriage counseling field in the late 1940s. Mudd visited the Kinsey Institute in Bloomington three times. In 1948 the NCFR's subcommittee on marriage and family counseling, chaired by Mudd, announced that Kinsey and his coworkers planned to write a volume on sexual adjustment in marriage. The same year, Kinsey joined Dickinson and the NCFR's Evelyn Millis Duvall on the AAMC's Library Committee, entrusted with updating Dickinson's list of suitable books on marriage, sex, and the family. On January 7, 1949, the AAMC held a special meeting, limited to invited members, to discuss the "clinical implications of the Kinsey Report for Marriage Counseling." Laidlaw requested that each member "come prepared to discuss briefly the influence of the Kinsey Report on his own thinking and its consequent influence on his counseling techniques."[52] Mudd arranged to have Kinsey speak in Philadelphia at the University of Pennsylvania in 1952 and at the AAMC's annual dinner meeting in 1953. Each year until his death in 1956, Kinsey lectured to Mudd's students in her course "Family Attitudes, Sexual Behavior and Marriage Counseling" at the University of Pennsylvania Medical School.[53]

In 1951 Kinsey asked Mudd to be "consulting editor" for his book on female sexuality. Even friends such as Abraham Stone noted that Kinsey's first volume on male sexuality had "hardly mentioned" the word "love," which did not even appear in the index.[54] Kinsey, mindful of this criticism, told Mudd, "We are particularly interested in having women go over [the volume on female sexuality]," and he thought Mudd was

Left to right: Robert Laidlaw, Alfred Kinsey, and Emily Mudd, ca. 1952. (Courtesy of the Arthur and Elizabeth Schlesinger Library on the History of Women in America, Radcliffe Institute for Advanced Study, Harvard University)

particularly well suited to do so, "with as much professional experience as you have had in dealing with other women."[55] Mudd had misgivings about some of Kinsey's terminology in the draft version of his 1953 volume, but on the whole, she warmly endorsed Kinsey's findings and his theoretical approach.[56]

Mudd's devotion to Kinsey's agenda was evident in her 1955 NIMH grant application to study "the impact of frigidity and impotence upon sexual behavior and attitudes of marriage partners." An earlier grant to study "marital adjustment" as an "aid to good mental health," funded by the U.S. Public Health Service, had provided the MCP with "a great deal of data" on sexual attitudes and behavior in individuals and married partners. In the follow-up NIMH project, Mudd and her University of Pennsylvania colleague Kenneth Appel wanted to analyze these data with a view to determining whether counseling that focused on "sexual attitudes" could shape "sexual functioning" within marriage. As Mudd admitted, the purpose of the NIMH study was to "cross-validate some of Kinsey's findings." As it turned out, Mudd's application was unsuccessful, likely due to the controversial nature of her subject matter, but it confirmed her deep commitment to Kinsey's research and its conclusions.[57]

Meanwhile, under the strain of his intense work schedule, Kinsey's health was already deteriorating when he became the target of an investigation by the House of Representatives in 1953. A special committee, chaired by B. Carroll Reece (R-Tenn.), had been created to investigate tax-exempt foundations. At the same time, the Senate was holding hearings, dominated by Senator Joseph McCarthy (R-Wis.), over what Reece called "the furtherance of socialism in the United States." The Reece committee was largely a response to mounting accusations in the press that Kinsey's two books "paved the way for people to believe in communism and to act like communists," as the Indianapolis Roman Catholic Archdiocese charged in 1954. Most of Kinsey's critics stopped short of accusing Kinsey of being a communist himself, but they tended to argue that his publications aided and abetted communists in destroying the moral foundations of marriage and the family. Citing Kinsey's book on the sexual behavior of women, Louis B. Heller (D-N.Y.) charged Kinsey with "hurling the insult of the century against our mothers, wives, daughters, and sisters."[58] Indeed, Kinsey's volume on female sexuality unleashed a heated reaction, notably from clergymen. For instance, evangelist Billy Graham described Kinsey's claim of high rates of female marital infidelity as "an indictment against American womanhood." Kinsey gave as good as he received: his second volume "seiz[ed] every opportunity to blame and ridicule traditionalist religion for its sexual prudery," in the words of historian R. Marie Griffith.[59] Kinsey was never shy about drawing battle lines between religion and science.

Kinsey was also reeling from accusations that his samples were not representative of the population.[60] In Los Angeles, Paul Popenoe claimed that Kinsey "did not get a fair picture of the female sex. He got a great collection of sophisticated, aggressive, exhibitionistic women who were eager to tell their stories. Apparently not more than 10% of his total was made up of happily married wives."[61] Psychoanalysts such as Lawrence Kubie questioned the reliability of interviewees' childhood memories about sexuality. Literary critic Lionel Trilling objected that Kinsey's willingness to equate the frequency of sexual acts with overall satisfaction was simply unwarranted. In *Time* magazine, liberal theologian Reinhold Niebuhr admitted that some clergymen's attitudes about sex were uninformed, but he added that "Christian teaching comes much closer than Dr. Kinsey to a true understanding of the place of sex in human relations."[62]

The Rockefeller Foundation was caught in the line of fire as Kinsey, its most controversial grantee, came under attack. By probing its tax-exempt status, the Reece committee likely hoped to intimidate the foundation, but by 1954, it needed little convincing. In 1952 the politically cautious Dean Rusk had replaced Allan Gregg as the Rockefeller Foundation's president, and two years later, he and the trustees had run out of patience with Kinsey. Neither Kinsey nor anyone from the Rockefeller Foundation was called to testify before the Reece committee, but with scant sympathy for Kinsey among trustees, the fate of his funding was sealed. Kinsey never recovered from the blow of losing his financial support, and he died two years later.

Emily Mudd was typical of the highly educated individuals who steadfastly supported Kinsey up to his death in 1956. Among Kinsey's defenders were sexologists, physicians, sociologists, psychologists, educators, journalists, lawyers, clergymen, and marriage counselors, many of whom were progressives united in the conviction that fast-moving twentieth-century events dictated the acceptance of a new set of scientifically grounded values distinct from the moral absolutes that had guided reformers in earlier eras.[63] Marriage counselors who defended Kinsey tended to oppose what Mudd called "the prudery and misinformation with which our culture has for generations surrounded sex," thereby "prevent[ing] an otherwise well-related couple from achieving sexual fulfillment."[64] Abraham Stone celebrated Kinsey for "tearing away most of the cobwebs of sex taboos and inhibitions" and "breaking up the hard surface of puritanism."[65] Some counselors, such as Paul Popenoe, rejected the contents of Kinsey's best-selling books, especially the one on female sexuality. Yet on the topic of Alfred Kinsey, Popenoe was out of step with the AAMC, as he was on so many other subjects.

To Robert Laidlaw, Kinsey's findings that children experienced sexual pleasure were groundbreaking and, as he told medical students at the

University of Pennsylvania in 1953, "a final blow to the old traditional concepts of childhood as being the age of innocence, where there is no conscious awareness of or preoccupation with things of a sexual nature."[66] Mudd was equally effusive about the implications of Kinsey's research: his volume on female sexuality was "a magnificent piece of basic research. . . . It and its companion volume give us the fullest set of facts we have at the moment on the subject of human sexual behaviour. . . . [T]he new Kinsey Report should bring happiness to far more people than it may hurt, and it could even change important aspects of our culture."[67] Kinsey showed the tremendous "complexity" surrounding the issues of premarital sex and marriage, Mudd wrote; "there are no simple answers [about sex] . . . I personally do not believe that any hard and fast recommendation of what is a 'healthy' attitude can or should be super-imposed on any individual against their own judgement and inclination." Yet her apparent nonjudgmentalism and her rejection of "impersonal criteria" to guide human behavior were belied by her conclusion—shared with Kinsey—that the customary definition of "normal" sexuality was outdated and positively injurious.[68]

Abraham Stone agreed with Mudd that the "outstanding research of Kinsey and his co-workers will be of inestimable value to the field of marriage counseling." Kinsey's studies of "the wide range of sex frequencies" made marriage counselors "more tolerant and understanding of the varieties in the patterns of human sex behavior." Stone also echoed Mudd's viewpoint that "information [about sexuality] alone, valuable as it is in adult education, is not sufficient in itself to change the sex behavior of an individual to any marked extent. It must be reinforced by the formation, or rather the re-formation, of attitudes, and it is to this purpose that the counselor must apply himself." This type of attitudinal modification was another example of therapism's stress on emotions over straightforward information as the key to happiness. In Stone's view, this adjustment had to start in the client's preschool years if a counselor hoped to change the sexual behavior of an adult client. According to Stone, counseling was only one part of a larger enterprise begun by Kinsey and dedicated to changing Americans' emotional makeup when it came to marriage and family life. Stone and his AAMC colleagues believed that, after Kinsey, marriage counseling would never be the same.[69]

Thus, Mudd, Laidlaw, and Dickinson, like Kinsey himself, were not just devout believers in scientific research as the best way to expand knowledge about human nature; they thought Kinsey's studies had a powerful social purpose. As one of Kinsey's coworkers claimed, his findings "might help people, help in counselling, in keeping people together and making adjustments."[70] Indeed, Kinsey had firm views on marriage counseling, stating in his volume on male sexuality that most marital advice amounted to counselors simply imposing their own social class–bound "intellectual eroticisms" on "lower-level clients."[71] Kinsey's comments might be read as a protest against class inequalities in American society, but it is more likely that he was reacting negatively to the standard marriage advice literature that existed back in the 1930s. He was merely urging all counselors to respect the principle of individual variation in sex, about which he felt very strongly. His views were similar to those of Mudd and her AAMC associates, who also insisted that there was no one-size-fits-all model of "healthy" sexuality and that counseling had to be tailored to the individual client, another core concept of therapism.

Long after his death, Mudd marveled that Kinsey had collected such "a great deal of material" on marriage "and the relationship field," and she revealed that she had hoped the two of them would write "a book on marital adjustment."[72] In fact, Kinsey withheld the statistics on pregnancy, contraception, and abortion gathered in his interviews because the AAMC had convinced him to do a separate book on those issues. According to historian Regina Markell Morantz, Kinsey's "special relationship" with the AAMC did not end with his death.[73] The so-called third Kinsey report, titled *Pregnancy, Birth and Abortion*, appeared in 1958 to much less acclaim than that accorded the previous two volumes. The 1958 book not only underlined Kinsey's longtime interest in contraception but also reflected the close ties between the AAMC and his institute. In 1959 Pomeroy and Gebhard hosted the AAMC at the Kinsey Institute. Pomeroy, who later went into private practice and served as AAMC president, represented a bridge between his Indiana University mentor and the field of marriage counseling.

The close connections among Kinsey, Mudd, Laidlaw, Dickinson, and other AAMC luminaries constitute the missing piece in the legend of Kinsey as a crusader for sexual permissiveness. The AAMC's efforts to put Kinsey's social engineering agenda into practice spoke volumes about the organization's elitist, secretive, paternalistic, and dogmatic orientation at a critical time in the fledgling field's development. In its later incarnations, the AAMC would continue to bear the Kinsey imprint as it struggled to reform married and family life in twentieth-century America.

lfred Kinsey's fate at the hands of the Reece committee was a reminder that in postwar America, the conflict over domestic communism was often intertwined with debates over marriage, the family, and the status of women. As the standoff between the USSR and the United States became increasingly bitter after 1947, a cultural cold war raged between sympathizers with the Soviet Union and resolute anticommunists who objected to any attempt to introduce collectivist policies that clashed with American values. Anticommunist cultural cold warriors were not always found on the right wing of the political spectrum; some, like the editors of the *New Leader*, were socialists who denounced "the Communist assault on the empire of the mind."[1] To opinion makers of the time, the cultural cold war was nothing less than a struggle for the hearts and minds of Americans. At stake for activists on both sides of the cultural cold war was the future of the nation's institutions—notably, marriage and the family.

Besides her many vital contributions to the marriage counseling field, Emily Mudd played an important role in the cultural cold war of the late 1940s. The event that best highlights her involvement in this struggle is her trip to Moscow on August 15, 1946, for a monthlong fact-finding mission designed to acquaint Mudd, her husband Stuart, and physician Robert Leslie, the business manager of the American-Soviet Medical Society (ASMS), with Soviet science and medicine. The Mudds were the last Americans to visit Stalin's USSR during the brief period when the Soviet Union and the United States were engaged in the friendly sharing of biomedical knowledge. The trip soon plunged the Mudds into the heated arena of early Cold War politics and scuttled Emily Mudd's efforts to convince U.S. policy makers to copy Soviet policies toward women, children, the family, and health care in general. Mudd, like

Kinsey and her colleagues in the AAMC, looked to the government as an instrument of change in the field of marriage and family living. In the process, the family, like physiology, psychiatry, and psychology, became a "Cold War battlefield."[2]

In their eagerness to reform American policies governing marriage and the family, it is clear that some individuals in the AAMC were willing to borrow blueprints from communist Russia. This penchant to adopt Soviet policies mirrored Emily Mudd's "determin[ation] to find in the Soviet Union what [she] thought was lacking in America," in the words of historian John Hutchinson.[3] In other words, Mudd saw the future of marriage and the family in the Soviet Union, and to her, it worked. She was a good example of what historian Kate Weigand has called "activist" American women who, though not necessarily members of the Communist Party of the United States of America (CPUSA), belonged to a "large progressive movement" between 1946 and 1956 that was centered on the party and struggled to change American attitudes and policies toward marriage, motherhood, and women's work. Their views about Soviet women were colored mainly by their own politicized interpretations of the status of U.S. women.[4]

When Emily Mudd boarded a Swedish airplane at New York City's La Guardia airport in 1946, she was embarking on a trip that would take her to numerous Russian schools, libraries, hospitals, orphanages, kindergartens, and day-care centers. She would meet dozens of Russian scientific and medical dignitaries in Moscow, Leningrad, and Georgia. She and her ASMS colleagues dubbed their trip the "Medical Mission to Moscow," a clear allusion to both *Mission to Moscow* (1941), a pro-Soviet best-selling book by former U.S. ambassador to the Soviet Union Joseph Davies, and the 1944 visit of U.S. scientists A. Baird Hastings and Michael B. Shimkin, called the "Medical Research Mission to the Soviet Union."[5]

Once the Mudds returned to the United States, they, like Ambassador Davies, sought to persuade audiences that the Soviet experiment deserved Americans' full sympathy. However, just as they arrived back on U.S. soil the Cold War began to unfold, and they soon became targets of anticommunist sentiment. Threatened with the loss of funding for their research projects, the Mudds resigned from the National Council of American-Soviet Friendship (NCASF), the parent organization of the ASMS, and they publicly denied ever being communists or participating in "subversive activities."[6] The ASMS itself, plagued by an abrupt drop in membership, folded in 1949, closing a dramatic chapter in the Mudds' lives and marking the beginning of a lengthy interruption in U.S.-Soviet collaboration in biomedical science. This chapter from Cold War history demonstrates how swiftly events can mobilize public and official opinion and hence how those who wish to influence policy making sometimes misjudge the temper of their times.

To date, scholars have paid little attention to these dramatic events in the history of Cold War politics. One historian has written that the ASMS in general and the 1946 Medical Mission to Moscow in particular were casualties of both rising anticommunism in the United States in the late 1940s and policy decisions by the Soviet Politburo regarding cooperation between U.S. and Russian medical scientists. As far as it goes, this is a reasonably accurate interpretation of the transition from collaboration in biomedical research to confrontation between the world's two superpowers in the post–World War II era.[7]

However, Emily Mudd's retrospective version of her brush with Cold War politics tends to stress her victimization, political naivete, and nonpartisan commitment to the mutual exchange of value-free medical information and the peaceful coexistence of nations in the dawning nuclear age.[8] Mudd may well have believed that by pooling their knowledge, U.S. and Soviet scientists could help build a better world. However, when it came to the Soviet Union, Emily Mudd was far from disinterested. She capitalized on the good press the Soviet regime enjoyed between 1941 and the onset of the Cold War in 1947 and sought to persuade Americans to follow Soviet policies. Mudd was inclined to agree with Henry Sigerist—Johns Hopkins University physician, ASMS cofounder, historian of medicine, and the most eminent apologist for Soviet medicine in the 1930s and 1940s—who argued that the West should copy the Soviet health care policy. As Sigerist put it in 1937, "socialism works in the medical field too."[9] Although the Mudds did not share Sigerist's socialist political views, the evidence strongly suggests that both before and after their trip to Russia, Emily believed that women in the Soviet Union were far more liberated than they were in the United States.[10]

Emily Mudd's road to Moscow began with the formative influence of her suffragist mother, but her personal experiences as a mother, laboratory assistant to her husband, and community activist further politicized her. As she recalled later in life, after the birth of her first child, she had to balance work and family:

> [I] experienced personally the question of nursing babies and working wives. . . . We had not worked this out in this country and I think never have, because a mother who wants to nurse her baby either has to give up her job or give up nursing the baby. So I gave up working for about three or four months and my husband got into quite a state at this because he needed the help so finally I said . . . well, I'd try going back to work and having somebody give the baby a bottle. The minute I went back to work I lost my milk.

She had to make private arrangements for her children's day care, and she was "always . . . in conflict as to what might be happening to them" while she was working. Thus, the issue of day care was highly personal for Emily Mudd, and when she visited communist Russia in 1946, she marveled at "how cleverly [the Soviets] worked that out."[11]

By the 1940s, then, Mudd had come to believe that U.S. policies toward motherhood, marriage, and women's work had to change substantially and that the profession of marriage counseling could be a vehicle for such Soviet-style reform. The historical background to Mudd's pro-Sovietism dated to the interwar period, when there was growing interest in improved relations between the Soviet Union and the United States. In the years after the 1917 Bolshevik Revolution, communist Russia enjoyed scant sympathy in America outside of radical political circles. However, beginning in 1933, when Washington extended diplomatic recognition to the Soviet Union, U.S. attitudes toward Soviet Russia grew more positive, especially as the international situation darkened due to the escalating threat of war in Europe. Thousands of scholars, scientists, intellectuals, educators, and artists traveled to the Soviet Union as guests of the All-Union Society for Cultural Relations with Foreign Countries (VOKS), founded in 1925. Many visitors liked what they saw in the Soviet Union and were eager to convey to others their belief that the Bolshevik experiment was succeeding.

By contrast, as Joseph Stalin tightened his political grip over the USSR, the Soviets became increasingly suspicious of contact with foreign dignitaries. This trend, predating Stalin's ascension to power in the late 1920s, resulted in the Soviet regime strictly controlling its scientists and exploiting such contacts to achieve propaganda victories on both the international and the domestic fronts. By the time of the signing of the Nazi-Soviet Non-Aggression Pact on August 22, 1939, VOKS was nearly moribund, and the Soviet state had erected formidable barriers against collaboration with foreign scientists.[12]

Relations between the United States and the USSR took an abrupt turn after the Nazi invasion of the Soviet Union on June 22, 1941, and America's entry into World War II the following December. With Soviet Russia locked in a life-and-death battle to defeat Hitler's Germany, Americans shipped enormous amounts of military aid as well as other forms of war relief, including medicine, food, and clothing. By 1943, the government, the press, and Hollywood were extolling the accomplishments of the Soviet people and heralding an age of peaceful coexistence between the two countries. Accounts such as Davies's *Mission to Moscow* praised the courage and determination of the Soviet people but tended to elide the grim reality of life under Stalin's rule.

The climate of official friendship between the United States and the USSR led to the formation of American organizations dedicated to maintaining warm relations with the Soviet Union, such as the National Council of American-Soviet Friendship, which began in 1938 as a small New York City group called the American Council on Soviet Relations. A three-day celebration in November 1942 of the twenty-fifth anniversary of the Bolshevik Revolution marked the launching of the NCASF. National and international dignitaries from all levels of government, as well as prominent clergymen, business leaders, university presidents, and trade union officials, attended the gala event in New York City.[13] Ultimately, the NCASF spawned about thirty local chapters across the country, as well as numerous special committees, including its Committee of Women (which the Mudds later joined). Worldwide, there were as many as sixty similar friendship societies.

The NCASF's stated purpose was to "promote better understanding and strengthen friendly relations between the United States and the Soviet Union as essential to the winning of the war, and the establishment of world-wide democracy and enduring peace." The NCASF leadership declared that the key to promoting U.S.-Soviet cooperation was the "education of the broad masses of the American people about the Soviet Union." Yet the NCASF found it difficult to distinguish between efforts to educate Americans about the Soviet Union and pro-Soviet propaganda intended to alter U.S. foreign policy regarding the course of the war and the postwar diplomatic settlement. Groups such as the America First Committee and the Friends of Democracy accused the NCASF of being the "Voice of Stalin in America." By the late 1940s, many Americans were suspicious of the fact that NCASF's "educational" efforts overwhelmingly denounced American but not Soviet positions.[14] In 1946 the House Un-American Activities Committee (HUAC) launched a formal investigation of the NCASF, and its two principal members were cited for contempt of Congress. In 1947 the NCASF was indicted for failure to register with the Subversive Activities Control Board, and in November 1947 the group was placed on the U.S. attorney general's list of eighty-two subversive organizations that federal employees were prohibited from joining.[15]

Meanwhile, an important event in early NCASF history occurred in 1943 when some group members, including Henry Sigerist, launched the American-Soviet Medical Society. Sigerist was born in Paris in 1891 of Swiss parents and received a medical degree in Zurich in 1917. Between 1932 and 1947 Sigerist taught medical history at Johns Hopkins University. His *Socialized Medicine in the Soviet Union* (1937) was an overwhelmingly positive account of health care in communist Russia, and his 1944 report on health care services in the Canadian province of Saskatchewan served as the basis for the provincial government's decision to provide free hospitalization for all citizens through tax revenues, the first step in North America toward Medicare.[16]

Sigerist, along with ASMS cofounder Robert Leslie and the AAMC's Abraham Stone, was keen to establish a working relationship with Soviet medical agencies and individuals. Sigerist later wrote, "We were at war; Russia was our powerful ally that had gained much experience in war medicine. Even the best of our medical libraries were poorly supplied with Russian medical literature. It was felt, therefore, that a group organized to exchange medical information and make Russian medical literature available to our doctors in English translation would perform a real service to the country."[17]

The ASMS was headquartered in the same New York City building as the American-Russian Institute for Cultural Relations with the Soviet Union, which U.S. Attorney General Thomas C. Clark labeled a "communist front" and a "subversive" organization in 1947.[18] Nonetheless, Sigerist protested that the ASMS had no "official support, either financial or moral," and no "political ties of any kind." Its main activity was publishing its bimonthly journal, the *American Review of Soviet Medicine*, which translated and reviewed the work of Soviet biologists and medical scientists (in 1948, its fifth and final year, it became a quarterly). The ASMS, working with Soviet officialdom, hosted several meetings where visiting Soviet physicians were given the opportunity to present their work. Stuart Mudd's University of Pennsylvania colleague, psychiatrist Kenneth Appel, spoke at the ASMS's annual meeting in Philadelphia in 1945. In denouncing nationalism and lauding international citizenship, Appel was telling the group's pro-Soviet audience what it liked to hear. New York oncologist Jacob Heiman, a CPUSA member, was the ASMS representative at the anniversary celebration of the USSR Academy of Sciences in Moscow in June 1945. One hundred twenty-two delegates from eighteen different countries attended the festivities, and on the final day, their Soviet hosts threw a lavish banquet in the Kremlin, attended by Stalin himself.[19]

Until 1946 there was no clear indication that the U.S. government disapproved of the activities of the ASMS.[20] Because the ASMS tended to focus on the fields of science and medicine and tried to avoid overtly political matters, it enjoyed a relatively uncontroversial reputation. However, once tensions mounted between the two superpowers, many ASMS members lost interest in Soviet medicine. According to Sigerist, this was a case of people trained in "scientific methods of thought" being swayed by political pressure. For example, Morris Fishbein, editor of the *Journal of the American Medical Association*, accused the ASMS of being "propagandists" for Soviet medicine. He asserted, "Competent physicians have found that the Russian standards of scientific achievements are below that of our own."[21] In early 1948 Sigerist vowed that the ASMS would carry on "in spite of all momentary difficulties," but by the end of the year, the ASMS was virtually defunct.[22]

Back in 1945, however, when the future of the ASMS looked much brighter, Stuart Mudd succeeded renowned physiologist Walter Cannon as president. No mere figurehead, Mudd plunged into the day-to-day operations of the ASMS, and toward the end of the 1940s he was still actively trying to revive the organization's fortunes, drawing Sigerist's warm admiration. Stuart Mudd took a leading role in planning the Medical Mission to Moscow and securing the official invitation from the VOKS. His ties to Alfred Newton Richards, dean of the University of Pennsylvania Medical School and later president of the National Academy of Sciences, proved to be crucial. Richards, whom Mudd described as eager to cultivate exchanges between U.S. and Soviet scientists, had also been instrumental in arranging the 1944 visit of Hastings and Shimkin.[23]

To the ASMS, the 1946 trip to Moscow represented an important step in the group's effort to build bridges between the scientific establishments of the two world powers. Yet the Mudds—particularly Emily— were predisposed to like much of what they saw of Soviet life. As she wrote two months before leaving for the Soviet Union: "I hope to establish friendly contacts with Russian women and learn something of the advances made in women's activities in the Soviet Union."[24] Mudd knew of the writings of NCASF stalwart (and later NCFR member) Rose Maurer, who in 1943 had published a book arguing that Soviet women were better off than their U.S. counterparts.[25] What Maurer had to say about Soviet women dovetailed with Mudd's own vision for women's emancipation, and Maurer's views no doubt affected Mudd's expectations of what she would witness in Russia.[26]

The ASMS delegation's visit coincided with the Soviet state's massive effort to rebuild the country in the wake of four years of total war against Hitler's Germany. Millions of Soviet soldiers and citizens had perished in the struggle against Nazism, and huge swaths of the nation's cities and countryside had been devastated. The Soviet leadership was also tightening its political grip on the everyday lives of Russian men, women, and children. The many Russians who had hoped that the Stalinist state would reward them for their enormous wartime sacrifices by easing the political terror of the late 1930s were bitterly disappointed after 1945.

America's atomic monopoly was another reason for the Soviet state to clamp down on the activities of its citizens, especially their dealings with representatives from the Anglo-American world. While frantically trying to develop its own atomic weapons, the USSR was engaged in a propaganda campaign to assert the superiority of Soviet medicine and science on the international stage. When Soviet scientists Nina Klyueva and Grigorii Roskin supposedly developed a breakthrough cancer cure, the state government trumpeted it as a counterweight to the success of the U.S. atomic bomb program. Thus, the Mudds and Robert Leslie arrived in Russia at a time when the Soviets were acutely sensitive about the issues of medicine and health and how they affected the country's image abroad. Indeed, while in the Soviet Union, Stuart Mudd toured Klyueva and Roskin's laboratory and described meeting the two scientists as "a high point" of the visit.[27] Concerned about public relations, the Soviet leadership was fully informed of the ASMS visit and was keen to exploit it for any propagandistic purposes it might serve.[28]

For her part, Emily Mudd was aware that the people she met and the conditions of life she encountered might not be accurate reflections of reality, but that did not stop her from forming a relentlessly positive view of Russian society. Maurer had advised her that if she wanted to get a true glimpse of Soviet life—particularly the nation's women—it was important to avoid the "big wigs" and talk to "the average Soviet woman."[29] Yet Mudd's Soviet contacts were overwhelmingly official and professional. If she was aware of the political repression and the likely staged quality of her tour of the Soviet Union, she showed no signs. She confessed that time and again she marveled at the number of women she encountered in a wide variety of professional capacities. "Wherever we went in Russia," the Mudds wrote in 1947, "we were impressed by the women workers and the amount of responsible and creative work they accomplished."[30] As she recalled thirty years later:

[Soviet] women were taking their place as essential and, obviously, had won the respect, admiration and cooperation of the men with whom they worked. In Leningrad we saw a large commercial vessel . . . freighter of some kind . . . that was completely manned by a crew of women, from the captain on down. We saw women lifting bales and baggage, storing it in the boat. We saw women rebuilding buildings that had been bombed in Moscow. We saw them climbing ladders to manmade scaffolds and putting in mortar between stones. All the street cleaners were women. There were women everywhere.

Two aspects of Soviet women's lives stood out: first, that even in "high-up institutions for research there seemed to be as many women at the level of top research as there were men," and second, that Russian women with children from all walks of life "participate[d] so continuously and actively with so little apparent conflict and tension" in Soviet society. The contrast with her own experiences as a mother and a career woman in the United States captured her attention.[31]

During the course of her visit, Mudd objected to virtually nothing about Soviet society, culture, or science. Although Soviet citizens certainly faced severe deprivations, their sufferings, the Mudds contended, were entirely due to the German invasion and had nothing to do with either the nature of Russian communism or Stalin's rule. To the Mudds, Soviet society from top to bottom was grimly determined to rebuild the nation and wanted only peace to accomplish this task. Given their pro-Soviet viewpoint, political dissent seemed scarcely imaginable in Stalin's Russia. How could there be dissent when, in the Mudds' eyes, working Soviet women with children enjoyed so many more rights than their sisters in the United States?

Armed with her positive impressions of Soviet women, Emily Mudd returned to America just as health care policy debates were heating up, especially over national health insurance. Americans' interest in national, publicly funded health insurance had begun mounting during the 1930s, when voluntary plans had failed to protect millions amid the widespread unemployment of the Depression. During World War II the Social Security Board drafted a bill that would have provided health insurance for all persons paying Social Security taxes, as well as their families, but the bill died in committee. Nonetheless, President Franklin Roosevelt had supported an "economic bill of rights," including a right to adequate medical care, and his successor, Harry Truman, proposed a single health insurance system, encouraging many Americans to believe that sweeping health insurance reform was imminent.

Yet, despite Truman's protests that his program was not "socialized medicine," opponents labeled government-sponsored health insurance "sovietism." In 1946 Senator Robert Taft (R-Ohio) proclaimed Truman's plan to be "the most socialistic measure this Congress has ever had before it." Organized medicine shared these sentiments. Truman promised in 1948 that, if reelected, he would push for national health insurance, and after his surprise victory, organized medicine mobilized to thwart health insurance reform. The American Medical Association (AMA) spent more than $2 million and hired a public relations firm to try to convince the public that their health care needs could be better met through voluntary insurance plans than "socialized medicine." The campaign paid off in the 1950 off-year congressional elections, when the AMA succeeded in defeating several candidates who had refused to renounce their earlier defense of national health insurance. By that point, the idea of national health insurance was widely and firmly equated with "sovietism."[32]

The national debate over day care also intensified in the 1940s—a cause in which Emily Mudd had a deep emotional investment. Child care was one of several issues linked to family policy, and it drew support from a handful of national luminaries, including First Lady Eleanor Roosevelt. In the midst of widespread unemployment in the 1930s, many male breadwinners found themselves out of work and reliant on their spouses' participation in the labor force. Some social workers, private charity nursery workers, and early childhood educators began to argue that the government had a responsibility to pay for day-care centers for children. A handful of reformers maintained that day care was a fundamental need for families from all socioeconomic classes and could be an educational experience, not just a custodial one. Nonetheless, as the 1930s unfolded, New Deal policy makers in Washington focused on male breadwinners in their attempts to construct a welfare state. Educators likewise appeared to be uninterested in making day care a part of the nation's public school system.

World War II proved to be an important watershed in the history of day-care policy. After December 1941, about 6 million women who had never worked outside the home eventually joined the workforce in war-related industries and services. Thousands of women enlisted in the military as nurses or joined the army's WAC or the navy's WAVES. The mobilization of women at home, at work, and in the armed services led various employers, government officials, social workers, and everyday

Americans to think about the need for publicly funded day care. As one editorialist asked: "after the boys come marching home, and they marry these emancipated young women, who is going to tend the babies in the next generation?"[33] People on both sides of the debate wrestled with some difficult questions: What is the relationship between motherhood and citizenship? Are marriage and motherhood the most satisfying jobs that women can do? Is motherhood chiefly a private obligation to one's husband and children? If not, what obligations do mothers owe the state?[34]

The idea of federal programs providing day-care facilities met stiff opposition from government officials and some faith-based communities. Prior to World War II, some women's groups described supporters of state-sponsored child care and even child labor laws as subversives obeying "direct orders from Moscow."[35] Little changed once the war began: a government pamphlet informed readers that Rosie the Riveter's labor was valuable, but only until her husband returned from war.[36] Opponents of public day care pointed out that the vast majority of mothers would be staying home for the duration of the war. They argued that day care "weaken[ed] family responsibility" and offered substandard care. Child development expert Arnold Gesell warned that day-care facilities for the children of working women followed the example of authoritarian nations such as Japan, Germany, and Soviet Russia, where the "values of the family" were secondary to those of the state. Others, including FBI director J. Edgar Hoover and the National Catholic Welfare Conference, praised full-time motherhood, discouraged government efforts to provide day care, and tended to prefer day care provided by one woman for several children in her own home rather than group-care situations. Unpaid mothering, they argued, was a patriotic task more important than work in a war industry.[37]

Despite these and other voices of opposition to public day care, some defense contractors such as Curtiss-Wright in Buffalo, New York, and Kaiser Industries in Portland, Oregon, opened nursery and day-care centers for their employees in an effort to recruit and retain women workers. Day-care activists often appealed to national priorities when they asserted that "the day nursery . . . is as sure a weapon as the gun on the battlefield." Some women's auxiliary groups within organized labor also advocated for day care, although much of the trade union leadership remained cool to the idea. Occasionally, voices such as that of journalist Susan B. Anthony II (grandniece and namesake of the nineteenth-century suffragist) were raised to defend public day care as a tool of women's emancipation, but if there was any official support for the policy, it was typically couched in terms of the nation's needs for women laborers during wartime rather than the educational needs of children or the emancipation of women.[38]

The need to mobilize women's wartime labor led Washington to halting policy reforms in this area. Federal funding for day care became a reality only thanks to a 1942 amendment to the 1941 Communities Facilities Act, known as the Lanham Act. Complaints soon arose over various features of the Lanham Act's day-care program, including the slow application process, the locations of some centers, and the low wages and training levels of nursery staff. Even at the height of the program in 1944, when funding supported roughly 3,000 nurseries, the Lanham program served only about 1 percent of all children under age fourteen with working mothers.

In Emily Mudd's hometown of Philadelphia, Lanham funds helped the city open twenty day-care centers, with a peak of 1,262 children in April 1945, even though the board of education had originally planned for thirty such facilities. One Philadelphia opponent of public day-care centers declared, "Mothers should be sent home to look after their children. The idea of day care centers is copied directly from Russia." Such resistance led the National Commission for Young People, a day-care advocacy group, to warn in 1943: "Here we have a great opportunity to build an efficient program of child care and we are letting it fail."[39]

As one historian has observed, the United States "was probably closer to having a national child day care policy in 1945" than at any time since.[40] Nonetheless, the return of peace in 1945 brought a cutoff of federal funds for day care; this sparked protests in Philadelphia and elsewhere, which pressured Congress into extending the funding until March 1946. In 1948 the *Philadelphia Bulletin* reported that the city's day-care program had had a "stormy history, punctuated by indignant mothers' marches on [the] City Council, skirmishes with the police, political recriminations and repercussions, and the like." When federal funding ran out, protesting mothers failed to convince the Philadelphia City Council to pay for the day-care centers, but the mayor stepped in and used his own budget to keep them operating. Thanks to expedients such as these, city officials were able to keep some of Philadelphia's day-care centers open for another twenty years. Yet by 1949, the issue had ceased to draw much media attention, likely because groups linked to the labor movement, which had helped organize the protests, had fallen on hard times.[41]

One such organization was the short-lived (1946–1950) Congress of American Women (CAW), a group that claimed 250,000 members in 1949. The CAW—whose motto was "ten women anywhere can organize anything"—was the official U.S. branch of the pro-Soviet Women's International Democratic Federation (WIDF), founded in Paris in 1945 by two communist leaders of the French resistance.[42] Like the NCASF, both the CAW and the WIDF routinely supported Soviet foreign policy during the early Cold War.[43] The CPUSA helped chart the course of the CAW virtually from its inception, as part of its efforts to depict communism as nothing more than "twentieth-century Americanism." Nationally known communists such as Claudia Jones, Eleanor Flexner, Betty Millard, and Elizabeth Gurley Flynn occupied key CAW leadership posts. Communist publications such as the *Daily Worker* repeatedly celebrated the CAW's goals and activities. The three major concerns of the CAW, following those of the WIDF, were international peace, child welfare, and the status of women. The CAW regularly identified with political causes involving women, such as state-supported day care, equal pay for equal work, and civil rights. The CAW's "Resolution on the Family" asserted that America needed "homes and playgrounds, not battleships. We need milk, bread, and meat, not atom bombs."[44] Although some of the group's members held traditional views about women's social roles, the organization tended to teach that discrimination, not biology or personal preference, kept women from participating fully as citizens in the workforce. Led by Susan B. Anthony II, the CAW lobbied for a national housing program and government-funded, twenty-four-hour child care.

By 1950, when the U.S. Department of Justice ordered the CAW to register as a foreign agent, many of its original members had left the organization, disenchanted by Soviet expansion in eastern Europe. At that point, the CAW had become largely communist dominated and focused on foreign policy rather than domestic issues. Its members voted to dis-

band in 1950, but in the meantime, thanks to the widening public perception that the CAW was a communist front organization, child day
care—like national health insurance—was broadly identified as a Soviet
policy.

In her own way, Emily Mudd helped conflate communism and day care
in early Cold War America. When she spoke out in favor of Soviet-style
day care, she was knowingly wading into a highly charged debate with
numerous political overtones, not the least of which was the mounting
opposition to anything that smacked of communist-inspired policy reform.

The ideas that the Soviet people stood loyally behind their govern
ment and that they enjoyed more constitutional freedoms and social security than Americans were the major themes of Mudd's numerous
public lectures after she returned to the United States, including events
at the American-Russian Institute for Cultural Relations in New York
City and the Philadelphia Council of American-Soviet Friendship in November 1946. In late 1946 Mudd told a reporter for the *New York Herald-
Tribune* that the Russian people were "far more unified in support of
their government than we are," and although they desired peace with
the United States, they would "willingly and patriotically fight another
war if that was the Kremlin's command."[45] Mudd's comparison of U.S.
and Soviet unity echoed a common refrain in postwar "progressive" and
communist circles; for example, the head of the Chicago chapter of the
CAW declared to the WIDF in February 1947 that, far from being united,
the United States was dominated by a reactionary and imperialist elite
accounting for only 10 percent of the population.[46]

Emily Mudd's venture into early Cold War politics, however, was devoted mainly to hailing the seeming advances of Soviet women and their
children. Mudd attributed the high visibility of women in the Soviet
workforce—including in the fields of science and medicine—to a com-
bination of wartime conditions and the superiority of the Soviet social
system. "Equal pay for equal work and no sex discrimination" reigned
in the Soviet Union, Mudd insisted, and women enjoyed "economic security." Thanks to Stalin's 1936 Soviet Constitution, they had "an equal
right with men to work, payment for work, rest, and leisure, social in-

surance and education, and . . . state protection of the interests of mother and child, pre-maternity and maternity leave with full pay, and the provision of a wide network of homes, nurseries, and kindergartens." Women's work had "authority, recognition, and honor equal to that of men." If living conditions for the vast majority of Russians were dismal, at least their "poorness [was] shared," she added.[47]

To Mudd, the Soviet system of institutions for war orphans and nurseries for the children of working women showed how highly the USSR regarded children and the "family unit." What particularly impressed her were the *yaslis*, which were "really day care centers set up adjoining every factory in Moscow."[48] In addition to providing working women with a vital social service, according to Mudd, the *yaslis* put children "always in groups and always with the idea that our life is part of the life of the country and our job is to be helpful, not to ourselves as an individual—not to find our individual identity; but our identity was found through relationship with the group and through dedication to improving the conditions in their country—the Soviet Union."[49] Thus, she favored a collectivist rather than individualist approach to defining the relationship between the state and its citizens.

Emily Mudd may have sincerely believed that women were better off in the Soviet Union than in the United States, but other American visitors came away with distinctly different interpretations of women's lives in the USSR. "Sure we have equality," a young Soviet woman told the *Women's Home Companion* in 1946, "equal rights to go out and kill ourselves working hard all day and then the right to come home and do all the housework and washing and cooking and shopping for food in the evenings. Besides getting the kids to bed." A reporter from the right-of-center *Washington Daily News* noted in 1947 that "the typical women of Russia . . . are the tens of millions who rise from childbirth to shovel snow, fell trees, work roads, sow, till, and harvest in the fields and pull their weight in industrial gangs. They are the mothers of Mother Russia—old at 30, as always silently, ploddingly, carrying a burden of the dark land they love." The *Washington Post* reported that the sight of Moscow women "with shawls around their skinny faces," jostling frantically at government stalls for unrationed bread, did not prove that "all Moscow women have to struggle for extra food or that all Moscow or Russia is underfed. But women do not usually struggle for a half loaf of

bread, as these women did, unless they or their families are hungry."
"Communist Russia boasts that its women have equal rights with men,"
another reporter wrote, "and they certainly have—particularly when it
comes to heavy work."[50]

On a broader scale, Emily Mudd agreed with Sigerist's advocacy of
preventive medicine and his outlook on the state's responsibility for
public health, or what one historian called Sigerist's overall "medical
totalitarianism."[51] Sigerist believed that the Soviet blueprint was worth
copying because it supposedly came closest to his ideal of state super-
vision over all aspects of medicine, a cradle-to-grave system of health
care that subjected individual lifestyle to complete state control. In 1947
Mudd, quoting Sigerist, wrote approvingly about the "general intent"
of Soviet medicine, which

> is to supervise the human being medically, in a discrete and
> unobtrusive way, from the moment of conception to the moment of
> death. Medical workers and medical institutions are placed wherever
> anyone, in the course of his life, may be exposed to danger. Medical
> supervision begins with the pregnant woman and the women in
> childbirth, proceeds to the infant, the pre-school and school child,
> the adolescent, and finally the man and woman at work.

"Emphasis in all phases," Mudd added in her own words, "is on the prevention of disease." While Mudd conceded that Soviet health care and
educational opportunities "are still far from guaranteeing a really acceptable standard of living," she added that the Soviets "continue[d] to
adjust to life," which ought to prove "provocative to other non-static
societies," presumably referring to the United States.[52]

The Mudds' many glowing testimonials in favor of the Soviet Union
coincided with the three-month-long visit of Vasilii Parin, head of the
medical section of the VOKS, vice minister of health for the USSR Academy of Medical Sciences, and the Mudds' host during their stay in the
Soviet Union two months earlier. Parin arrived in the United States on
October 16, 1946, having been invited by the American embassy in
Moscow on behalf of the U.S. surgeon general. At the time, both governments seemed keen to exchange biomedical information. Parin
toured several universities and clinics, and during his visit to Philadel-

phia, he stayed at the Mudds' home. On December 21, 1946, Parin also joined Stuart Mudd at the third annual meeting of the ASMS.

When Parin left the United States in January 1947, events were moving swiftly in Moscow. Unbeknownst to the Mudds and the ASMS, the Politburo (under Stalin's firm direction) had decided to end Soviet contact with Western scientists. Parin was charged with being an American spy and, in typical Stalinist fashion, abruptly disappeared into the prison system.[53] His fate signaled that a chill had descended on Soviet-American scientific relations, and the Mudds' window of opportunity for reversing public policy on women's issues was closing rapidly.

Meanwhile, the Mudds' effusive comments about the Soviet Union were drawing hostile attention from domestic sources. Mainly because of Leslie's membership in the CPUSA and Sigerist's warm praise for the Soviet Union dating back to the 1930s, the FBI had been investigating the ASMS. In the eyes of the U.S. intelligence community, the Mudds' close identification with both the ASMS and the NCASF was reason enough to suspect them of "un-American" activities. Other observers detected a distinct whiff of pro-Sovietism surrounding the Mudds. Some colleagues at the University of Pennsylvania called Stuart Mudd "Dr. Muddski."[54] As a reporter commented in January 1947, after Emily Mudd spoke at Bryn Mawr, "Some might have felt that her account was one-sided in expressing the advantages of the Russian educational and recreational system and not the disadvantages."[55] Shortly thereafter, *Collier's* magazine withdrew its offer to print Mudd's article on her positive impressions of Soviet women and children.[56]

The final chapter in the history of the Medical Mission to Moscow was written in late 1947 when Dean Alfred Richards informed Stuart Mudd that an anonymous donor intended to withhold his contribution to the university as long as the Mudds' names remained on the letterhead of the Philadelphia NCASF. On December 5, 1947, Stuart wrote a contrite letter to Richards, stating that although they still believed in the contribution of Soviet science to "world peace" and "the possibility of friendship" between the two superpowers:

> I assure you that neither Mrs. Mudd nor myself is, has been, or ever
> expects to be a Communist, or in any way a willing participant in
> subversive activities. We are thoroughly in sympathy with the

European Reconstruction Plan of the American government and believe that the misrepresentation of American motives in the Soviet press and by the political representatives of the Soviet government and the obstructive tactics employed by these political representatives are abominable.[57]

Stuart Mudd then wished the Philadelphia NCASF well but informed the group that he and Emily were withdrawing their memberships. He explained that because "the research work of my department, and also of the Marriage Council of Philadelphia is dependent on grants-in-aid received . . . from government sources," the end of such funding would "cripple . . . our professional work." (In July the MCP had received a U.S. Public Health Services grant for a research project titled "The Promotion of Marital Adjustment in Men and Women as an Aid to Good Mental Health.")[58]

Emily too asked that her name be stricken from the letterhead of the NCASF Women's Committee. "As part of my professional work is in research from which grants are received from government sources," she reasoned, "I do not feel that I have any right personally to jeopardize the funds for the family counselling work for which I have a responsible position." She must have felt attacked from all sides. Earlier that year, the Philadelphia assistant district attorney had tried to block the MCP's incorporation on the pretext that it was a private abortion clinic. Mudd always suspected that the Roman Catholic Church was behind this campaign to discredit the MCP. As a result, the MCP changed its name from "Marriage Counsel" to "Marriage Council" when some lawyers protested that "counsel" made it sound as if the group was a legal body. When that change failed to win city hall approval, the MCP incorporated in the neighboring state of Delaware. Mudd liked to depict local Catholic opposition to the MCP as religious bigotry, but in all likelihood it was tied to her public admiration of Soviet life. Philadelphia was a hotbed of anticommunist politics, uniting both Democrats and Republicans in a campaign to forestall any reforms that resembled "sovietism."[59]

In reflecting on this turn of events, Emily Mudd was certainly correct that U.S. attitudes toward the Soviet Union—which had been friendly only three years earlier—were becoming increasingly negative in 1947. Nonetheless, like her husband and their colleagues in the ASMS and the

NCASF, she maintained that American anticommunism was largely to blame for the situation. With memories of her Medical Mission to Moscow still fresh in her mind, she continued to view the Soviet Union through rose-colored glasses—a prime reason that she failed to solve the policy challenge of balancing work and family for American women.

The failure of the Medical Mission to Moscow was only a minor setback in Emily Mudd's ascent in the field of marriage and family counseling. If, by the late 1940s, her plans to use the Soviet blueprint for publicly funded day care, greater work opportunities for women, and a state-run system of health care in twentieth-century America were in shambles, other opportunities soon opened up. Her flirtation with Stalinist family policy notwithstanding, in the 1950s she became the unofficial spokesperson for marriage and family counseling in America, admired and liked by virtually everyone in the movement.

The question remains, however: did their tour of the USSR in 1946 make the Mudds "fellow travelers" in both the literal and the figurative senses? Although some ASMS and NCASF members belonged to the CPUSA, there is no evidence that the Mudds did. Nor, as the FBI discovered, was there a shred of evidence that the Mudds were engaged in any espionage on behalf of the Soviet government.[60] If they were sympathetic toward the USSR, their willingness to speak out in defense of Stalin's Russia could be traced to the barrage of pro-Soviet propaganda to which the American public had been exposed during the war years rather than any pro-communist ideological presuppositions. As World War II wound to a close, it was easy for many Americans to believe that U.S. attitudes toward the Soviet Union had changed and that drawing comparisons between the two countries that favored the Soviet Union would not be a liability.

However, Emily Mudd's views on Soviet women were largely the product of her own disenchantment with the status of women in the United States. As she told an interviewer in 1974:

My interest [in the Soviet Union] was to try to interpret to professional and lay groups in this country the kinds of facilities which were made routinely available to working women and for the care of the children of working women in the Soviet Union, because we had nothing of the kind in the U.S. at the time. I felt that this was where our social order fell down drastically. . . . In the Soviet Union [women] had to work and they had these marvellous day care centers.[61]

As we have seen, Mudd was drawing on her personal experience as a working woman, and she was certainly right that the U.S. "social order" provided nothing similar to the Soviet day-care system. However, identifying one's own country's shortcomings is one thing; it is quite another to compare it invidiously with a murderous, totalitarian regime with a radically different official ideology. Having actually visited the Soviet Union, she had few excuses for being swept away by propaganda about the nature of Soviet women's lives. The key factor appears to have been the Mudds' active participation in the ASMS, many of whose members belonged to the CPUSA or came from socialist backgrounds, like Sigerist, Heiman, Leslie, and the Stones. As Kate Weigand has argued, it was hard to miss the communist influence exerted on "progressive" groups engaged in fostering closer relations with the Soviet Union. If the Mudds shared a common mind-set, it was certainly close to the "communism is twentieth-century Americanism" attitude that was so widespread in left-of-center circles in the late 1940s.[62]

By repeatedly celebrating aspects of Soviet society, Emily Mudd served Soviet purposes. In the shadow of the United States atomic monopoly, the Soviets were scrambling to "dull its brilliance in the eyes of the world community." Thus the Mudds' positive statements about Soviet life and Soviet health care had a distinct "symbolic value as a propaganda counter-weight to the U.S. nuclear bomb," in the words of historian Nikolai Krementsov.[63] The Mudds ended up as mouthpieces for Stalinism not because they were communists but because they wholeheartedly believed that women were much better off in the Soviet Union than in the United States.

When Stalin and the Politburo decided in early 1947 to end all cultural relations with the United States, the ASMS's usefulness ended. As Sigerist and Leslie ruefully admitted, the VOKS refused to answer their letters. Yet to the Mudds and the ASMS executives, the chief blame for Soviet behavior lay not with ulterior motives in Moscow but with the bad faith of the U.S. government. In this respect, they were conforming to the standard NCASF response as the 1940s came to a close: if international tensions were on the rise, it was Washington's fault, not Moscow's. Their overemphasis on America's culpability was just another example of their misreading of history and current events and their propensity to prefer Moscow's social policies to Washington's.

Yet in another sense, Emily Mudd and the AAMC were solidly on the side of history as the 1950s dawned. They may have been scarred by anticommunist and anti-Kinsey attacks, but these trials and tribulations were only temporary. In the early 1950s America's "permissive society" was taking shape, laying the groundwork for the launch of marriage and family counseling as a profession of "secular priests."[64] On the horizon were the exploits of William Masters and Virginia Johnson, whose research began, as Mudd put it, "where Kinsey left off."[65] The AAMC itself, a group known for its "counseling" ethos, increasingly defined its practice as "therapy." The chief significance of the notion that communism was twentieth-century Americanism lay not in the penalties endured by some AAMC members but in the willingness of its key figures to follow the example of one of the worst totalitarian regimes in history in order to forge a therapeutic outlook that rejected the traditional norms of gender, sex, marriage, and family. When Emily Mudd reflected in the 1970s how far America had come in her lifetime, she was simply acknowledging that what appeared to be highly contingent in the 1940s had become a historical reality by the time she retired from professional life.

mily Mudd's brush with anticommunism may have been personally uncomfortable, but as events revealed, neither she nor the field of marriage and family counseling suffered any long-term professional setbacks. During the 1950s the acceptance of marriage and family counseling steadily spread, as did many of its core therapism principles. The field received a boost when Mudd's MCP became affiliated with the University of Pennsylvania Medical School. By 1956, the MCP was one of three accredited marriage counseling training centers in the United States. The number of college courses on marriage preparation continued to grow: in 1955–1956, 630 colleges and universities offered 1,027 different courses on marriage and the family.[1] Research on marriage and the family benefited from corporate and government funding. Clergymen increasingly received formal training in marriage and family counseling at seminaries and other religious educational institutions. On the West Coast, Paul Popenoe's appearances on radio and television exposed millions to the new field. In 1963 Popenoe's home state of California became the first to pass a licensing law for marriage and family counselors. It took until 1974 for marriage counselors to found their first independent journal, but by then, both they and family therapists had come of age as professional groups, and the therapeutic outlook they championed enjoyed widespread affirmation. Indeed, in the 1960s and 1970s practitioners ceased calling themselves counselors and increasingly referred to themselves as therapists. Rather than teaching people what to do, they preferred to define themselves as professionals who taught people what to feel.

Yet, as steady as this progress appears in retrospect, it masks the turmoil that racked the field in these years. Relations between the AAMC and the NCFR were uneasy at best. The viewpoints of outspoken therapists such as Albert Ellis and Carl Rogers often clashed with those of educators, researchers, and counselors. Some clergymen worried that adopting secular theories about counseling might undermine core religious doctrines. Younger practitioners bridled when the AAMC refused to open up membership to individuals with less formal qualifications. In the words of two later leaders in the field, in the 1950s and 1960s marriage counseling "was always richer in enthusiasm and commitment than in consensus or clarity as to its nature."[2] Despite the turbulence of these years, however, wider trends such as the presence of veterans on college campuses, the growth of a consumer society, and the expansion of the media, to say nothing of the energetic efforts of the profession's spokespeople, steadily fostered a belief in the therapist outlook.

In 1948 the American-Soviet Medical Society was fading fast into oblivion, but what Emily Mudd called the AAMC's "golden years" were just dawning.[3] That year the AAMC took an important step when it and the marriage counseling section of the NCFR issued a joint statement on standards for counselors based on academic training, clinical experience, and personal qualifications. The subcommittee that prepared the report was a veritable who's who of marriage counseling pioneers, including Emily Mudd (who chaired the committee), Robert Latou Dickinson, Robert Laidlaw, Ernest Burgess, Lester Dearborn, Lena Levine, Abraham Stone, and Rabbi Sidney Goldstein (the NCFR's fifth president). The report stressed what many of the field's spokespeople had been saying for years: the scientific study of relationships—"that which makes possible getting along with one another individually and in groups"—was critical if humanity was to survive. This belief had given birth to marriage and family counseling, but with about 300 counseling centers in forty of the forty-eight states operating under a plethora of diverse agencies and institutions, the field was in disarray. Additionally, the report said, "the present stage of knowledge does not furnish adequate evaluation of the effectiveness of counseling," but this failed to dim the confidence of people working with families or married couples. "The essential next step," the committee concluded, was "the establishment of high professional standards for future full-time marriage and family counselors, uniform in basic minimum requirements."[4]

But establishing licensing standards for marriage counselors in the absence of accredited, college-based training programs was easier said than done. Thus, the prestige and legitimacy of the field received a much-needed boost in 1952 with the MCP's affiliation with the University of Pennsylvania. The MCP, already known as the foremost community center for research and training in marriage counseling, became the functional clinical and teaching unit in the Department of Psychiatry's newly created Division of Family Study. Firmly dedicated to the service side of marriage counseling, Mudd knew that the success of the field depended on the academic credentials of its leaders. Thus, back in 1936, she had obtained her master's degree in social work. "I realized for myself," she admitted years later, "that if I was going on to a recognized leadership role as director of the marriage counseling service— that had the respect of the professional medical community and other professionals—that I really needed to go for a doctoral degree."[5] Undeterred by her time-consuming duties as a mother of four and as a marriage counseling activist, Mudd received a Ph.D. in sociology from the University of Pennsylvania in 1950.

Meanwhile, beginning in 1943, various foundations provided funding to the MCP for research, including Ortho Pharmaceutical, a subsidiary of Johnson and Johnson (the medical device manufacturer incorporated in 1887). Robert Dickinson was largely responsible for arranging the two-year Johnson and Johnson grant, which was earmarked to study "the relation of premarital counseling to marriage adjustment," a topic in which Dickinson, Dearborn, Kinsey, Mudd, and others in the field were vitally interested due to their visceral opposition to the accepted belief in chastity before marriage. The Kinseyites in the AAMC believed that by teaching that premarital sex did not damage prospects for a happy marriage, counselors could take a giant step toward overthrowing what AAMC member Robert Harper called "medieval concepts of sex."[6]

The MCP received additional funding from the William T. Grant Foundation, established in 1936. The Grant Foundation, which tended to support mental health care research, desired to fund training for marriage counseling at the MCP, the Menninger Clinic in Topeka, Kansas, and Detroit's Merrill-Palmer School, a center of research and training in child development. Because the foundation wanted one of the centers it funded to be connected to a university medical school, and because, at the time, only the MCP had any realistic prospect of such affiliation, the foundation's "velvet glove" tactics paved the way for that to happen. The MCP became the first marriage counseling clinic to be officially affiliated with a U.S. university, and Mudd became only the third woman appointed to the faculty of the University of Pennsylvania's Medical School. Thanks to this link, the MCP was poised to lead the field for the next twenty years.

Among the University of Pennsylvania faculty who approved of this link was psychiatrist Kenneth Appel, a stalwart MCP board member since its earliest days. Appel also helped launch the Joint Commission on Mental Illness and Health (JCMIH) in the 1950s. One of the central motivations behind the JCMIH was "the need to examine the resources with which individuals and our society promote mental health and prevent mental illness. New ways must be sought to achieve these objectives."[7] The commission's final report, released in 1961, was a landmark document in the history of U.S. psychiatry. It articulated the increasingly popular viewpoint among American psychiatrists that their main concern should be addressing the needs of the "worried well"—that is, those "psychologically troubled individuals" who suffered from everyday problems of living—not the seriously and chronically ill who had been diagnosed with schizophrenia or manic depression. Psychiatrists were encouraged to "provide every person with the chance to develop a personality or character of sufficient strength to cope with the stresses life imposes upon him." Such an open-ended aim, combined with the prospect of steep government investment in treatment and rehabilitation programs and services, was music to the ears of many marriage and family counselors, who saw themselves as the first line of defense against the "stresses" that sapped the emotional strength of American families.[8]

Emily Mudd described Appel (a close family friend) as a man with "a broad-based curiosity . . . and an unusual amount of imagination," which enabled him to "straddle" both currents in psychiatry—the psychoanalytically oriented faction, and the group that treated people with severe mental disabilities.[9] "The origin of my own interest in marriage counseling," Appel wrote in 1957, "was my discovery of the extent to which marital maladjustment appeared in patients, masquerading or expressing itself unconsciously in unhappiness, vocational ineffectiveness, alcoholism, psycho-somatic symptoms, nervous illness, mental disease, and even suicide."[10] Appel fervently believed that improving the nation's mental health depended to a great extent on preventing psychological disorders that arose due to family and marital troubles, and he envisioned marriage and family counseling as a key weapon in the struggle to make Americans happier.

Mudd's friendship with Appel was indicative of the warm relations she enjoyed with other powerful University of Pennsylvania officials. It certainly helped that her husband was chairman of the university's Microbiology Department. The dean of the medical school was a pediatrician whose first patient had been the Mudds' first child. The Mudds were also on friendly terms with Alfred Newton Richards, the university's vice president for medical affairs. These connections, the product of similar social backgrounds and viewpoints, were key reasons behind Mudd's success in launching three elective courses in marriage counseling for medical students at the University of Pennsylvania, including the first university course in U.S. history to have the word *sexual* in its title. Despite the medical school's insistence that it be an elective rather than a required course, that it be offered late in the afternoon, and that it be open only to senior students, 95 of the 110 eligible students showed up.

Then, in a startling break with tradition, the medical school promoted Mudd in 1956 from assistant to full professor, bypassing the associate professor level. Mudd and Appel had anticipated that the university's "gynephobia" (Appel's term) would scuttle any chance of promotion. Yet, according to Mudd's husband, who was present at the faculty meeting where her candidacy was discussed, her promotion was "unique in the annals of our medical school." The chairman of the promotions committee informed the faculty that Emily Mudd was "not only the leading Marriage Counselor in the country but that she invented the discipline." When he recommended that she be promoted to full professor, "surprised silence" followed, broken only when Stuart Mudd said: "Dr. Mudd has been a good researcher and a good teacher. I think she is a good man for the position." Once the laughter subsided, the motion to promote her was carried. Emily Mudd's promotion, in a day and age of discrimination against women in academia, proved the old adage that who you know is as important as what you know.[11] Yet it was also a tribute to the esteem in which people held her: the attitude seemed to be that if Emily Mudd was in favor of marriage counseling, that was good enough for the university's medical faculty.

The claim that Mudd had "invented" marriage counseling was hyperbole, but her ascent through the ranks of University of Pennsylvania faculty was a good example of the impressive strides the field was taking on the East Coast. On the West Coast, marriage counseling was enjoying a somewhat different kind of success, fueled in large part by the growth of the country's colleges and universities and the expansion of communications technology in the twentieth-century United States.

After World War I, movies, radio, advertising, the record industry, and the marketing of paperback books fostered an unprecedented mass culture that helped break down divisions among social classes and ethnic groups. Mass culture elevated individuals such as baseball player Babe Ruth and aviator Charles Lindbergh to the status of national celebrities. Many social groups still clung to inherited values and revered family traditions, and conservative faith-based groups, such as evangelicals, exploited the radio in particular to spread their religious messages. But by the Depression, it was clear that, overall, the new media were having a homogenizing cultural effect by creating wider audiences who seemingly shared the same tastes and attitudes.

In the post–World War II era, Hollywood took a leadership role by choosing psychological or psychiatric themes for many of its movie story lines, thanks in part to lobbying by the American Psychiatric Association. Films such as *The Snake Pit* (1948), *The Three Faces of Eve* (1957), and *Freud* (1962) cast doubt on traditional methods of treating mental illness, such as institutionalization, or introduced new concepts of psychological disease, such as multiple-personality disorder. Yet they were all largely supportive of the image of the psychiatrist as a kind of compassionate seer whose use of psychotherapy could have a liberating impact.[12] The final scene in Alfred Hitchcock's thriller *Psycho* (1960) features a psychiatrist who explains the motives behind the murderer's horrendous crimes, thus emphasizing how experts trained in the psychological sciences could unravel mysteries of the mind that had baffled earlier generations and terrified present-day society.

Counselors recognized the effects of the printed media on young

Alfred Kinsey lecturing at the University of California–Berkeley, 1949. (Courtesy of the Kinsey Institute for Research in Sex, Gender, and Reproduction)

Americans' attitudes toward married life. As the editor of *Redbook* informed Gladys Groves in 1953, the magazine coveted material on marriage because "so many of *Redbook*'s readers are young married couples," and many of the husbands were attending college thanks to the Servicemen's Readjustment Act passed by Congress in 1944 (commonly referred to as the GI Bill).[13] Prior to World War II, colleges had frowned on married undergraduates and often forced them to live off campus. After the war, when almost 2.25 million ex-servicemen crowded onto 2,000 campuses, postsecondary institutions were pressured to build housing for married students and find jobs for their wives.[14] The influx of veterans of World War II and the Korean War (1951–1955) altered the atmosphere on campuses. The presence of married men living with their wives was a blow to the traditional sex-segregated ethos of American colleges. Having lived away from home for years and having experienced the emotional excitement of war, ex-servicemen also brought a worldly curiosity to a host of issues—notably, sexuality. Thus, when Alfred Kinsey addressed college students at the University of California at Berkeley in 1949, it was an overflow crowd.

The percentage of college-aged Americans who actually attended college almost doubled between 1940 and 1960, and they were a key segment of the expanding audience for media coverage of marriage and courtship. In 1953, however, Henry Bowman of Stephens College admitted that only 2 percent of all college students took a marriage course.[15] The popular media, which hired marriage experts as advice columnists and publicized research findings related to marriage, widened the audience for such information. Young people were already predisposed to be interested in marriage, given the powerful "human mating" impulse, but according to Ernest Groves in 1940, "the widespread attention now given to marriage problems, especially in popular literature," was highlighting "the problems of marriage" rather than the benefits. "Instead of lessening the desire for marriage on the part of American young people," Groves wrote, "the material that appears in newspapers, magazines, and popular books has tended to make them conscious of the difficulties of marital adjustment, and this has increased their incentives for counsel." Radio promised to be even more influential. Groves warned that radio's "dangers are even greater than those of popular literature. . . . Much of it is under commercial sponsorship, and this will tend to emphasize a highly dramatic and appealing type of discussion, which can be extremely hazardous."[16] Groves remained hopeful about the educational potential of radio, but in a refrain that still echoes in the twenty-first century, he lamented that the media could be exploited by unqualified people with no legitimate claim to expertise. By serially reporting stories about marriage, the burgeoning media were making Americans more uncertain about their matrimonial destinies and more inclined to seek professional guidance, rather than empowering them with the knowledge they needed to make informed choices about matrimony. In the words of David Mace, a leading Cold War marriage counselor, "contemporary culture" bred "higher expectations of marriage and anxiety about attaining them."[17] By fostering a gnawing insecurity about "human mating," the media were paving the way for therapism's ascendancy in the form of Americans' reliance on experts to meet their high expectations for fulfillment in marriage.

The coming of television in the 1950s introduced a powerful new medium of popular culture and accelerated the rise of therapism. Television's arrival coincided with an unprecedented economic boom. In the mid-1950s the average American had twice as much real income to spend as in the prosperous 1920s, as well as more leisure time to spend that income. Most workers enjoyed at least two weeks of vacation each year. Economist John Kenneth Galbraith warned in *The Affluent Society*

(1958) that Americans, spurred by mass advertising, were frantically buying consumer goods, such as automobiles and dishwashers, and plunging into debt. Millions of Americans were still mired in poverty, but the rising life expectancy, combined with the perception of material progress, convinced many people that their quality of life would only get better.

The first television set was invented in 1926, but it did not become a staple consumer product until after World War II. Television's impact was enormous; by 1956, the average American was watching five hours of television per day. In 1951 a family counselor told the *New York Times* that "watching television in the living room every night after dinner is as much a ritual in many homes today as evening prayers in the parlor were in another era."[18] As Americans bought TV sets by the millions, debates raged over whether television distorted reality, but few disputed its power to affect viewers. Television proved to be an ideal medium for the therapeutic outlook. As Robert Bellah and his colleagues wrote in 1985:

> Television is much more interested in how people feel than in what they think. What they think might separate us, but how they feel draws us together. Successful television personalities and people are thus people able freely to communicate their emotional states. We feel that "we really know them," and the very consumption goods that television so insistently puts before us integrate us by providing symbols of our version of the good life.[19]

Advertisers exploited the new medium by flashing image after image of fashionable consumer items, from refrigerators to cars. Advertising and marketing strategists on Madison Avenue were using the findings of psychologists to craft their sales campaigns, prompting author Vance Packard to call their approaches "mass psychoanalysis."[20] Industry was busy trying to compel all viewers to desire the same goods and services, thus homogenizing American society.

Situation comedies and action dramas quickly emerged as the most popular television programs. However, daytime fare, which included quiz shows, soap operas, and variety talk shows, also caught on rapidly, thanks to the millions of women who were home raising their families.

The first TV talk show was Phil Donahue's local Dayton, Ohio, program, which introduced its first guest on November 6, 1967. By the 1980s, the no-holds-barred talk show, featuring a parade of people admitting to emotional afflictions or crippling addictions, was a staple of daytime television. In the words of historian Eva Moskowitz, the talk show's arrival in the late 1960s brought the language of therapism "out of the church basement and into American living rooms and offices."[21]

However, the close connections between television and therapism date back even further. The popular *House Party*, which started as a radio program, aired on television from 1952 to 1969, making it the longest-running daytime variety show ever. It began when an advertising agency representing General Electric (the show's first sponsor) pitched the idea of an audience participation program with Art Linkletter as the host. *House Party*—a blend of consumerism and bland, wholesome entertainment that included quizzes and celebrity interviews—became an instant hit. One critic lamented Linkletter's "imperishable banality," but his easygoing, nonthreatening mannerisms put his guests at ease, particularly the children he interviewed during the popular segment called "Kids Say the Darnedest Things." To the millions of women who made up three-quarters of his afternoon audience, Linkletter was a friendly presence in their lives.[22]

A favorite guest on *House Party* was the AIFR's Paul Popenoe, whose appearances on the show vividly demonstrated the blending of consumerism and marriage counseling in the 1950s. Whether he was explaining the mysteries of individual personality or the differences between men and women, Popenoe helped make marriage counseling a consumer product that seemed as desirable as any new household appliance. NCFR executive director Ruth Jewson described Popenoe's TV appearances as "unbelievably bad," but his lack of scientific sophistication may have been the very thing that enabled him to appeal to a broad audience.[23] In a decade when growing affluence increased the income and the leisure time of millions of families, Popenoe's message was that marriage counseling was one of many new and exciting services Americans needed. The fine line between addressing real needs and stimulating demand for products and services was gradually fading in an age of rapidly changing communications technology.

Popenoe's genial TV promotion of marriage counseling as a scientifically based consumer service was a decided asset because it helped overshadow the deep cleavages in the field in the 1950s. The stark divergence of opinion was largely due to the AAMC's Kinseyites, who mobilized to disseminate the Indiana professor's viewpoints to the diverse groups and individuals in the NCFR through its journal *Marriage and Family Living* (initially launched by the NCFR in 1938 and titled *Living*, it was renamed in 1941). The AAMC's activism precipitated a fight with the NCFR, and the wounds took years to heal. By the 1970s, the interests of the two groups would dovetail once again (as they had briefly in the 1940s), but in the mid-1950s the marriage and family counseling field was bitterly divided—notably, over sex. Kinsey's AAMC admirers had taken to heart his urgings to use marriage counseling as a vehicle for revolutionizing Americans' sexual morals, but many of their professional counterparts in the NCFR balked at engaging in what psychiatrist Walter Stokes approvingly called a "cultural engineering project" designed to overturn "irrational prejudice" and the "dogmas of mystical philosophy."[24]

The NCFR-AAMC clash in the early 1950s can be traced back to the separate histories of the two groups. Due to the pronounced overlap in membership, the two groups sometimes held joint meetings, but there were significant differences between them. Whereas the AAMC, with its origin in the eugenics and birth control movements and its evolving links to the Kinsey Institute, purposely limited its membership to counselors who shared the same basic viewpoints, the NCFR welcomed a more eclectic membership from a variety of occupational backgrounds. In contrast to the AAMC's few dozen members, the NCFR grew from several hundred members in 1938 to more than 2,000 in 1950. By 1945, nineteen regional and state conferences were affiliated with the NCFR. As one NCFR member put it in 1953, the AAMC was "a kind of New York–Philadelphia closed shop," whereas the NCFR was "a strange organization with a strange assortment of active members."[25] Another member noted that the NCFR was full of "many warring elements . . . whose basic points of view are rather farther apart than East and West."[26] The Right Reverend Monsignor John O'Grady, secretary of the National Conference of Catholic Charities, sat on the NCFR's board of directors and was NCFR president in 1951–1952, but no Roman Catholic clergyman belonged to the AAMC. The NCFR may have had its "warring elements," but compared with the AAMC, it was a model of diversity.

Bad relations with the AAMC could not have come at a worse time for the NCFR. It was in turmoil over its paltry finances and the departure of stalwart Evelyn Duvall as executive secretary. It was also in the midst of reevaluating its organizational function and rewriting its constitution and bylaws, a soul-searching process that, if nothing else, indicated widespread dissatisfaction with past practices. To NCFR president Robert Foster, the time had come to end the group's dominance by Ernest Burgess, who had largely run the organization from his home institution, the University of Chicago. The group had to decide, Foster wrote in 1952, "the extent to which the National Council is going to be an extension of Burgess, or whether the National Council is going to be something that represents the membership and the people who have some concern and interest throughout the states. . . . I think the time does come in the growth of an organization when it needs to emancipate itself from mama and papa, papa in this instance, and really grow up."[27] One step in that direction was moving the NCFR's headquarters from Chicago to Minneapolis in 1955.

Thus, the NCFR was at a crossroads when the bitter power struggle broke out between it and the AAMC, eventually severing relations between the two groups in 1954. The conflict was over the contents of the journal *Marriage and Family Living* (*MFL*). In 1950 *MFL* began publishing a section on marriage counseling, thanks to a $2,500 subsidy arranged by Robert Laidlaw, who became one of the journal's associate editors. Laidlaw spearheaded a faction of individuals with dual memberships in the AAMC and NCFR who fervently hoped to make *MFL* a mouthpiece for Kinsey's findings. Laidlaw "wanted to put more things in about sexual behavior," Mudd disclosed, which "the more conservative editors felt was not appropriate for their journal."[28] As guest editor of the summer 1953 issue, Robert Harper also wished to use the journal as a forum for "forthright" articles "regarding the need for re-examination of our sex attitudes and sex codes as an inescapable prerequisite to the achievement of democratic marital and familial relationships." Harper tried unsuccessfully to get Kinsey to author an article about "the laws and attitudes concerning sex deviations," a topic Kinsey had been studying for some time.[29]

The matter came to a head in April 1953, during a debate over premarital sex at an AAMC meeting in Columbus, Ohio. Premarital sex was a hot-button issue among counselors in the 1950s, harking back to the controversy over Lester Dearborn's comments in 1934. In the 1950s some counselors and physicians continued to teach that "chastity until marriage" was "a valid standard" of morality and mental hygiene because "the too early development of the habit of stimulating sex desire by petting or other physical means may impair happiness in marriage."[30] Robert Dickinson was typical of the Kinseyites in the field who derided this viewpoint as "all-out 'chastity,' with no drawbacks."[31]

At the crux of the debate, reproduced in the pages of *MFL*, were the comments of Walter Stokes, "the foremost advocate of liberal attitudes toward sexuality as a vital part of whole lives," in the words of Aaron Rutledge.[32] In a full-fledged attack on the sex values of "the Hebraic-Christian religious system and Western culture in general," Stokes approvingly cited Kinsey's studies, which supposedly showed "a remarkable correlation between active, overt childhood sex expression and later life sex potency." Stokes claimed that his own clinical experience had taught him "the unhappy relationship of childhood chastity . . . to adult frigidity and impotence in marriage."[33] Stokes argued that the link between childhood sexuality and adult sexuality applied to both girls and boys.

It soon became evident that the AAMC and the NCFR did not agree over what constituted suitable material for *MFL*. In reaction to Stokes's comments and those of other participants in the debate, irate members wrote to NCFR president Robert Foster and threatened to end their subscriptions to *MFL* because of its "objectionable" and "pagan" contents. The president of Nazarene College in Idaho told *MFL* editor Gladys Groves, "To put it simply, I am unalterably opposed to any blanket approval of pre-marital or non-marital relations," and he referred to Stokes's "abrupt and sweeping, though uninformed, relegation of Christianity and Christian morals to the ash heap of unwholesome myth."[34] One NCFR member complained that *MFL* conveyed the "impression that marriage counselors are in reality sexologists."[35] To the NCFR's leadership, the prospect of losing *MFL* subscriptions was calamitous. As Foster stated in 1952, *MFL* was "the best avenue of interest and publicity for us, more so even than having star speakers going around the country making speeches."[36]

The main fallout of the split was the NCFR's decision to forgo the $2,500 AAMC subsidy—a difficult choice, given the NCFR's finances. By declining the subsidy, the NCFR was bowing to the moral attitudes of many of its members. To other NCFR members, the spectacle of practitioners disagreeing over such sensitive ethical issues could only undermine public confidence in their claims to expertise. Psychologist Dorothy Dyer, who became NCFR president in 1954, worried about the public relations fallout:

> [The NCFR is] an organization intended to provide a wiser-than-thou guidance to people looking for "expert" direction in something as basic to individual happiness and social welfare as marriage and the family! And how can laymen help but laugh when doctors disagree in such an organization? And if they know anything about the personal and private conduct of some of the people still allowed to pontificate in the NCFR and its Journal? The American family and the American people deserve something better than that—if they are paying much attention, which I sometimes doubt![37]

Dyer, like many other NCFR members, believed that the field in general and the NCFR in particular were at a critical turning point and that such open spats could only weaken confidence in a young profession determined to influence public opinion.

The acrimonious dispute over the editorial direction of *MFL* was just one sign of the field's flux and the diversity of outlooks during the 1950s. According to Emily Mudd, AAMC meetings in the 1950s were marked regularly by "considerable disagreement and controversy."[38] Consensus about a range of issues, including divorce, proved highly elusive. Historian Kristin Celello has argued that "marriage experts" generally endorsed the view that "a failed marriage was strong evidence of individual shortcomings, primarily on the part of the wife."[39] Similarly, Stephanie Coontz has written that experts, like the rest of society, saw divorce as "a failure of individuals rather than of marriage."[40] Indeed, the majority of Americans may have taken a dim view of divorce, but experts certainly did not. "The momentary flood of veterans' divorces" in the postwar years, according to Stanford University's William J.

Goode, was evidence that "incompatible matings" were a sign of the times. The urbanization of American society, Goode alleged, was producing "an emotional hunger . . . , a lesser willingness to wait through a long engagement period." Women who experienced "momentary irritations" in marriage were more tempted than ever to choose careers over marital commitment. Yet, far from condemning these trends or denouncing divorce, Goode recommended that "incompatible" spouses "be advised to divorce quickly."[41] The unofficial motto of Emily Mudd's MCP was "save persons, not marriages."[42] In 1955 Robert Harper lamented the "let's-keep-people-married bias," which he detected in many of his colleagues.[43] In his 1956 presidential address to the NCFR, Judson Landis maintained that his research showed that "the children from chronically unhappy homes not broken by divorce were worse off in their development than children from divorced homes." He asserted that "the past and present feeling . . . that divorce must be prevented for the sake of the children" was outdated.[44] In 1959 Walter Stokes admitted, "I have long since ceased to think of myself as primarily a servant of the marital institution or relationship."[45] According to Aaron Rutledge, writing in 1963, the practice of counselors recommending divorce had "reached gross proportions." In Rutledge's words, "many individual psychotherapists . . . naively accept as true the distorted out-pourings of the mate who consults them first, and in a half hour to several sessions recommend divorce as the only solution. . . . Some individual therapists are all too quick to trigger a divorce."[46] These utterances are just some of the many examples of the field's willingness to not just tolerate divorce but positively approve of it.

Besides their permissive attitudes toward divorce, leading counselors in the 1950s preached that the traditional division of labor between men and women no longer applied in the postwar period. Los Angeles psychiatrist Judd Marmor stated in 1951 that "democratic equalitarianism" was transforming the family, sweeping away the "Old World pattern of authoritarianism." The "psychologically healthy woman can be legitimately self-assertive in her inter-personal relationships as well as an active participant in the sexual partnership." A woman's "horizon" was not "limited to motherhood, any more than that of man is expected to be limited to fatherhood." Marmor, who in 1973 was instrumental in having homosexuality removed from the American Psychiatric Association's official list of mental disorders, believed that every woman had a right and a responsibility to develop herself to her full potential. The "regimented patterns" of the past were an obstacle to self-fulfillment, Marmor asserted. To Marmor, this version of the therapeutic outlook was nothing less than the march of democracy, a liberation from what Robert Harper called the "rural, authoritarian, superstition-dominated family values of another age."[47]

Judson Landis largely concurred with Marmor when he wrote, "With the changing roles of men and women it is inaccurate to speak of 'women's work' and 'men's work' as far as families are concerned." Landis did not exactly call for women to work outside the home, but his condemnation of the popular view that "the mother rears the children and the father earns the living" mirrored the mounting opinion that marriage had to change to meet the shifting needs of both women and men.[48] Overall, marriages were moving in a more "democratic" direction in the 1950s. As middle-of-the-road entertainer Pat Boone sang in 1958, marriage was "a fifty-fifty deal."[49]

Debates over the permissibility of divorce and the changing roles of men and women were closely tied to what Harper called the "nebulosity" of the exact nature and identity of marriage counseling in the 1950s. Ernest Groves, an early advocate of professionalization, wrote in 1944 that "the time seems ripe for projecting marriage and family counseling as an independent profession, with its own specialized training program." Groves, like others in the fledgling field, was unhappy that many troubled Americans went to untrained counselors for help. Even though he was a high-profile AAMC member, Groves argued that a much bigger "national organization" was preferable to a small interest group headquartered in the Northeast, which is what the AAMC had become. When the NCFR and the AAMC collaborated in 1948 to explore the possibility of establishing licensing standards for counseling, it appeared as if Groves's aims would be realized, but the friction between the two groups in the early 1950s scuttled those efforts. Here, too, Alfred Kinsey's influence over the AAMC was partly responsible. Kinsey's opinion that an enlarged AAMC would end the kind of intimate meetings he had attended over the years was a powerful obstacle to professionalization. Groves's hope for a bigger, more populist organization united on the basis of clear-cut training and licensing criteria faded in the face of AAMC "elitism."[50]

The field's failure to professionalize in the 1950s dismayed NCFR president Robert Foster, director of the Menninger Clinic's marriage counseling service in Topeka, Kansas. Foster expressed a typical concern when he observed in 1949 that marriage counselors appeared to be "anything under the sun from gynecologists to dog catchers." In 1953 he complained that "everybody in God's heaven seems to be a specialist in family life education from the psychiatric social worker and psychiatrist, to the educator to the domestic relations judge, the minister, and even I think, the iceman, if there are any left."[51] The ambiguous nature of the field was a by-product of its counseling orientation: if counseling involved primarily the didactic dissemination of practical knowledge to clients, not the in-depth psychological analysis of individual personalities, then countless people from a range of occupational backgrounds related to marriage and the family, including psychology, social work, home economics, and the ministry, felt entitled to dispense advice. Everyone with an opinion about marriage seemingly felt like a "specialist" in the field, but if everyone was a specialist, there was no way to convincingly argue that a single group possessed unique expertise. Drawing firm professional boundaries between AAMC members and all those who claimed to have knowledge about marriage and family matters was far from easy, and it vexed practitioners.

Emily Mudd was often at the forefront of efforts to define the distinctive nature of marriage counseling. She wholeheartedly believed in some of therapism's core principles, such as the notion that "each person is unique and needs to be helped to his own solutions." However, she went to great lengths to draw firm distinctions between counseling and "methods in psychiatric or psychoanalytic treatment," as well as the techniques of psychologist Carl Rogers, who pioneered "non-directive," client-centered therapy. In counseling, according to Mudd:

> Interviewing is face to face (a time lapse of at least several days and usually a week occurs between interviews), and . . . explanations are limited to conscious and near-conscious material. The counselor refrains from interpretations of highly symbolic

material; insistence on free association is absent, and comments on dream material are not made except where the meaning is obvious from the manifest rather than the latent content. In general, the counseling is designed to keep the treatment from entering the realm of the deep unconscious. The chief distinction between psychiatric treatment or analysis and marriage counseling is one of depth—depth of transference, of the worker's comments, and of the material reviewed by the client.[52]

The counselor's focus, she maintained, was "the relationship between the two people in the marriage, rather than, as in psychiatric therapy, the re-organization of the personality structure of the individual."[53]

In counseling, the marriage was the patient, rather than either partner. In Abraham Stone's words, it was "quite possible for a marriage to be sick even though both partners are well." Unlike psychoanalysts, who believed that therapists should not work with more than one partner in a marriage, counselors often found it advantageous to see both partners. As Kenneth Appel remarked, the counselor "needs to see both sides of the situation to get things in proper perspective."[54] Fifty years later, two therapists observed that counselors "stayed close to couples' presenting problems, provided advice and information, e.g., about the biological aspects of marriages. . . . A marriage counselor's approach was typically very focused, very short-term, and quite didactic." In contrast to a therapist, a marriage counselor was more a teacher than an adventurer into "the realm of the deep unconscious."[55]

Mudd's eagerness to differentiate between counseling and therapy may have stemmed from her faculty position at the University of Pennsylvania Medical School and the fact that 31 percent of AAMC members were physicians in 1955. She was acutely aware that her colleagues in organized medicine were lukewarm about a new group of self-proclaimed experts presuming to perform therapy. According to future AAMC president William C. Nichols, in the 1950s and 1960s the medical profession imposed a "stranglehold" over the whole field of therapy, and physicians tended to oppose attempts to recognize nonphysicians as legitimate therapists.[56] Mudd was in an awkward position: she owed much of her professional prestige to her husband's standing at the university, yet she was spearheading an emerging occupational group that many in psychiatry and related medical fields viewed as competition for a potential patient pool numbering in the millions. The professional stakes over the precise distinction between counseling and therapy were high.

Mudd also preferred the "counseling" label because, in the words of one psychologist, "many members of the public are willing to go to someone who is called a 'marriage counselor' rather than someone who is called a 'psychotherapist.'"[57] In the 1950s the term *therapy* still connoted a service dispensed by a licensed physician to people who were clinically "sick." Yet, over the next quarter of a century, the stigma surrounding therapy as a treatment for people with mental disabilities faded due to the growing belief that therapy could also help individuals deal with the emotional problems of everyday life.

By siding with her counterparts in organized medicine on the issue of marriage counseling, Mudd discovered that, in twenty years, she had gone from radical pioneer to defender of the professional status quo. In its early days, the AAMC had attempted to define a professional identity with a circling-the-wagons strategy that denied admission to any self-taught counselors. Only like-minded counselors with recognized clinical experience could hope for admission. Social connections mattered too; current members had to sponsor prospective members, and, as in college fraternities, members could be "blackballed." "Meetings of the young organization were reminiscent of European professional society gatherings," William Nichols remembered, where individuals gathered informally and behind closed doors to discuss collegially preapproved topics.[58] In 1963 the AAMC's executive directors proudly claimed that membership had "come to be prized as an honor not easily won." One member recalled, "When I applied for membership in 1964, I had two master's degrees, a doctorate, and an appropriate post-doctoral internship. I was admitted as an Associate-in-Training and had to wait three years to be advanced to full membership. That was standard for the times."[59] The AAMC leadership evidently believed that strict membership criteria would bar amateurs as well as minimize differences of opinion within the ranks, especially from those who wanted marriage counseling to be more "therapeutic."

However, the AAMC's "closed-shop" mentality that limited membership to sharply defined social circles in Philadelphia and New York

City came under attack in the 1960s as a new wave of practitioners challenged this approach to professionalization. The first challenge came from Carl Rogers, a pivotal founder of therapism. Rogers, born in 1902 in suburban Chicago, was almost single-handedly responsible for replacing the term *patient* with *client* in nonpsychiatric settings. Rogers and his coworkers were the first to use unedited transcripts of audio-taped therapeutic sessions for clinical instruction purposes. Thanks to Rogers, organized medicine's monopoly over the concept of therapy gradually slipped out of its hands, and the therapeutic relationship became a "democratic" enterprise between equals.[60]

As a young man, Rogers believed he was destined for the clergy, but he left the seminary when his religious doubts multiplied. He later rejected the "Protestant Christian tradition" that, he claimed, "has permeated our culture with the concept that man is basically sinful, and only by something approaching a miracle can his sinful nature be negated."[61] By contrast, Rogers was an indefatigable believer in human goodness and the individual's ability to "progress toward becoming increasingly his or her own self."[62] "There is no beast in man," Rogers wrote; "there is only man in man."[63] Between 1945 and 1947 Rogers, a professor at the University of Chicago, ran a campus counseling center where he developed his theories of client-centered, nondirective therapy, which cast the therapist as a facilitator rather than a leader of the counseling session. "In counseling of this sort," Rogers wrote in 1944, "the deeply significant activities are those of the client; those of the counselor are only such as will make it easier for the client to guide himself." According to Rogers, nondirective counseling was "fully consistent with the highest achievements of democratic living" because it bestowed "the right on the individual to guide his actions in areas as personal as marriage."[64] Rogers, like Robert Harper, Judson Landis, Judd Marmor, and other marriage counselors, was an early exponent of therapy's "democratic side": the notion that, by helping individuals "grow" personally in any direction they chose, therapy is crucial to the smooth functioning of a free nation. Therapy in this view is more than simply an individual choice: it is tantamount to a civic duty that helps all of society.[65]

When he presented his views at an AAMC meeting in New York City in 1952, however, Rogers encountered opposition from those who held to the original counseling ethos. As psychiatrist Lena Levine sternly reminded him, "We are very much concerned here with the difference between counseling and psychotherapy." Rogers rejected a firm distinction between the two; it was not possible, he claimed, to say, "To the left, this is counseling, and to the right, this is psychotherapy. . . . People will keep moving across it all the time."[66]

A second challenge came from the most outspoken of the Young Turks in the field, psychologist Albert Ellis. Born in 1913 in Pittsburgh, Pennsylvania, Ellis was the founder of rational emotive behavior therapy (REBT), which is based on the theory that individuals' emotional reactions are determined not by events in their lives but by their own beliefs, in which case individuals should accept reality as distinct from what they think about it. In 2003 the American Psychological Association voted Ellis the second most influential psychotherapist of the twentieth century; Rogers ranked first, with Sigmund Freud trailing in third place. Kinsey got most of the headlines as a sex pioneer in Cold War America, but Ellis, author of *Sex without Guilt* (1957) and an advocate of "open marriage," deserved almost as much credit for his determined efforts to liberalize attitudes by defending publishers of sex-related materials, alleged sex offenders, and gay liberation.

A regular participant at AAMC meetings in the 1950s, Ellis "used to make our hair stand on end," in Emily Mudd's words.[67] Ellis was never shy about expressing his unconventional ideas; he asserted that Western society "clung to the idea that virginity and chastity are sacred to God— which idea, of course, was largely a Hebrew and early Christian rationalization for the socio-economic realities of the ancient world"—in other words, hopelessly outdated.[68] Ellis's view that "any man or woman who can only enjoy face to face intercourse . . . is as much a pervert as the homosexual and the sadist" drew predictable outcries from counselors who believed that "the complete satisfaction expressed in the orgasm belongs only to coition between husband and wife."[69]

Ellis's opinions about the differences between counseling and therapy were perhaps less hair-raising but equally unconventional and adversarial. He contended that, based on his reading of the reported case histories in *MFL*, much of what passed for marriage counseling was in actuality psychotherapy. Ellis had a point. In his view, contrary to what some defenders of the counseling model maintained, people who sought counseling suffered from emotional disturbances, required repeated counseling over a lengthy period, and consequently often achieved "better insight into themselves as well as into their relations with each other." Counselors had to face the fact that they practiced "a special kind of psychotherapy" that was distinct from orthodox psychoanalysis. Ellis's comments failed to change the minds of Emily Mudd and other eminent counselors in the 1950s, but they were a harbinger of important shifts that would occur in the field in the 1970s. By that time, marriage counseling would be redefined as a form of therapy in which clients went "much deeper into themselves and gained considerably more self understanding" than in simple counseling, in Ellis's words.[70]

If AAMC and NCFR members of the 1950s debated whether they practiced counseling or therapy, on another front, the field was in agreement. The one issue on which counselors were mostly united was the conviction that America's clergymen were ill equipped to advise their parishioners about matrimony and family matters. Some early pastoral counselors shared this opinion and dedicated themselves to correcting the situation, but many clergymen worried that in the rush to improve counseling skills, core theological doctrines would be sacrificed. Other clergy saw the ambitions of marriage and family counselors as "secular invasions into soul caring."[71] These concerns, however, did little to slow therapism's steady march into pastoral counseling (and many other aspects of American society).

Pastoral counseling was conquered by the therapeutic viewpoint as a broad tide of religiosity swept 1950s America. Rates of church attendance were at their highest in U.S. history. Evangelical and fundamentalist churches experienced remarkable growth, as did the Roman Catholic Church. Between 1942 and 1956 the percentage of Americans who said they belonged to a church jumped from 50 to 65. Sales of the Bible increased 140 percent between 1949 and 1953. Evangelist Billy Graham organized revival meetings that were so big they had to be held in football stadiums.[72] Most Americans wanted church weddings, and in 1940 three-fourths of all marriages were solemnized by a priest, a minister, or a rabbi; between one-half and two-thirds of all Americans attended a church or a synagogue.[73] Surveys showed that in the 1950s, 42 percent of Americans who sought help for personal problems consulted their clergymen, and people who consulted their clergymen did so mainly because of marital problems. This situation rankled many marriage counselors, who accounted for only 10 percent of all generic marriage counseling performed in the United States.[74] As long as America's clergy exerted a firm grip over the nation's hearts and minds, marriage and family counselors would have to play second fiddle. To correct this imbalance, groups such as the AAMC dedicated themselves to convincing clergy that their theological training left them poorly prepared to advise laypeople.

The ambitions of marriage counselors were matched by the efforts of some clergymen to professionalize pastoral counseling in accordance with developments in psychological theory. Prior to World War II, a handful of Protestant ministers were so impressed with the growth in psychological knowledge that they developed programs in clinical pastoral education, but their intention was not to offer psychological counseling to their parishioners. That changed when the United States entered World War II and the need for military chaplains increased. As a result of their war experience, veterans were inclined to consult clergymen when grappling with problems adjusting to civilian life. Likewise, after the war, millions of predominantly young, white, Protestant Americans bought homes in the nation's suburbs, began families, joined churches, and sought advice from their clergymen, based on the mounting belief that counseling could drastically improve the quality of their lives.[75] In his 1956 best seller *The Organization Man*, sociologist William Whyte reported that middle-class, suburban Americans placed enormous emotional strains on their clergy. One minister reported that "so many young people around makes counseling my main worry. I simply haven't time for any more. . . . But the thing is, you feel you can do so much in a place like this. . . . These young people have all their adjustments to make at once, and you feel you can do so much for them. No case seems hopeless, and you're tormented by the thought that how you help them will be important for years to come."[76] Thus, Americans' churchgoing tendencies helped reinterpret religion as "God's psychiatry." Opinion makers such as the Reverend Norman Vincent Peale and Rabbi Joshua Loth Liebman taught that psychology and psychiatry enabled people to achieve "peace of mind" and practice "positive thinking." "The new piety" sweeping the nation's suburbs in the 1950s "hailed the psychological benefits of faith," according to historian E. Brooks Holifield, and blurred the boundaries between religion and psychiatry. The arrival of "religion as personal therapy" marked a decisive turn in the nation's history.[77]

The authoritative Joint Commission on Mental Illness and Health (JCMIH) called for amplified efforts to improve mental health, and because it recognized the widespread impact of pastoral counseling, it recommended the "collaboration of certain of the theological groups" in evaluating "the nature, extent, and quality of this counseling."[78] Although growing numbers of marriage and family counselors endorsed the spirit of the JCMIH's 1961 report, these counselors agreed on two things: (1) they had to convince Americans to consult them rather than clergymen on matters of mental well-being, and (2) pastoral counseling was largely amateurish and rooted in out-of-date theological doctrine.

As Ernest Groves complained back in 1940, "The pastor is drawn toward literature that seems to be especially Christian on account of its vocabulary, when what he needs is the insight of science."[79] In 1947 the *Journal of Clinical and Pastoral Work* and the *Journal of Pastoral Care* were launched. "Training of ministers for counseling should take account of the Standards for Marriage Counselors adopted in principle by the American Association of Marriage Counselors," an *MFL* author tersely noted in 1950.[80] That same year, the journal *Pastoral Psychology* began publication, featuring articles by Carl Rogers, psychiatrist William Menninger, anthropologist Margaret Mead, and clergyman Joseph Fletcher, whose theory of "situation ethics" stated that ethical decisions in medicine should be based solely on an individual's patient's particular condition and circumstances, not on absolute values or rules. *Pastoral Psychology*'s editor was theologian Seward Hiltner (his wife served briefly as NCFR executive secretary in 1953). In 1957 Aaron Rutledge complained that "the clergy see an overwhelming amount of marital stress, but most seminaries continue to offer inadequate training in this area." In Rutledge's opinion, "one of the glaring inadequacies" of existing pastoral training was a lack of "knowledge and skills for dealing with sexual problems." Still, he was heartened by the "major progress in recent years."[81]

By 1955, roughly 75 percent of all seminaries either ran their own clinical training programs or sent their students elsewhere for such training. Universities received funds from the government and private foundations to develop new programs in pastoral counseling. Jobs for pastoral counselors opened up not only in teaching and training institutes but also in general hospitals, state mental hospitals, Veterans Administration hospitals, prisons, and reform schools. Indeed, Harry Emerson Fosdick declared in 1960 that a "good minister cannot now escape personal counselling. . . . It is in the air."[82] The formation of the American Association of Pastoral Counselors in 1963 capped a period of breathtaking growth that few could have imagined twenty years earlier.

Emily Mudd and the MCP were trailblazers in the training of clergymen to perform marriage and family counseling. Mudd wrote that "the church offers as great a potential as a mental health resource for adults as does the school for children." Beginning in 1947 Mudd's MCP offered specialized training in marriage counseling at the postgraduate level for persons in the ministry who had already earned graduate degrees in their own discipline and had some experience in face-to-face counseling. By 1964, about half of the 125 accredited divinity schools in the nation offered courses in pastoral care, yet there were no specialized university-based training programs for divinity school faculty. That changed between 1964 and 1969, when Mudd's MCP received NIMH funding to support a training program for seminary teachers of pastoral care. As Mudd put it, "This experiment will bring general recognition of the importance of extending theological education to include an understanding of human behavior based on scientific studies."[83]

A priest who trained at the MCP approvingly observed: "The most basic effect [of the training] has been the separation of the parson from the person. . . . I came to Marriage Council with my personal self so subsumed by the professional self of the priest that I was not a real person at all. What is emerging, not without labor pains, is a personal self increasingly capable, not simply as a carrier of priestly function, but as a very human person."[84] A rabbi described his 1961–1963 stint at the MCP: "During these two, rather painful learning years I progressed from a strongly defended, feeling denying person, to one who, according to my final evaluation, could work helpfully with clients and keep my personal feelings and biases from greatly affecting my counseling."[85] His characterization of the nonjudgmental attitudes taught by the MCP reveals that Mudd's clinic was teaching its students to leave their religious "biases" at the door and practice a value-neutral form of counseling—a core tenet of therapism. As Hilda Goodwin, the supervisor of training and counseling at the MCP, observed in 1964, a clergyman in training "may find himself having to reassess his moral judgments, and perhaps his whole ideal of the marriage relationship." The counselor's task was to recognize that "within each of us [is] a desire for growth and maturity" and a capacity to make "responsible choices."[86] The judgmental concepts of sin and guilt had no place in a clinical setting that encouraged the "separation of the parson from the person."

Pastoral counseling not only led to a liberalization of religious doctrine; it also had a "subversive" impact on gender roles in the 1950s and 1960s, in the words of historian Susan Myers-Shirk.[87] Two factors stood out: women seemed more likely than men to approach their clergymen for help, and Carl Rogers exerted a huge influence over pastoral counseling in its early years.[88] Relying on Rogers's nondirective and client-centered method, Protestant pastoral counselors cultivated a non-judgmental style that avoided giving advice to counselees and encouraged them to make their own choices. Thus, theory and clinical realities shaped the viewpoints of pastoral counselors. Their willingness to acknowledge the personal autonomy of their parishioners led them to question the "domestic ideal in which fathers served as breadwinners and mothers stayed home with the children."[89] More subversively, Seward Hiltner acknowledged that the "democratic and anti-authoritarian implications of the nondirective approach" made it difficult for clergymen to remain orthodox "in the realm of faith and morals." Hilda Goodwin warned that clergymen who were "committed to a belief in the sanctity of marriage, or whose faith prohibits divorce," would find pastoral counseling training "especially difficult."[90] Psychoanalyst Doris Mode expressed doubts about "the permissive atmosphere" of a Rogers-inspired, client-centered encounter: a pastoral counselor who passively "place[s] no blame" was a therapist who "abandons all values of his own." "If God were not judgmental," Mode wrote in 1950, "there would be no meaning to life, and if he were not loving, there would be no fulfillment."[91] In 1962 a Roman Catholic pastoral counselor proclaimed that "as long as the pastor is functioning as a clergyman, he cannot practice client-centered therapy. . . . To practice as [a] client-centered coun-

David Mace giving a corsage to his wife, Vera. (Courtesy of the National Council on Family Relations)

selor, he must, for the time being at least, renounce his priestly role. As a pastor he can be permissive within limits, but he cannot and should not be neutral in religious and moral matters."[92] Nonetheless, these objections to Rogerian counseling failed to stem a swelling tide that would result in therapism's takeover of pastoral counseling.

Regardless of their inroads into pastoral counseling, the 1960s did not immediately usher in sweeping changes for marriage and family counselors. Indeed, a brief period of retrenchment occurred, marked in October 1960 by the hiring of David Mace and his wife, Vera, as AAMC "joint executive directors." In 1938 David Mace, a Methodist minister and a native of Scotland, had helped form the National Marriage Guidance Council of Great Britain.[93] The Maces were close friends of Emily

Mudd, who had arranged for their two daughters to travel to the United States to escape the London Blitz during World War II. In 1949 the Maces joined their daughters in the United States, and shortly thereafter, with Mudd's spiritual support, they became Quakers. David Mace took a position as professor of human relations at Drew University in Madison, New Jersey, and he sometimes referred doctoral students in theology to do fieldwork for Mudd's MCP. After resigning from Drew in 1959 to accept a three-year contract with the International Council of Churches, Mace was summarily fired when he officiated at his daughter's wedding to a Hindu. Mudd then arranged for the University of Pennsylvania to hire him as an adjunct visiting professor of marriage counseling. In 1961 Mace became NCFR president, thus holding concurrent leadership positions in both the AAMC and the NCFR.

During the 1950s and 1960s David Mace was a regular columnist on married and family life for *McCall's* and *Women's Home Companion* magazines. He later taught at the Bowman Gray School of Medicine at Wake Forest University. He and Vera collaborated on thirty-three books, including *The Soviet Family* (1963), which, like Mudd's early writings on the Soviet Union, generally praised communist Russia for its policies on marriage and the family.[94] His acceptance of the AAMC executive directorship not only indicated his rising stature in the field but also strengthened Emily Mudd's grip over the group. Mace may not have been Mudd's mouthpiece, but the close overlap in their viewpoints guaranteed that her sway over the field remained strong into the late 1960s.

The Maces' success in building up the National Marriage Guidance Council of Great Britain was crucial in the AAMC's decision to hire them and signaled that the financially strapped group had reached a crossroads, as had the field in general. As part of an overall cost-cutting exercise, the AAMC's New York City office was closed and the organization's headquarters was moved to the Maces' home in New Jersey. Mudd came through with a three-year, $24,000 Pathfinder grant from Clarence Gamble, and additional financial aid came in the form of a $10,000 grant from the Mary Biddle Duke Foundation to fund a New York City referral service for marriage counselors. The Pathfinder grant gave the Maces some breathing space, allowing them to fend off attempts to relax the AAMC's clinical experience requirements for membership. As they noted in 1961: "Our board is emphatic in regarding the AAMC as an elite, a professional association. . . . It is obviously far more important to stress high standards than to build up a large membership. . . . By lowering our membership standards we could easily sweep into our ranks large numbers of people whose dues would enable us to balance our relatively modest budget."[95]

The Maces also tried to shift the field's orientation back to Emily Mudd's original vision of linking marriage counseling to reproductive freedom. As program chair for the NCFR annual meeting in Salt Lake City, Utah, in August 1961, David Mace organized a plenary session panel discussion on abortion and birth control. When executive director Ruth Jewson objected, Mace replied that "the really crucial and inadequately examined area of difference in the religious field is in the connection between sex and reproduction."[96] Emily Mudd could not have put it any better.

Yet the grants provided only a brief respite from the AAMC's ongoing troubles. A new age in the history of mental health beckoned. The mounting taste for therapism had unleashed forces in American society that threatened to leave the AAMC and the NCFR far behind. For the AAMC, the 1960s were a time to catch up or close up shop.

*W*hen noted psychiatrist William Menninger sat down with President John F. Kennedy in the Oval Office on February 9, 1962, the entire history of U.S. mental health care was at a turning point. As Kennedy listened in his familiar, old-fashioned-looking rocking chair, Menninger quickly got down to business. He challenged Kennedy to seize "leadership" of the movement in psychiatry that focused on the "most neglected area of all health causes": mental health. "We want somebody of your stature who will stand up with us and be counted," Menninger told Kennedy.

Menninger already knew that no U.S. president had taken a bigger personal interest in mental health issues than Kennedy. The president's sister Eunice was an active board member of the Menninger Foundation, and his eldest sister Rosemary had undergone a lobotomy, a surgical procedure that destroyed the nerve tracts to and from the frontal lobe of the brain. Yet, when Kennedy readily accepted the psychiatrist's challenge, even Menninger was pleasantly surprised.

Kennedy kept his word. On February 5, 1963, he sent a special message to Congress on the issue of mental health. He called on the country to adopt a "bold new approach" to mental health, replacing "the cold mercy of custodial isolation" with "the open warmth of community concern and capability." Later that year, on October 31, Kennedy signed into law the Community Mental Health Centers Act, which earmarked $150 million for the construction of treatment centers where people could receive mental health services outside the walls of state hospitals. Kennedy's signature unleashed the federal government's first peacetime initiative in mental health policy.[1]

To the public at large, the act seemed to come out of the blue, but to marriage and family counselors, it was a vindication of their efforts dating back to the 1930s. Historically, the field had stressed that counseling was an important weapon in the battle to prevent psychological disorders: the more counseling Americans received, the better their mental wellness. The emphasis on prevention embodied by the newly constructed community mental health centers emboldened a younger generation of counselors to forge a new professional identity in the 1960s. Central to attempts to professionalize was the overthrow of the old counseling model and its replacement with a more therapeutic orientation. As Albert Ellis and Carl Rogers had argued, distinguishing therapy from counseling behind the closed doors of a practitioner's office was often little more than a rhetorical exercise anyway. The younger cohort of counselors increasingly coveted the designation "therapist" in the wake of Kennedy's 1963 act, and for the next forty years they assiduously preached the therapeutic gospel that each and every American deserved better emotional health.

The efforts of marriage and family counselors were aided by emerging countercultural movements that often linked the ideals of self-realization and personal autonomy to political causes that challenged many of the country's established institutions. The burgeoning media—notably, television—helped spread the notion that experts could unlock the mysteries of marriage and the family and apply techniques that would allow everyone to achieve the happiness they deserved. By the end of the twentieth century, few Americans dissented from the marriage and family therapy field's viewpoint that personal psychological health was a vital national goal.

Yet, while much was changing in the 1960s and into the 1970s, much also remained the same. The seeds of therapism had been sown by the first generation of counselors such as Mudd, Laidlaw, Dickinson, Groves, and Dearborn, who had taught that scientific knowledge could empower individuals to seek emotional self-fulfillment inside or outside the boundaries of marriage. If, as the 1980s dawned, practitioners preferred to define their activities as therapy rather than counseling, it did not mean that they utterly rejected the legacy of their predecessors. Emily Mudd may have thought Ellis's ideas were "hair-raising," and she certainly opposed the "primarily non-medical" trajectory of the AAMC by the early 1970s, but she had laid the groundwork for the ascendancy of therapism a quarter century earlier.[2] Continuity and discontinuity blended together in the history of twentieth-century marriage and family counseling.

As the AAMC closed ranks in the early 1960s, it was nonetheless evident to many counselors that the occupational status quo was obsolete. Even David Mace, a defender of the AAMC's "old guard," believed that popular expectations of marriage and family life were changing dramatically. To Mace, by 1964, a "shift of emphasis on contemporary culture [had occurred] from the concept of marriage as mainly concerned with familial goals to a concept which focused in interpersonal fulfillment and satisfaction."[3] According to Mace, the days of married people subordinating their own desires to their family duties were quickly coming to an end. By the close of the decade, the Maces had left their AAMC posts for newer professional pastures. They were touting the first ever "marriage enrichment" retreats for couples. The therapeutic revolution in marriage and the family was under way.

Nothing better signals the shift from counseling to therapy than the idea of marriage enrichment (ME). Before ME, as David Mace explained, counselors "dealt only with marriages in trouble." Yet in 1962, he and his wife, Vera, started attending Quaker-organized retreats for married couples in Kirkridge, Pennsylvania, where they came into "close touch with many 'normal'" husbands and wives. This proved to be a revelation for the Maces, who discovered that "many of these normal couples were settling for relationships that were far short of their inherent potential." According to the Maces, ME empowered these "normal" couples to enjoy the "relationship-in-depth" they desired and hoped for. ME retreats enabled couples to topple "the taboo"—"hitherto unrecognized as such," they hastened to add—that blocked married couples from "sharing their intra-marital experiences with each other." Such retreats were the ideal settings for couples to overcome the "strictness that goes far beyond [the taboo's] usefulness in our changing society." ME differed from standard marriage counseling because it included couples who seemingly had no "serious problems." To the Maces, it was time to open up marriage to the scrutiny of others and expose its secrets to the world. A huge segment of the married population would benefit from baring its soul in this way. With the right kind of guidance, this population could enjoy the relationships they allegedly deserved. Ending marital unhappiness was giving way to the aim of achieving marital happiness—an infinitely open-ended goal.[4]

The Maces went on to found the Association for Couples in Marriage Enrichment in 1973, and they devised a "tool-kit for couples to use as they carry out the adventure of 'growing a marriage.'"[5] ME dovetailed historically with similar initiatives associated with the United Methodist Church and the Christian Family Movement (CFM). Founded in 1948, CFM was a lay Catholic organization that endorsed the idea of "marriage encounters," during which Catholic couples would meet to discuss their marriages. One couple attested that after eight years of marriage and six children, they "fell in love again . . . by the end of the first day [of the encounter] we had discovered each other for the very first time."[6] However, if the basic methods of ME and CFM encounters were similar, their aims were different. CFM urged Christian couples to "reorientate their married lives along apostolic lines." The Maces and ME, by contrast, were "not asking that people be put under pressure to marry, or to stay in marriage."[7] Their advocacy of "a long overdue overhaul of our concepts about marriage" invited "radical changes" not just to counseling but also to the way husbands and wives interacted with each other, with their families, and with other married couples. In requiring "interpersonal competence" in marriage, and in calling on state and federal governments to end their traditional "'hands-off' policy" regarding marriage, Mace and the ME movement were arguing that marriage was no longer a private matter; it was everybody's business. Marital self-fulfillment was an exercise in democracy. ME, in other words, highlighted the blurring of boundaries between personal freedom and societal expectations characteristic of therapism.[8]

The ME movement was merely one of many dramatic changes in American society as the 1960s drew to a close. Gays, women, African Americans, Native Americans, and college students staged strikes and protests against poverty, pollution, the Vietnam War, and racial and sexual discrimination. The anger of many protesters was captured in the words of Meredith Tax, a radical feminist who declared that women had had their "mental and emotional feet bound for thousands of years."[9] Just as ME was a challenge to long-standing attitudes toward marriage, so countercultural protests were targeting a range of other institutions throughout U.S. society, from the Pentagon and General Motors to organized medicine and some of the nation's most prestigious universities. College students, showing their defiance of authority, occupied university buildings, shouted down professors and administrators, and often clashed with security or police. In 1964 Luther Terry, the U.S. surgeon general, issued his report on smoking and health that alerted the nation to the risks of cigarettes and ushered in an era of bitter litigation against the country's powerful tobacco companies.[10] A slew of best-selling books in the 1960s attacked America's other bellwether industries. Rachel Carson's *Silent Spring* (1962) was a stinging indictment of the chemical industry and helped launch the modern environmentalist movement. Ralph Nader's *Unsafe at Any Speed* (1965), a key document of the consumer rights movement, accused automobile manufacturers of neglecting safety and putting lives at risk. *The Doctors' Case against the Pill* (1969),written by Barbara Seaman, vigorously warned of the health risks of the oral contraceptive pill, winning her a reputation as the "Ralph Nader of the birth control pill."[11]

Discontent, often bitter, soon morphed into malaise as inflation, unemployment, defeat in Vietnam, the oil crisis, the Watergate scandal, and the backlash against the Great Society reforms of the 1960s continued to undermine the country's faith in its traditional elites and institutions in the 1970s. Few institutions endured more criticism than organized medicine. Historian Paul Starr has written that the "mandate" enjoyed by the medical profession in the first half of the twentieth century abruptly came to an end in the 1970s.[12] Countless Americans began to question whether clinicians, researchers, hospitals, and medical schools should run their own affairs as they saw fit. A barrage of bad publicity led to a drop in doctors' public esteem (from 72 to 57 percent approval) between 1965 and 1973.[13] In 1974 a U.S. Senate investigation confirmed a lot of fears when it disclosed that more than 2.4 million unnecessary operations were performed each year in the United States, causing 11,900 deaths and costing $3.9 billion. In his book *Medical Nemesis* (1975), Austrian-born ex–Catholic priest Ivan Illich went so far as to claim that the medical establishment itself was a threat to public health. According to historian Edward Shorter, a "postmodern" patient emerged during these years, one who was highly suspicious of medical diagnosis and treatment yet prone to interpret the aches and pains of everyday life as symptoms of bona fide disease.[14] Growing numbers of patients viewed their relationships with their doctors as adversarial rather than cooperative, and they demanded that doctors pay more attention to patients' perceptions of their illnesses. In 1972 the American Hospital Association issued a Patients' Bill of Rights, including the right to informed consent and to considerate and respectful care. The American Medical Association quickly followed suit, declaring in 1973 that patients needed to agree with the treatment options offered by their physicians. By the mid-1970s, the public reputation of physicians had badly frayed.

The attack on organized medicine occupied center stage in the women's movement. Female activists denounced the paternalism of male doctors and the harm done to women by the health care industry. Women's groups demanded that the medical profession admit more women into its ranks and called on women to take their health into their own hands through self-medication and improved public health programs. The campaign in favor of gender privacy and empowerment led to publications such as *Our Bodies, Ourselves,* a best-selling self-help manual on women's health first published in 1971. These and other attacks inspired many women to give credence to their own emotions as they struggled to understand their mental health, rather than deferring to what their (mostly male) physicians told them. A female psychologist urged women to "deepen our contact with our feelings. Our first concern must not be with whether these feelings are good or bad, but what they are. Feelings are a reality." These psychological notions were indebted to the client-centered theories of Carl Rogers, and they often formed the basis of consciousness-raising sessions in which women used group discussion to explore common emotions. A member of the New York Radical Women, a group formed in 1967, stated that with consciousness-raising, "we always stay in touch with our feelings."[15]

A key document of the women's movement that attacked the institutions of marriage and the family was Betty Friedan's *The Feminine Mystique* (1963). Based on the findings of her own survey of former Smith College classmates, Friedan claimed to have discovered "the problem that has no name," which she described as a "strange stirring, a sense of dissatisfaction, a yearning" that suburban women in mid-twentieth-century America were feeling. Taught to "seek fulfillment as wives and mothers," these women were haunted by the "silent question—'Is this all?'" As one housewife told Friedan: "I can take the real problems; it's the endless boring days that make me desperate." In *The Feminine Mystique* Friedan lamented "the dull routine of housework" and argued that women's genuine self-actualization was achieved outside of the home and the family. The solution to "the problem that has no name" was "work," according to Friedan, "the work important to the world . . . the work that used [women's] human abilities and through which they were able to find self-realization." Friedan urged women not to give up their dreams of education and their "right to participate in the more advanced work of society."[16]

Friedan proudly adopted the mantle of revolutionary, but she was not quite the pioneer she claimed to be. Long before she and other figures of the women's movement began talking about "the problem that has no name," Emily Mudd was advocating for reforms aimed at achieving women's equality in the home, the workplace, and society as an antidote to married women's lack of fulfillment. Scholars have shown that Friedan's views about the status of American women dated back to her involvement in postwar, left-wing, labor movement politics.[17] Years earlier, Mudd drew on many of the same political sources in her efforts to document women's conflicted feelings about work and motherhood.

Friedan was scathingly critical of what passed for marriage advice in the mainstream women's magazines of the day such as *Redbook* and *Good Housekeeping*, and she accused Freudian psychoanalysis of being an "obstacle to truth for women in America today and a major cause of the pervasive problem that knows no name."[18] Among the "millions of words" written about women, Friedan alleged, there was "no word" that described their fierce longing for self-esteem and self-fulfillment.[19] Emily Mudd, in Friedan's eyes, was little better than a defender of the traditional theory that women's happiness depended on their "adjustment" to marriage.[20] Yet Friedan was wrong about Mudd in particular and about marriage counseling in general: neither was an apologist for the "feminine mystique." Nor, as historian Eva Moskowitz has shown, did popular women's magazines of the 1950s ignore the unhappiness of housewives: time and again their stories acknowledged the frustrations, yearnings, and anger married women felt as they tried to live up to the domestic ideal.[21] Friedan's theory that marriage and family counselors

in the early 1960s only taught women that they should adapt to the realities of life as wives and mothers was incorrect.[22]

Friedan's claim in *The Feminine Mystique* that she spoke for all women
was similarly inaccurate. In 1962 more than two-thirds of the women
surveyed by University of Michigan researchers agreed that most of the
important family decisions should be made by the "man of the house."[23]
When *McCall's* ran her article titled "The Fraud of Femininity," the magazine was deluged by letters from angry readers who objected to
Friedan's message that housewives' lives were "empty, wasted, and full
of frustration." One reader wrote that she was "a proud and fulfilled
wife, mother, daughter, sister, daughter-in-law, and friend; trying to live
up to my purpose of being here on this earth . . . and I am sick, sick, sick
of reading just this type of article." Another wrote that after marrying
at age nineteen and leaving college, "no statistic can convince me that
my life is empty and that my work is not 'serious' and important to society." Friedan and her sympathizers argued that her book was welcomed by countless women who shared her opinion of women's
emotional lives, but many other women dissented, complaining that
they were "tired of hearing about the poor little housewife who is
trapped, frustrated, guilty, wasting her life, unappreciated, dependent,
passive, and whatever else she is called."[24]

If Friedan was harsh in her criticism of postwar psychology, she
nonetheless relied heavily on popular psychological theories to justify
her attacks on the "feminine mystique." As an undergraduate at Smith
College, Friedan had majored in psychology, and she also studied under
Freudian psychologist Erik Erikson at the University of California at
Berkeley. In New York City she underwent psychoanalytic treatment and
explored, among other things, what she described as her hatred of her
mother. In calling for women to rebel against the domestic ideal, Friedan
enlisted the views of Abraham Maslow to explain the condition of the
"forfeited self," whereby women were allegedly expected to conform to
"an image that does not permit them to become what they now can be."[25]
Maslow, a professor of psychology at Brandeis University from 1951 to
1969, taught that people should engage in "self-actualization," a process
by which individuals explored new ranges of motivations on the road
toward realizing their humanity. Maslow was not politically radical, but
for activists in the women's movement, his ideas helped account for the

deeply conflicted feelings so many of them harbored. The use of Maslow's theories was one example of the way feminist activists exploited psychology to uncover "who had power, who did not, and why," in the words of historian Ellen Herman. Numerous feminists warned against "thinking that women's liberation is therapy," but in the struggle to achieve greater freedom for women, many in the movement found it difficult to distinguish between psychology and politics.[26]

Thus, Friedan's book revealed that the countercultural attacks on the domestic ideal were Janus-faced, owing as much to events in the 1950s as to radical shifts in mind-set in the 1960s. Friedan mischaracterized much of marriage counseling prior to the 1960s, and she either overlooked or simply did not know that Emily Mudd had described "the problem that has no name" back in the 1940s, albeit with less panache and publicity. Dazzled by her impressions of women's status in the Soviet Union during her 1946 tour, Mudd had argued that work outside the home would enable women to overcome the psychological turmoil caused by the "conflicting values" of motherhood and selfhood. In January 1946, even before she visited the USSR, she told a McGill University audience in Montreal that women longed to "participate actively in the worthwhile work of the world" and that the "Soviet experiment" had demonstrated that women can take on "responsibility outside the home, that women can master 'men's' professions, that masses of women can be intelligently concerned with large issues, national and international." However, according to Mudd, "in our present American culture women are forced to hurdle the barriers erected by the denial of the principle that women can give equal value in creative work." "Our way of life," she maintained, has taught every woman "to approach her experiences through the back door of a special relation to man, receiving bounties, even the gift of life from him." By contrast, Soviet women deserved the "gratitude" of American women for "disproving so many of the time-hallowed contentions concerning women's naturally inferior role in society."[27] In placing a high value on the work performed by Soviet women outside the home, Mudd was seeing them chiefly through the prism of her own experience as a working mother in America who—as she admitted—felt conflicted herself. Yet it was evident that she was discussing the same psychological condition Friedan would claim to have discovered fifteen years later.

In a revised 1955 version of her 1946 lecture, Mudd came even closer to describing "the problem that has no name" when she asserted that "the criteria held by society in regard to the duties of the married woman were so inimical to the development of her inner life" that she felt "helpless, frightened, and confused."[28] Although both Friedan and Mudd inhabited fellow-traveling circles in the late 1940s, *The Feminine Mystique* did not associate women's emancipation with the status of women in the Soviet Union, as Mudd had. Mudd had relied on Rose Maurer's writings on Soviet women, as well as those of Sophie Drinker, a member of the MCP's board.[29] Drinker's *Music and Women* (1948) praised women's contributions to the history of music, and Friedan personally invited Drinker to join the first board of the National Organization for Women (NOW), which Friedan helped found in 1966. Thus, although there were dissimilarities in their approaches, Friedan and Mudd both had radical pasts that they later downplayed. They shared a belief in marriage's severe psychological and mental risks for women. They both contended that marital social conventions produced emotionally stunted women and that work outside the home was the most effective path toward self-realization. Each in her own way—Mudd in her powerful influence over marriage counseling, and Friedan as a best-selling author and founder of NOW—helped blur the lines between politics and psychology as the women's movement began its ascent during the Cold War. Both Friedan and Mudd reinforced the reliance of countercultural movements—notably, the women's movement—on the creed of therapism.

One crucial difference between Mudd and Friedan was Mudd's emphasis on what she called the "spiritual power of sexual intercourse."[30] By contrast, Friedan tended to stress women's equal protection under the law and equal opportunity in education and employment. To Friedan, "sex in the America of the feminine mystique is becoming a strangely joyless national compulsion," and she condemned "the endless flow of manuals describing new sex techniques."[31] She shared NOW's opposition to Hugh Hefner's *Playboy* magazine, with its pictorials of nude women and its celebration of the "*Playboy* lifestyle" based on sexual promiscuity and consumerist gratification. Once it hit the newsstands in November 1953, *Playboy* championed "sexual liberation" and supported the legalization of abortion, birth control, and sex education, but critics argued that Hefner's aim was not to emancipate women but to make them more sexually available to men. Friedan and NOW particularly objected to *Playboy*'s glorification of consumerism as a means of men's liberation from responsible masculinity, whereas media depictions of female consumers often cast them as "happy housewives, idiots, and sex objects," in the words of one activist.[32]

The conclusions Friedan drew from Kinsey's writings also differed from Mudd's. Friedan hailed Kinsey's finding that the most sexually fulfilled women tended to be college educated and professional. To her, Kinsey's data confirmed her theory that the core problem was not sexual dysfunction but a lack of educational and professional opportunities.[33] For Friedan, lack of sexual fulfillment did not account for the feminine mystique; it was the other way around.

Mudd, in contrast, always believed that a key precondition to the emancipation of women was the use of science to overturn long-standing sexual mores. In the past, she affirmed, "modesty, decorum, and restraint were superimposed as essential values with little or no recognition of the normal biological urges of physically healthy, active men and women."[34] Mudd viewed twentieth-century history as a chronicle of progress during which "the repeal of reticence" about sex benefited women. Whereas Friedan thought Americans' interest in sex was "a strangely joyless national compulsion," Mudd was convinced that there was almost no such thing as too much talk about sex. Mudd believed that scientifically grounded sex education—and lots of it—could eliminate the guilt that emotionally crippled countless Americans. To Mudd, medical schools were key institutions in this educational campaign, and she foresaw the MCP assuming a leadership role in this endeavor. In 1968 the MCP launched the Center for the Study of Sex Education in Medicine, with the aim of promoting courses in human sexuality in U.S. medical schools. By 1974, 106 medical schools included sexuality in their curricula, up from 3 in 1960—a "laudable achievement," bragged an MCP official in 1975.[35]

Mudd's willingness to defy age-old attitudes toward sex explains her close and lengthy collaboration with sex researchers William Masters and Virginia Johnson. Just as she was a fervent, early backer of Kinsey,

Mudd was also one of the first to rally support for their findings. Even before she retired from the MCP in 1967, she had become a keen advocate for the kind of sex therapy and research pioneered by Masters and Johnson:

> Just as the two major Kinsey reports have proved of enormous value to counselors through the past decade or more, so I am confident that the Masters-Johnson findings including their clinical research in marital sexual adjustment will prove of continuous value through the decade ahead, in helping counselors to help their clients. . . . It is to be hoped that as the Masters-Johnson findings seep down in various ways from the professional to the non-professional level, they will have a directly beneficial effect on the majority of citizens. There will always be some whose religious or cultural inhibitions, biases, and prejudices motivate them to reject novel approaches to intimate areas of men's behavior. These men and women may be unable to accept the constructive potentials for human welfare resulting from research and study the methods of which they find unacceptable. In spite of such attitudes toward the discovery of new facts, exploration into the unknown will, I am confident, continue in all areas of man's behavior.[36]

Thus, to Mudd, Masters and Johnson were vital contributors to the brand of therapism she had been championing since the 1930s—an agenda with broad, social liberationist aims. Like David Mace, Mudd was on the lookout for the next new wave in the history of marriage and family counseling, and she thought she had found it in the work of Masters and Johnson.

The careers of Masters and Johnson unfolded against a background of events that signaled the rising power of the media and the educated elite to shape public opinion. University of Pennsylvania psychiatrist Harold Lief, Mudd's successor at the MCP, referred to "our Hollywood–Madison Avenue culture which overstimulates sexual appetite and yet surrounds sex with tantalizing mystery."[37] According to the national mass media, the country was in the midst of a sexual revolution in the 1960s. *Time* magazine's January 24, 1964, cover story proclaimed a "second sex revolution" (the first had been in the 1920s).[38] Virginia Johnson noted that in the mid-1960s, "the floodgates opened" for women's magazines. "All of a sudden the whole magazine—every single magazine—was being sold on the basis of sex. A little food, a little fashion, a little parenting, and all the rest is sex, so the media actually created the concept of a revolution."[39] Johnson was on to something: the evidence indicates that a sexual revolution in behavior—notably, premarital intercourse—had started in the 1940s and was well under way in the 1950s. According to historian Alan Petigny, "World War II clearly helped to usher in an age of sexual liberalism." What changed in the 1960s was the broadening acceptance of a message that mental health elites—including marriage and family counselors—had been trying to spread in the 1950s. The message, in Petigny's words, was "to ease up sexually."[40]

Opinion makers in the psychological sciences were not the only ones advocating a relaxation of sexual morality. Liberal churchmen such as Joseph Fletcher and Joshua Loth Liebman openly speculated about the psychological harm of guilt feelings and sexual repression. The biggest impact of mental health experts in the 1950s and 1960s was not to launch an actual sexual revolution; it was to help create a cultural climate in which Americans could feel less guilty about the sex they were having. Whether they truly felt less guilty is difficult to determine, but over the coming decades, millions of Americans learned a language that asserted that a scientific and value-neutral attitude toward sex was good for overall emotional health.

Highlighting the first chapter in the cultural history of the sexual revolution was the founding of *Playboy* magazine. Hugh Hefner's first *Playboy* editorial in 1953 declared that the new magazine would fill "a publishing need only slightly less important than the one just taken care of by the Kinsey Report."[41] *Playboy* encouraged men to enjoy the bachelor lifestyle, especially the opportunities for sexual gratification outside of marriage. Hefner was a vocal critic of the theory that sex had to be confined to marriage, and he urged adult men to "throw off the shackles of sameness and security." At *Playboy*, Hefner stated, "We don't believe in the old taboos and the old sacred cows." That included marriage, which, according to the "*Playboy* philosophy," simply imposed the "fetters of conformity" on men.[42]

Helen Gurley Brown's *Sex and the Single Girl*, published in 1962, essentially extended the *Playboy* revolution to women. Brown's advice book celebrated the "single girl" and validated her choice to remain unmarried for as long as it took to enjoy life before settling down. The "single girl," in Brown's view, was not defined by housework or child care. She was entitled to enjoy her independence and her sex life. The stigma surrounding spinsterhood, Brown argued, had seen its day.[43]

Two years later, in 1964, physician Mary Calderone founded the Sex Information and Education Council of the United States (SIECUS). Calderone, born in New York City in 1904, graduated from the University of Rochester in 1939, and between 1953 and 1964 she served as the medical director of Planned Parenthood Federation of America. From 1964 to 1982 she toured the country as the head of SIECUS. Like Alfred Kinsey, she was a polarizing figure. One fan called her "the High Priestess of Orgasm," but an opponent dubbed her "Typhoid Mary."[44] In founding SIECUS, Calderone sought to provide Americans with accurate information about sex; it was time, she maintained, to end the silence surrounding the topic. The strong philosophical kinship between SIECUS and the AAMC was reflected in SIECUS's membership list, which featured numerous familiar names associated with both the birth control and the marriage and family counseling movements: Emily Mudd, Robert Laidlaw, Sophia Kleegman, Aaron Rutledge, David Mace, William Genné, Harriet Pilpel, Evelyn Duvall, Wardell Pomeroy, Harold Christensen, and Robert Harper. Harold Lief of the MCP was a SIECUS cofounder. Calderone herself belonged to NCFR, and she and Ruth Jewson, the NCFR's executive director, were good friends with many mutual interests in sex education.[45] Other NCFR members who were involved in SIECUS's founding were Wallace C. Fulton, Lester A. Kirkendall, and Clark E. Vincent.

A Quaker like her friend Emily Mudd, Calderone insisted that sex was for pleasure and that no one should pass moral judgment on other people's sexual choices. She and other SIECUS officials cultivated a public image of scientific neutrality about values, but as one SIECUS member reminisced, this was simply a "clever tactic" to avoid being "blown out of the water" by opponents who accused SIECUS of preaching a new set of norms. Calderone's scientific mantle slipped when she exclaimed that she was really "trying to . . . free people—free a society, really, not

Mary Calderone. (Courtesy of the National Council on Family Relations)

people, a whole society—from the horrible incubus that we've been carrying for years of looking upon sexuality as evil instead of a gift from God."[46] Yet that freedom came with grave responsibilities: hailing the separation of sexuality and "reproductivity" as a giant step forward for humanity, Calderone—drawing on fashionable worries that population growth consumed nonrenewable natural resources—argued that human beings' use of their sexuality and reproduction would determine whether the species survived.[47] Sexual liberation was less about choice than about the individual's duty to the welfare of humanity.

Calderone's attempt to popularize what she called "the civilized concepts of human sexuality" in the 1960s coincided with the rise to national and international notoriety of William Masters and Virginia Johnson. Calderone wrote, "As far as I'm concerned not the most important but the only important contributions to our knowledge of physiology and psychology of sexual functioning have come from the studies

Wardell Pomeroy simulating an interview with Kinsey Institute staff member Jean Brown. (Photograph by William Dellenback. Courtesy of the Kinsey Institute for Research in Sex, Gender, and Reproduction)

of Bill [Masters] and Gini [Johnson]."[48] There were several connections between them: Calderone's husband, Frank, a leading official of the World Health Organization in its formative years, sat on the board of the Masters and Johnson Institute. Masters, who served on the SIECUS board of directors, received the SIECUS Award in 1972.

Like Alfred Kinsey, Masters and Johnson profoundly shaped the national conversation about sex. The media hailed them as the couple who took up "where Kinsey left off." *Harper's* magazine called them "the Sex Crusaders from Missouri."[49] Yet their fame rested on more than that. Masters and Johnson, like Kinsey, were researchers, but unlike Kinsey, they also claimed clinical expertise as therapists. Whereas Kinsey presented himself as a pure scientist, Masters and Johnson combined both research knowledge about sex and clinical techniques for making sex better. Just as importantly, the presence of Virginia Johnson as an equal partner was newsworthy in itself and caught the attention of countless people who had never identified scientific expertise with a woman.[50] Johnson denied that she was a "lady liberationist," but like Calderone and environmentalist Rachel Carson, she blazed a path for women who wanted to be taken seriously as scientists.[51]

William Howell Masters, born December 27, 1915, in Cleveland, Ohio, received his medical training at the University of Rochester under George Corner, one of Kinsey's mentors. Though intrigued by Kinsey's work, Masters followed Corner's advice and delayed his sex research until he was nearly forty years old, a husband and father of two children, and professionally established as a respected obstetrician and gynecologist. In 1954 Masters persuaded Washington University in St. Louis, where he was on the faculty of the medical school, to provide him with laboratory space and equipment to study male and female sexual inadequacy. Masters enjoyed the backing of Ethan Shepley, the university's chancellor, much like president Herman B. Wells of Indiana University was a staunch defender of Kinsey's research. In 1956 Masters hired Virginia Eshelman Johnson, a sociology student and twice-divorced mother of two, as his research assistant. Johnson never acquired a college degree but soon advanced to the position of research instructor. Before long, she and Masters were collaborating as virtual equals. In 1964 they founded the independent, not-for-profit Reproductive Biology Research Foundation (RBRF) in St. Louis, adjacent to the university's medical school. (The RBRF was renamed the Masters and Johnson Institute in 1978.) Their first two books, *Human Sexual Response* (1966) and *Human Sexual Inadequacy* (1970), were runaway best sellers and were translated into more than thirty languages. The Playboy Foundation, founded in 1965, poured $300,000 into the RBRF (it also funded SIECUS). In 1968 Masters reciprocated by calling *Playboy* "probably the single most important source of sex information in America today."[52] In 1970 Masters divorced his wife, and the next year he married Johnson.

By the time Masters and Johnson married, they had become the darlings of the media: customarily robed in white laboratory coats for publicity photos, he was the balding, bow-tied Sphinx and she was the enigmatic, smiling Mona Lisa. Although they described their work as experimental and cutting edge, they were also a throwback to the typically optimistic American belief that the mysteries of life could be solved by science and a hardy, can-do attitude. They were featured in mainstream magazines such as *Time, Life, Newsweek*, and *People*, and *Playboy* repeatedly sang their praises. As far as the media were concerned, there was not a hint of un-Americanism about Masters and Johnson. In 1975 *Newsweek*'s Shana Alexander called them the "Ma and Pa Kettle of sex therapists."[53] In 1977 an excerpt from *Human Sexual Inadequacy* was published in the staid *Saturday Evening Post*.[54] The arrival of television talk shows and news programs also boosted the profile of Masters and Johnson, who appeared on *Meet the Press, The Mike Douglas Show*, and *The Phil Donahue Show*. Phil Donahue "would call us constantly" about appearing on his show, Johnson remembered.[55] TV producers could count on Masters and Johnson to talk openly about sex—a surefire way to boost ratings.

Their star continued its ascent until 1980, when two psychologists alleged that their research was seriously "flawed by methodological errors and slipshod reporting."[56] When Masters and Johnson began to claim that they could cure homosexuality in the early 1980s, they sparked a fierce backlash from gay activists. In 1988 Masters drew fire when he asserted that the AIDS virus was running rampant throughout the heterosexual community. Meanwhile, feminists such as Shere Hite attacked both of them for alleging that women's sexual pleasure was restricted to vaginal intercourse. Masters and Johnson divorced in 1992, and when their institute closed down in 1994, few seemed to notice. The media coverage of William Masters's death due to complications from Parkinson's disease on February 16, 2001, was a faint reminder of their heyday.

What historians have neglected is the important role Masters and Johnson played in the evolution of marriage counseling. Thanks largely to them, therapism conquered sex, and sex therapy became a widespread practice. It was not just that Masters and Johnson helped popularize the notion of sex therapy; according to the *Boston Globe*, they possessed the "Rx for marital sex ills."[57] *Time* magazine stated in 1970 that they were engaged in "repairing the conjugal bed," and Masters told readers that "the greatest form of sex education is Pop walking past Mom in the kitchen and patting her on the fanny, and Mom obviously liking it."[58] Johnson told *Playboy*, "We think the renaissance of sexuality will strengthen [marriage], not weaken it," although as a thrice-married woman, she was hardly a poster girl for the institution.[59]

In their opposition to Freudian notions of female sexuality, Masters and Johnson—like Kinsey—were part of a backlash against psychoanalytic psychiatry that was gaining momentum in the 1960s. This would culminate in the victory of the "St. Louis School" of biological psychiatry by the time the third edition of the American Psychiatric Association's *Diagnostic and Statistical Manual of Mental Disorders* was published in 1980. One-third of the task force created to revise the second edition of the *DSM* had trained at Masters's Washington University.[60] Samuel Guze, a distinguished psychiatrist with the St. Louis School, sat on the RBRF board. Correctly sensing the challenge to psychoanalysis posed by Masters and Johnson, psychiatrists such as Natalie Shainess of New York City attacked their work. On November 17, 1970, Shainess testified before a House of Representatives subcommittee that Masters and Johnson's research was "scientifically unsound," was "grossly dehumanizing," and "opened the door 'from on high' to pornography at every level of society, and through virtually every medium. . . . And there is virtually no piece of pornographic literature, film or anything else that doesn't somewhere acknowledge a debt to William H. Masters."[61] Shainess and other critics condemned Masters and Johnson for their use of surrogate sex partners—notably, prostitutes—to overcome sexual inhibitions and their use of mechanical equipment to study sexual responses in women. "They're selling joyless sex," Shainess charged.[62]

Masters and Johnson championed the therapeutic viewpoint that sexual dysfunction was caused not by the individual's intrapsychic conflicts—as in psychoanalysis—but by what they called "the sexually restrictive culture into which we were born."[63] Their research on the anatomy and physiology of sex clashed with the Freudian emphasis on the psychology of sexuality. Johnson later admitted, "I'm so anti-Freudian," and she asserted that psychoanalysis "was a perfectly ridiculous bunch of stuff. Utterly idiotic, ridiculous stuff."[64] Masters and Johnson's basic theory was that scientific research could unlock the biological mysteries of sex, that sexual inadequacy was at the root of marital failure and that it could be cured, and that people were victims of the religious taboos society inflicted on them. Their beliefs bolstered the emerging therapeutic outlook of Cold War America.

There were strong connections between the fields of sex therapy and marriage and family counseling. In 1961 the AAMC received a $10,000

grant from the Mary Duke Biddle Foundation, thanks to James H. Semans, the husband of Mary Duke Biddle Trent Semans, heiress of tobacco magnate and Duke University cofounder Benjamin N. Duke. In
1956 Semans, a Duke University urologist and AAMC member, had developed an innovative technique for curing men of premature ejaculation.[65] In *Human Sexual Response*, Masters and Johnson presented a
variation on this method. Although admirers of Masters and Johnson
traced their attempts to cure premature ejaculation to Johnson's emphasis on meeting women's sexual needs, Masters and Johnson couched
their therapeutic effort in terms of its potential to improve the quality
of marriages.[66]

Emily Mudd's career also highlighted the links between sex therapy
and marriage and family counseling. She first met Masters and Johnson
in the 1950s, and she invited Masters to lecture on sex in her marriage
course at the University of Pennsylvania. In 1958, thanks in large part
to Mudd's efforts, Masters and Johnson spoke at the AAMC's annual
meeting in New York City. Their high estimation of Mudd's work was
evident in 1961 when Masters told her:

> [We] would be particularly interested in the approach of the
> Marriage Council to the therapy of the sexually maladjusted family
> unit. Since so much of what we have already developed at a basic
> science level has obvious clinical application, we are particularly
> interested in present concepts of therapy. We are also obviously
> interested in the physiologic and psychologic background on which
> your therapeutic considerations are based. In short, we need
> educating in clinical therapy.[67]

By that point, Mudd, Masters, and Johnson were on a first-name basis.
Masters and Johnson lectured at the AAMC in 1964 and also at the
Merrill-Palmer Institute. "Masters became very popular with the mar-
riage counseling group," in Mudd's words, and the AAMC helped him
and Johnson book lectures "all over the country." Mudd visited the
RBRF in St. Louis, and, as she later remarked, "I became very fond of
Virginia Johnson."[68]

After a SIECUS meeting in 1969, Masters took Mudd out for dinner
and asked her to help set up a training program for the male-female

therapist teams that the two St. Louis sexologists believed were best suited for their style of therapy, which they called the "dual-sex team approach." Mudd agreed to work with University of Michigan psychiatrist and former president of the American Psychiatric Association Raymond Waggoner in screening trainees from around the country. Between 1970 and 1972 Mudd and Waggoner spent time in St. Louis engaged in the effort, but the challenges were stiff: at least one member of each two-person team had to be a physician, and finding men and women who could work together as sex therapists, whether married or unmarried, proved to be difficult. Involving two therapists rather than just one also made it too expensive for most of the population.[69] To make matters worse, Masters needed funding to continue the pilot project beyond the first two years, but shortly after his application to the NIMH was approved, President Richard M. Nixon cut government funding for mental health, which effectively terminated the RBRF training program. Mudd stayed on as an RBRF board member until 1978, but Masters and Johnson never landed either a large government grant or a corporate grant.[70] To psychiatrist Robert Kolodny, a longtime coworker of Masters and Johnson, the RBRF's lack of funding was explained by "the Master's equation: sex, plus research, equal controversy."[71]

The impact of the Masters and Johnson dual-sex team approach to the training of marriage therapists may have been limited, but the overall effect of their work was to hasten the end of marriage counseling's brief flirtation with psychoanalysis and its prevalent belief that therapy should be restricted to individuals. Prior to the 1960s, some psychoanalysts had been interested in the relations between spouses in troubled marriages; for example, in 1931 Clarence Oberndorf had resurrected the notion of *folie à deux*, introduced by nineteenth-century French psychiatrists to describe how two seemingly healthy individuals could share neuroses. Psychoanalyst Bela Mittelman later conducted simultaneous interviews of two or more persons (usually married couples)—called conjoint therapy—because he was struck by how partners' stories about their relationship differed. (The term *conjoint therapy* was coined in 1959 by psychiatrist Don Jackson.) Yet Freud himself and leading U.S. psychoanalysts such as Lawrence Kubie viewed "concurrent analysis of husband and wife . . . as unwise." Kubie argued that "one or the other [partner in conjoint therapy] is likely to lose his confidence in the impartiality of the analyst and the analysis of the patient will suffer accordingly."[72] Another psychoanalyst captured the opposition to conjoint or family therapy when he remarked in 1967: "I am not primarily involved in treating marital disharmony, which is a symptom, but rather in treating the two individuals in the marriage." In the eyes of some in the marriage counseling field, psychoanalysis also ran counter to the emerging belief in nonjudgmentalism, the notion that each partner's perspective was equally valid. The psychoanalytic focus remained on the individual, not on the relationship, and the therapist was presumed to be "the pivotal agent of change."[73] The difference between the notion that the analyst was the central person in therapy and Carl Rogers's belief in the egalitarian, nondirective nature of the therapeutic relationship was glaring.

The rise of family therapy also helped speed up the decline of psychoanalysis in marriage counseling circles. For years, marriage counselors and family therapists had coexisted in groups such as the NCFR, and according to one founder of family therapy, "the therapy of marital disorders" was "the core approach to family change."[74] Most family therapists actually spent the bulk of their time working with couples rather than with multigenerational families. Family therapy's ascendancy was largely a reaction to what some therapists perceived as the grave shortcomings of individualized psychiatric treatment, which tended to trace psychological and behavioral dysfunction to problems solely within the individual, whether biological or psychodynamic in nature. Family therapy had blossomed in the 1950s when psychiatrists and psychologists, dismayed at biochemical research's lack of progress in identifying the causes of schizophrenia, turned their attention to the possible family origins of the disease. For a brief time, some psychiatrists argued that bad mothering was responsible for what was deemed to be an epidemic of emotionally crippled children. In 1953 one psychoanalyst defined a schizophrenic as someone "who is reared by a woman who suffers from a perversion of the maternal instinct."[75] This theory of the "schizophrenogenic mother" quickly gave way to the belief that schizophrenia and other disorders originated in the family and its communication. The NIMH's Lyman C. Wynne, a key founder of family therapy, was one of the first to conduct meetings with the parents of schizophrenic patients. Another was John Bell, a Clark University psychologist. Bell recalled that a British colleague was "having the whole family of the patient come in. . . . It was a startling thought to me," Bell confessed. "Nobody was doing a thing like that [in 1951]—but it sounded appealing. I decided to try it myself."[76] Forty years later, a family therapist told an audience of clinicians:

> It's hard, I suppose, for you to imagine the enormous opposition to working with whole families in those early days . . . (e.g., the child psychiatrist who said to me at a professional meeting, "Doctor, you are doing a very dangerous thing, bringing parents and child together in the same treatment room."). Once we presented our findings [about families] to the local psychoanalytic society in Philadelphia and they proceeded to tell family jokes.

Therapists who attended gatherings of the American Psychiatric Association or the American Psychological Association "would meet in corridors and say surreptitiously, 'I'm seeing families. How about you?'"[77]

"Look, these parents aren't to blame for these kids' psychopathology," Wynne and his fellow researchers concluded on the basis of their family sessions. Thus, the family ceased to be viewed as a "noxious influence."[78] Wynne "took families off the hook," one psychiatrist observed.[79] Yet, in trying to deflect blame from parents and families, Wynne dodged the question of what distinguished a healthy family from a sick family. By endeavoring to make families with schizophrenic children seem normal, he ran the risk of making other families look like breeding grounds for illness.

In 1962 a major milestone in the history of family therapy was reached when *Family Process*, the field's first major journal, was founded. *The Atlantic*, *Scientific American*, and *The Nation* hailed the discovery that disturbed families adversely affected children. "Schizophrenia may be perceived as one kind of attempt to handle the human fear of being unloved," *The Atlantic* noted. *Time* also celebrated Wynne's work and reprinted an excerpt of a conversation between a child and her parents:

> DAUGHTER: Nobody will listen to me. Everybody is trying to still me.
> MOTHER: Nobody wants to kill you.

FATHER: If you're going to associate with intelligent people, you're going to have to remember that "still" is a noun and not a verb.

To Wynne, such children tended to develop "an underlying feeling of meaninglessness and pessimism about the possibility of finding meaning in any experience or behavior." And that, Wynne added, "is enough to drive anybody crazy."[80] No matter how much Wynne tried to take families "off the hook," he and his colleagues left the impression that people got emotionally sick because of their toxic home environments.

The arrival of "systems" theory, a pillar of therapism, was an important event in the rise of family therapy. "System approaches," a New York City psychologist wrote in 1997, "developed in large part as a reaction against the perceived limitations of therapies that attributed psychological and social dysfunction to problems solely within the individual, whether these were viewed as biological, psychodynamic or behavioral in nature."[81] Systems theory, first popularized by Georgetown University psychiatrist Murray Bowen, was "a more holistic way to look at complex phenomena," such as the interrelatedness of family members. The theory stated that no individual could be understood in isolation and that all family members formed an interacting "system." Systems theory rejected the notion that any single family member was a "patient." Changing just one member without changing the others did not solve the problems that had driven the individual to seek therapy in the first place. Systems theory gained wide acceptance in family therapy circles in the 1970s, when therapists increasingly emphasized individual desires over the challenge of preserving marriages. A 1983 AAMFT task force defined marriage and family therapy "as the professional application of marital and family system theories and techniques in the diagnosis and treatment of mental and emotional conditions in individuals, couples, and families."[82] As late as the first decade of the twenty-first century, it was still viewed as the linchpin of most family therapy.[83]

In the early years of family therapy, Virginia Satir was a teacher and practitioner who helped lay the cornerstones of therapism—notably, the idea of self-esteem. In the opinion of two therapists writing in 2002, there was "no doubt that the charismatic Virginia Satir was the most visible and influential popularizer of family and marital therapy among

Tom Snyder and Suzanne Somers in a publicity photo for NBC-TV's National Love, Sex, and Marriage Test, *which aired on March 5, 1978. (Courtesy of the National Council on Family Relations)*

both professional and lay audiences from the mid-1960s until about the mid-1970s."[84] Described as "a heavily credentialed expert in the field of marriage and family counseling," Satir starred in NBC-TV's *National Love, Sex, and Marriage Test*, which aired on March 5, 1978, and was hosted by talk-show personality Tom Snyder and actress Suzanne Somers.[85]

Once called "the Columbus of Family Therapy" or the "Mother of Family Systems Therapy," Satir was born in 1916 in Neillsville, Wisconsin. She began working with families in 1951, and in 1959 she cofounded the Mental Research Institute in Palo Alto, California. After 1966 she

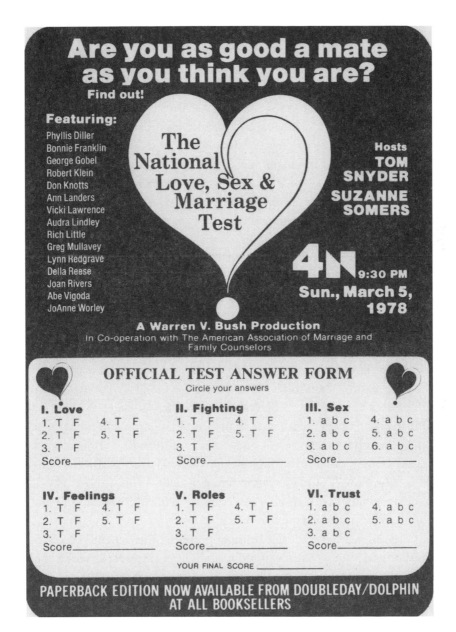

NBC-TV's National Love, Sex, and Marriage Test. *(Courtesy of the National Council on Family Relations)*

served briefly as the first training director at the Esalen Institute in Big Sur, California, a hot springs spa for emotional healing and spiritual introspection visited by the likes of Abraham Maslow, folk singer Joan Baez, George Harrison of the Beatles, poet Allen Ginsberg, science fiction writer Ray Bradbury, architect Buckminster Fuller, and mythologist Joseph Campbell. Maslow called Esalen "the most important educational institution in the world." In 1968 a *Life* magazine reporter attended an "advanced encounter workshop" at Esalen and observed participants "interpersonally relating, interacting, honing, and venting our feelings about one another with generous doses of what to me was a new currency: the gift of seeing ourselves as others see us, technically known as feedback."[86] The emphasis on self-insight through feedback was a crucial aspect of Satir's approach to therapy.

An NIMH grant in 1962 enabled Satir's Mental Research Institute to offer the first formal family therapy training program, with Satir as its training director. Thanks to her best-selling books *Conjoint Family Therapy* (1964), *People-Making* (1972), and *Helping Families to Change* (1975), Satir stood out as the foremost female clinician in her field. Her advocacy of the emerging concept of self-esteem was evident in her poem of the same name: "I am me . . . I have the tools to survive, to be close to others, to be productive. I am me, and I am OK." To Satir, the first aim of marriage therapy was "not to maintain the relationship nor to separate the pair but to help each . . . take charge of himself."[87] How one perceived the self and others, and how one related to others, formed what Satir called the "couple's system." Self-actualization, increased self-awareness, and clarity of self-expression were the ultimate aims of couples therapy, not salvaging marriages.

Often identified with the "human potential movement" involving Maslow and Rogers, Satir lectured to audiences around the world. "She can fill any auditorium in the country," a colleague told *Time* in 1985, three years before her death from pancreatic cancer. Satir's success as a spokesperson for marriage and family therapy occurred in the face of some resentful male practitioners who "patronized or insensitively put her down," one colleague recalled.[88] Some found her views "naïve and fuzzy," but her legacy matched that of any of her contemporaries.[89]

⬅⬆⬆

The surging family therapy movement of the 1960s overtook the AAMC at a time when the marriage counseling field was adrift. In the words of two therapists, by the end of the twentieth century, family therapy had "not merely incorporated, merged with, or absorbed marriage counseling and psychoanalytic couple therapy; it had engulfed, consumed, and devoured them both."[90] In the mid-1960s only 25 percent of AAMC members identified themselves primarily as marriage counselors. The varied occupational backgrounds of AAMC members made for "scattered loyalties."[91] Given the AAMC's pronounced family planning origins, it is understandable why the organization lacked direction in the late 1960s. In the wake of cases such as *Griswold v. Connecticut* (1965), in which the U.S. Supreme Court overturned a Connecticut law prohibiting the use of contraceptives, AAMC members who straddled the birth control and marriage counseling movements likely believed they had finally achieved victory in their struggle to win reproductive rights. A new raison d'être for the group was therefore in order. The Supreme Court's defense of a "marital right to privacy" seemingly opened new vistas: counselors need no longer restrict themselves to dispensing advice about "planned parenthood" and other practical challenges of marriage and family life. They could imagine themselves as therapists engaged in the reconstruction of the family itself.

When the organization changed its name to the American Association of Marriage and Family Counselors (AAMFC) in 1970, this signaled the group's increasing interest in family therapy. Eight years later, reflecting practitioners' growing preference to call themselves therapists rather than counselors, the group became the American Association for Marriage and Family Therapy (AAMFT). The word *therapy* carried professional significance; by the 1970s, the term *counselor* "evoked images of folksy advice givers."[92] William C. Nichols, a pivotal leader in family therapy's takeover of marriage counseling, later recounted that "counseling in the mind of many people connotes a rather superficial approach to human conflict."[93] *Therapy*, by contrast, implied a rigorously scientific and multidimensional approach that examined individuals' extended relations with other people, groups, and institutions.

William Nichols, born in 1929 in Fayette, Alabama, spearheaded many of the noteworthy changes that occurred during marriage and family therapy's crucial transition period between the mid-1960s and the 1980s. Nichols's background in the family therapy field dated back to the mid-1950s, when he was in training at Kentucky's Central State Psychiatric Hospital. One day, he watched as workmen tore down the fence surrounding the hospital; the administration of new antipsychotic medications to hospitalized patients made such security unnecessary. This taught him that "treatment was moving toward recovery and/or rehabilitation," he remembered more than half a century later, and "that the family and society played a role in the outcome of the treatment." In 1957 Nichols attended the American Psychiatric Association conference, where "a few psychiatrists and psychologists daringly admitted that they were working with families, instead of doing therapy only with individuals"—an experience he called a "coming-out" event for him and other budding therapists.[94]

After obtaining a doctorate at Columbia University, Nichols did postdoctoral work at Detroit's Merrill-Palmer Institute, which, "under the leadership of Aaron L. Rutledge," Nichols recalled, "essentially provided intensive training in psychodynamic therapeutic work." In 1966, at the annual NCFR conference in Minneapolis, Nichols spoke on a panel about Merrill-Palmer's clinical training program and was later stopped by a colleague who exclaimed: "My God! You're talking about therapy. I gotta talk to you."[95] Over the next thirty years, Nichols helped facilitate the merger of the marriage counseling and family therapy fields, and in the process, what he called "classical marriage counseling" largely vanished. By the late 1970s, the AAMC "had become a family therapy organization."[96] Or, in the words, of an AAMC president, "marriage counseling had evolved into a subsystem of family therapy."[97]

Nichols, like others in the field, was appalled at the state of marriage counseling in the 1960s. As he observed in 1973, marriage counseling "virtually was an inchoate mass." The marriage counseling movement, he wrote, was "galloping off in all directions like a herd of wild horses in some of its parts and languishing in a torpid state in others." The AAMC, according to Nichols, was riddled with "elitism," making it feel like an exclusive club that zealously monitored who gained admittance. Restrictive admissions policies kept membership low and virtually guaranteed that the AAMC would be chronically short of money. Debates raged over the nature and aims of marriage counseling. Who qualified to practice marriage counseling? Was counseling really therapy? Which theory about marriage counseling was right? Nichols's task, as he saw it, was to bring "order out of chaos," and an important first step was overhauling the AAMC and regulating the field through certification and licensing.[98]

As early as 1940, Ernest Groves had warned that the greatest task facing the new profession was the marginalization of all competitors who, in his opinion, exploited "the growing desire" for courtship and marital counseling. "The only possible protection must come from a more general education of the public," Groves wrote, "that they may realize the responsibilities that belong to the counselor. This will lead to a demand for a standard of ethics which alone can safeguard counseling."[99] Twenty years later, pressure to regulate the field escalated due to a national scandal over unlicensed counselors. In 1962 the *Saturday Evening Post* dispatched reporters posing as clients and found that "the marriage counselor field is infested with quacks, phonies, and incompetents." As the *New York Times Magazine* explained, "anybody—tinker, soldier, sailor, or the girl next door—can tell other people how to run their marriages, [and] charge from $1 to $50 per hour for the service and function free of the law, because there isn't any law" regulating the practice. Two reporters posing as a married couple found a counselor in the Los Angeles phone book who described himself as "Dr. A. Donahji, Ph.D., D.D.N.S., Founder—Palace of Brmhayati." Donahji wore a turquoise turban and a surgical smock, and his waiting room featured "worn oriental rugs, battered couches," and huge portraits of himself and Jesus Christ. The national press exposé of individuals such as Donahji coincided with an investigation by the California Assembly to determine the need for legislation in the marriage counseling field. Testifying before an assembly committee in 1963, Donahji admitted he was really Don Wilson of Girard, Kansas, and that he had awarded himself his Ph.D. and doctor of divinity degrees.[100]

More troubling were accusations of sexual harassment. Aaron Rutledge reported that a midwestern psychiatrist, expelled from a local medical society for having sex with several patients, promptly relabeled himself a marriage counselor and reverted to his old practices. A Van Nuys, California, woman with marital problems picked a counselor out of the phone book and discovered that he wanted her to disrobe during treatment. A Los Angeles counselor was caught performing illegal physical examinations of his clients and offering "services" to relieve their "sexual frustrations."[101] Inspired by these and other complaints, California enacted legislation in 1963, becoming the first state to crack down on bogus counseling.

The rising field of sexology also jeopardized the reputation of marriage counseling. The 1967 founding of the American Association of Sex Educators and Counselors (renamed a decade later the American Association of Sexuality Educators, Counselors, and Therapists [AASECT]) and the appearance of the *Journal of Sex and Marital Therapy* (1975) were signs that interest in sex therapy was escalating. Helen Singer Kaplan, a New York City psychiatrist born in 1926 in Vienna, Austria, was dubbed the "Sex Queen" because she was a vocal cheerleader for the popular 1960s notion that people should enjoy sexual intercourse as often as possible. One historian has called Kaplan's contributions to sexology "politically reactionary," but her theories and techniques of sex therapy urged women to question society's demands that they be subservient and dependent.[102] A pioneer in sex therapy who rivaled the influence of Masters and Johnson, Kaplan was a coeditor of the *Journal of Sex and Marital Therapy* and founded the first clinic for sexual dysfunction located at a medical school (the Payne Whitney Clinic at the New York Hospital–Cornell Medical Center). She rejected Masters and Johnson's theory that a team of two therapists was preferable, but she—like Masters and Johnson—helped integrate the practices of sex therapy and marriage counseling.[103]

Yet the mainstreaming of sex therapy triggered mounting concerns about the unregulated nature of the field. William Masters decried what he called a wave of "phony sex clinics," numbering between 3,500 and 5,000 nationally. Masters and Johnson's *Human Sexual Inadequacy* (1970), the first comprehensive textbook of sexual problems and therapeutic methods, was likely the biggest reason for the explosion in the number of clinics and treatment centers dedicated to curing sexual dysfunction. However, with that stunning growth came a crescendo of complaints about professional fraud. "The current field of sexual therapy," Masters wrote in 1974, "is dominated by an astounding assortment of incompetents, cultists, mystics, well-meaning dabblers, and outright charlatans." In 1973 a media consultant in New York City launched a chain of clinics called Male Potency Centers of America, prompting a journalist to quip that sex therapy was "America's greatest cultural contribution after jazz."[104] Survivors of bogus sex therapy often ended up at the Masters and Johnson Institute, according to Masters, complaining about therapists who had tried to seduce them or whose methods had failed abysmally. Like marriage counselors, sex therapists could operate in most states without any government controls or regulatory mechanisms.[105] In 1972 the AASECT began to establish certification procedures and a code of ethics, but as late as the end of the twentieth century, the field of sex therapy was still largely unregulated.[106]

"Sexology on the defensive," proclaimed *Time* magazine in 1983, and although some of sexology's proponents blamed its problems on the "conservative political climate" during Ronald Reagan's presidency, many of its difficulties derived from its own claims that it constituted a rigorous field. "It was not always easy," the *New York Times* reported in 1983, "to separate the science from the more questionable fare," whether in terms of research or clinical practice.[107] The proliferation of "quack" sex therapists and marriage counselors was worrisome to the AAMC for three reasons: the potential harm to clients, the risk of discrediting the entire field and its claims to expertise, and the unwanted competition in an already crowded marketplace. The solution lay in stiff licensing requirements designed to keep "phony" practitioners from advertising as certified counselors and to establish marriage and family therapists as legitimate mental health professionals. Such steps were designed to stake out professional territory against "quacks" and rivals in psychiatry, psychology, family medicine, and clinical social work, as well as to qualify the field for insurance reimbursement and expand employment opportunities. In short, by the 1970s, marriage and family therapists were convinced of the need to organize as an interest group with lobbyists, money, and friends in high places.

The AAMC took the formation of the California Association of Marriage and Family Counselors (CAMFC) as another sign that the occupational status quo was unacceptable and the field needed to reorganize professionally. After California passed its regulatory legislation in 1963, the CAMFC was created, and its membership quickly grew to 1,300 licensed counselors. At the time, the AAMC had only about 500 members, and many CAMFC members were bitter about being refused admission to the AAMC because they had only master's degrees. One AAMC board member remarked in 1966 that the AAMC had "no real future" unless it found a way to "open its ranks and find a place for at least the better part of these [CAMFC] people." Later attempts to merge the AAMC and CAMFC failed, but in the meantime, the AAMC was encouraged to alter its standards and admit more members. By 1972, AAMC membership had more than tripled since the early 1960s. People of color were rare in the AAMC, but the percentage of women in the group's ranks doubled from 20 percent in 1962 to 40 percent in 1972.[108] Nichols rejoiced that the AAMC's former "elitism" was dead and that the group was financially sound. He had helped bring the AAMC back from the brink of extinction.[109]

The evolution of marriage counseling into marriage and family therapy began with a crucial series of AAMC meetings between 1966 and 1972. At the 1967 meeting in Anaheim, California, David and Vera Mace, two of the last holdovers from marriage counseling's past, resigned from the AAMC. Later that year, in Washington, D.C., the AAMC paid tribute to its first twenty-five years of existence. Yet the mood of the conference was conflicted; in Nichols's words, it "was the last hurrah of the old organization. Although it would take several years to bury the corpse, the marriage counseling part of the association's history was breathing its last."[110] In 1970, in New York City, the AAMC's board of directors decided to "go for broke" rather than disband in the face of formidable fiscal woes. The organization changed its name to the AAMFC, and the influx of family therapists pushed the membership over 1,000. The resulting increase in membership dues eased the group's money worries.

Over the next decade, the field's coming-of-age was marked by three significant developments. The first key event was the launching of a distinctive marriage and family counseling journal. Since the NCFR had asserted control over *Marriage and Family Living* in the 1950s, counselors had tended to publish in other journals, such as *Family Process* or *Family Coordinator*, but the AAMC had no journal it could call its own. In 1971 an AAMFC official asserted, "There was consensus that a most important issue is the development of a journal."[111] When funds became available in 1973, Nichols stepped down as editor of *Family Coordinator* and assumed that post for the new publication, called the *Journal of Marriage and Family Counseling* (renamed the *Journal of Marital and Family Therapy* in 1978).

The second important event involved the AAMFC in a high-stakes battle over government reimbursement for services. By 1966, Congress had passed legislation that created the Civilian Health and Medical Program of the Uniformed Services (CHAMPUS), which extended medical benefits to the families of servicemen. Thanks to Senator Robert F. Kennedy (D-N.Y.) and his concerns about the stresses endured by military families, marriage and family counselors were recognized as providers under CHAMPUS. However, in the wake of an inquiry conducted by Senator Henry "Scoop" Jackson (D-Wash.), the Department of Defense eliminated reimbursement for marriage, family, and pastoral counselors in 1975. After negotiations failed, the AAMFC sued the government for reinstatement.[112] On March 25, 1976, a Washington, D.C., district court reinstated marriage and family counseling benefits and recognized the AAMFC's clinical membership standards as appropriate qualifications for those who performed marriage and family counseling. In achieving this victory, the AAMFC convinced the courts and other consumer and mental health organizations that marriage and family counseling was a legitimate form of mental health care. From the standpoint of pure power politics, "the AAMFC David had taken on the Goliath of the Department of Defense and won," in Nichols's words. "The new kid on the block" had arrived.[113]

Accreditation was the third notable achievement of the 1970s, and here too, Nichols played an instrumental role. At issue was this question: was marriage and family counseling a discipline in its own right, or merely "an amalgam of psychology, social work, and pastoral counseling"? Nichols spearheaded the AAMFC's application for accreditation to the U.S. Office of Education by writing the first accreditation manual for the field and scripting a model curriculum for graduate programs in marriage and family counseling. The road to victory, reached in October 1978, was far from smooth. The American Family Therapy Association (AFTA), a group founded in 1977 and made up largely of psychiatrists, argued at Health, Education, and Welfare (HEW) hearings in 1978 that the AAMFT (newly renamed) should not serve as the accrediting body in the field. HEW rejected AFTA's point of view, a ruling that did nothing to mitigate the bitter feelings between the two organizations.[114] Nonetheless, an AAMFT member exulted: "This is an historic occasion! For the first time, family therapy has been officially recognized!" An AAMFT lawyer wrote that the panel's decision was the most important event in the group's history.[115]

By the time the AAMFT moved its headquarters from California to Washington, D.C., in 1982, relations between it and the government had grown closer. Thanks to the AAMFT's efforts, the profession had gained recognition as one of the foremost mental health groups. Traditional distinctions between family and marriage counseling had faded away, and therapy had replaced counseling as the field's chief practice. In a few short years, therapism had blossomed as a new outlook on life with its own moral terminology. The change in language from *counseling* to *therapy* was more than symbolic: it signaled that the nature of the field's practice differed substantially from that of Emily Mudd and her cohort. Lost amid celebrations over the field's strides in the 1980s, however, was the fact that Mudd's generation had laid the foundations for marriage and family therapy years earlier.

When "Miss X" visited the University of Pennsylvania's MCP in 1968 for a "premarital consultation," she was no stranger to its staff. Her first visit had been in 1963 as a newly married woman whose husband had been impotent since their wedding night. Divorced in 1965, she had been dating a man for six months prior to her 1968 visit, and although she had decided not to marry him, she hoped the MCP's counselors could help her determine whether she was "a good risk for any man."

At first glance, Miss X had it all: a graduate of the University of Pennsylvania, she was described as "a tall, most attractive, 24-year-old Jewish woman" who was "profitably employed in a job which she likes" as a "fashion coordinator for a newspaper." Yet she longed for "a more authentic existence." Her concern derived from the "recurring patterns regarding the men she dated"; she was "tired," she said, "of dating weak men who eventually let her down." Prior to her 1968 visit she had been engaged to a man with a "marvelous personality," but she broke it off after "a smashing courtship." She was back to dating "casually" when she sought "help in my problems at relating."

Initially, Miss X's life history appears to confirm the MCP's ideology that relationship problems between men and women stemmed chiefly from issues of sexual inadequacy. As one of the counselors noted, there was "a lot of confusion in her psychosexual development which could be helped by therapy." Yet other details from her background defied the MCP's standard narrative. Although her husband had been impotent, there was no evidence of sexual incompatibility with her ex-fiancé. Instead, they had fought over finances (she made more money than he did). She was perceptive enough to observe that her beauty and brains were attractive to men, but the men drawn to her were "weak because I put out something which they read as strength and independence."

What she really "admire[d]" were "men who are able to take command." She complained about her parents, especially her mother, who
was "always passing judgment on her dates . . . usually negative." Her
father was remote: "He never told me I was pretty," she lamented. She
viewed herself as "refusing to adhere to the demands and standards"
her parents set. Describing herself as "a loner," Miss X "alternat[ed] between being a stylish high class seductress and a low-keyed lap dog," in
the judgmental words of her counselor. The counselor continued:

> She is a dramatic self-presenter who is highly dissatisfied with her
> pattern of relating to date. There has been some visible progress in
> counseling and she shows some willingness to want to move off the
> magical level of dependency in order to become a person she would
> be happier being. . . . She evidences a trait disturbance of the
> passive-dependent sort, and her own behavior is alien and
> uncomfortable to her.

Her "role confusion" kept her from making a breakthrough and becoming a happier person, but sex seemed to be a secondary factor at best.[1]
    What happened to Miss X is a mystery, but her case history illustrates
several important aspects of marriage counseling as it evolved during
and after the cultural turmoil of the 1960s. Most MCP clients were white
and college educated, came from affluent backgrounds, and, like their
parents, tended to see heterosexual marriage as a life goal. Yet the breakdown of gender norms across American society meant that the MCP
and other counseling services were seeing more and more career women
like Miss X. Counselors were also beginning to see people who spoke
the language of therapism, which emphasized personal growth and individual autonomy. Miss X's therapist continued the paternalistic tradition in counseling but also sought to "move [her] off the magic level
of dependency in order to become a person she would be happier
being." There was no pretense at the MCP that clients were being counseled to fit into assigned marital roles. Counseling was morphing into
therapy, and the goal was to enable clients to achieve "a more authentic
existence."
    Thus, as early as the Watergate era, the field of marriage counseling
was engaged in redefining itself as therapy. In the process, the AAMFT

was well on its way to becoming a powerful presence in the mental health care field in particular and American society in general. Yet these professional gains also thrust the field into the "culture wars" that raged in the 1970s, pitting Americans with strongly held moral visions against one another.[2] Just as the field's leaders imagined themselves shaping mainstream attitudes and behavior to fit a therapeutic template, political forces that contested counseling's ascendancy were on the upswing. The resulting clash of moral standpoints delayed the triumph of therapism but ultimately failed to defeat it.

Conflicts over moral politics were nothing new to marriage counselors. In the 1950s the AAMC's Kinseyites had clashed with other counselors over sexual mores. Ten years later, permissive viewpoints about sex were waxing, and leading the campaign to overturn conventional sex values was Wardell Pomeroy (1913–2001). Born in Kalamazoo, Michigan, Pomeroy cast long shadows in marriage and family counseling circles during the turbulent 1960s and 1970s. During his years as a high-profile researcher at the Kinsey Institute (1943–1963), he was an exceptionally hard worker and, thanks to his interviewing skills and his ability to get "sex shy" people to divulge their sexual histories, a valuable member of Kinsey's team. A coworker described Pomeroy's personality as "zip and zap and snap-crackle-pop."[3] Yet his real interests lay in clinical therapy, notably, sex therapy.[4] In 1963 he left the Kinsey Institute and set up a private practice in marriage counseling and sexual psychotherapy in New York City with the help of Robert Laidlaw and others in the field.[5] Like Kinsey, Pomeroy subscribed to the goal of sexually liberating American society. Unlike Kinsey, Pomeroy was a therapist, so he was poised to play a pivotal role in the AAMC. As AAMC president (1969–1970), a member of the board of directors (1971–1972), and chair of its finance, admissions, and long-range planning committees, Pomeroy "saw the futility of attempting to operate [the AAMC] on a 'shoe-string' budget," in William Nichols's words. Pomeroy was instrumental in rebranding the AAMC as the AAMFT and easing the academic requirements for applicants in order to expand the group's membership. "Probably no other member is as responsible as Wardell Pomeroy, Ph.D., for moving the AAMC out of elitism and starting it on the way toward becoming a large and relevant organization," according to Nichols.[6]

Pomeroy's interest in sex therapy was personal as well as professional. Though married with children, he had a busy extramarital sex life, a fact that became legendary at the Kinsey Institute. A handsome man with considerable charm, he slept with hundreds of people of both sexes, though he preferred women. One AAMFT member confessed that she "felt something salacious . . . some attempt to live vicariously through others' experiences . . . with Wardell," an interest that went "beyond the professional interest in sex research and treatment."[7] A friend who rejected his advances commented that Pomeroy "fucks everybody." "Sex is fun, why not?" countered Pomeroy.[8]

Controversy continued to swirl around Pomeroy after he left the Kinsey Institute. When he became AAMC president in 1970, he was already a lightning rod for criticism. According to the American Library Association, his two books, *Boys and Sex* (1968) and *Girls and Sex* (1970), were among the top 100 books Americans sought to ban in the 1990s. The publication of *Boys and Sex*, a book intended for adolescents and their parents about a range of topics including masturbation, homosexuality, and preadolescent sex play, helped drive a wedge into the ranks of the AAMC.[9] Some California marriage and family counselors, under the leadership of James Rue, did not dispute Pomeroy's freedom to write his books, but they insisted that he should step down as AAMC president. When Pomeroy refused to resign, Rue lodged a formal complaint with the AAMC, alleging that Pomeroy had violated its code of ethics. In 1970 the board of directors threw out Rue's request, but controversy over Pomeroy flared again in 1972.

Pomeroy was chiefly responsible for the showing of graphic films of heterosexual and homosexual behavior at the AAMFC's 1972 meeting at New York City's Waldorf Astoria hotel. The theme of the conference was "Human Sexuality in Life and in Therapy," and prior to the meeting, members had been strongly encouraged to bring their spouses or conjugal partners because of "the erotic nature of the films," a gesture some found patronizing. The conference's format included the "viewing of explicit state-of-the-art teaching films on human sexuality," according to Nichols.[10] Discussions in small sensitivity training groups followed. One therapist complained to Emily Mudd that the conference was an indication of "the direction the organization is taking. . . . [P]rofessional ethics are being re-examined to the extent that sex relations with one's clients could be deemed 'therapeutic.'. . . [C]ounselling for 'swingers' is a possibility. . . . [N]ational meetings are preceded by 'touch-feely' sessions, etc., etc."[11]

At the final plenary session of the 1972 meeting, James Rue—by then AAMFC vice president—vehemently denounced the proceedings. According to Nichols (who was there), Rue began by uttering, "Jesus Christ is my saviour!" Pandemonium ensued: as Rue spoke, angry members "began shouting at him and shaking their fists, including one fellow who started down the aisle toward the rostrum, waving his arms and indignantly proclaiming his outrage."[12] On June 7, 1972, Rue announced his resignation from what he called "the anti-family" AAMFC, citing an "'ominous trend' which had been eating at the very fiber of the association." According to Rue, recent AAMFC meetings had "ridiculed those who believe in monogamous marriage and the stability of family life." He cited the meeting at the Waldorf Astoria as an example:

> [There was a] large display of erotica supplied by the Community
> Sex Information and Educational Service of New York which
> promotes abortion, freedom of sex, and ridicule of large families.
> They even had posters to this effect hung around the hall. One
> could also buy life-size, soft, pliable models of penises and vaginas
> to make it much easier to masturbate. . . . I found the first [group]
> session to be a "touch and feel" of the sexual areas of the person
> next to you. It was explained that this would put you in a "free"
> mood for the raw sex scenes to be seen throughout the three days.[13]

In September 1973 Rue invited AAMFC members to join a new, breakaway organization—the National Alliance for Family Life (NAFL), which would defend "the values inherent in marital and familial commitment." By 1974, the NAFL had its own journal; a board of directors that included entertainers Art Linkletter, Pat Boone, and Danny Thomas; and more than 1,000 members.[14]

By accusing the AAMFC of "demeaning the Judeo-Christian values of marriage and the family," Rue may have been declaring a culture war on the group's leadership, but he represented a segment of the field that had grown uneasy about the direction of the AAMFC. Rue was hardly a lone voice, having been elected AAMFC vice president for 1971–1972. At the time of his conflict with the AAMFC executive, he was also general director of Paul Popenoe's AIFR, head of the Sir Thomas More marriage and family counseling clinics in Southern California, and president of the CAMFC. In addition, he was chair of the CAMFC committee that was then in merger negotiations with the AAMFC (despite its regional nature, the CAMFC had as many members as the entire AAMFC). Rue's acrimonious departure from the AAMFC was a clear sign that divisions over the moral politics of counseling were taking shape in the early 1970s. These fault lines would only get deeper in the years leading up to Jimmy Carter's overwhelming defeat in the 1980 presidential election.

Rue's allegations that his family values clashed with those of prominent AAMFC members were supported by the field's evolution during the 1970s. Numerous practitioners agreed with former NCFR president F. Ivan Nye that the task for the future was to help free families from "the dead hand of traditional practice."[15] Nichols and many of his colleagues, though unwilling to accept gay marriage, amplified the permissive ethos of the early marriage counselors. According to Nichols, "The notion that the chief aim of marriage counseling is to 'save the marriage' regardless of the nature of the marital relationship" had largely been consigned to the dustbin of history.[16] Indeed, by 1980, "divorce therapy"—designed to help couples and families "negotiate the stages of the divorce process"—had become "a component of systemic family therapy."[17]

The changes in counseling advocated by Carl Rogers and Abraham Maslow, as well as the backlash against Freudian psychoanalysis, inspired feminist therapists in the 1970s to attack what they alleged were male biases about gender roles and female sexuality. Both Maslow and Rogers had helped shift the focus away from counselors and the notion that patients should "fit existing social norms" and toward clients and their achievement of "self-actualization" and emotional fulfillment. Therapists such as Lena Levine and Phyllis Chesler argued that men in the field were bound by "society's role prescription for women" and "the value judgment that underlies it: that women are basically inferior to men." Male therapists, like their counterparts in general medicine, were accused of relying on "feminine and masculine stereotypes" that bolstered the unequal status of women in society. Many of the charges in the 1970s that marriage counseling was "strongly weighted toward maintaining 'traditional' marriage" ignored the field's evolution in the post–World War II era, but more important, they encouraged many practitioners—male and female—to view themselves as constructive agents for reforming the status of women.[18] According to one family relations researcher in 1976 (citing the work of Nichols), "marital counseling appears to be an ideal therapeutic setting" where couples can benefit from a form of "consciousness-raising" that breaks down gender stereotypes.[19] This was the viewpoint of Betty Blaisdell Berry, the national coordinator of NOW's Task Force on Marriage and Family Relations from 1968 to 1973; she championed the "egalitarian form of marriage" as "a pioneering step into the society of the future."[20] Villanova University professor Rachel T. Hare-Mustin urged that family therapists jettison the "normative concepts of the traditional family and idealized conceptions of family relationships," which presumably still dominated the field in the late 1980s. "Feminist theory" offered "an alternative construction of reality provided by a different lens. Feminism is futurist in calling for social change and changes in both men and women."[21] If feminist counselors did not emulate Emily Mudd by looking to the Soviet Union for the blueprint for "social change," they nonetheless kept alive her dream of marriage counseling as a tool for liberating women and the rest of society in the latter years of the twentieth century.

These antitraditional directions in family counseling theory help account for the field's support for the Equal Rights Amendment (ERA). First proposed in 1923, the ERA guaranteed equal rights for women under the law and was widely viewed as having direct consequences for marriage and the family. In 1972 the ERA was passed by both houses of Congress and went to the state legislatures for ratification, where it fell short of the required thirty-eight states by the 1982 deadline. Leading the campaign to defeat the ERA was Phyllis Schlafly, a St. Louis author, housewife, and constitutional lawyer who argued that the ERA would destroy the American family.[22] Schlafly was a brilliant organizer and a wily expert at public relations. The ERA was "anti-family, anti-children," Schlafly contended, the agenda of "women's libbers" who depicted "the home as a prison, and the wife and mother as a slave."[23] High-profile ERA proponents, such as *Ms.* magazine cofounder Gloria Steinem, former congresswoman Bella Abzug, and Christie Hefner (Hugh Hefner's daughter), did little to help their cause when they sometimes linked abortion and gay rights to ratification of the ERA.[24]

Both the AAMFC and the NCFR backed the ERA. To Nichols, the ERA assured "the equitable treatment of females [which] is essential for the well-being of not only women but also for children of both sexes and for the improvement of marriage."[25] He also acknowledged that the "NCFR essentially has been on the liberal side of [the contraception] issue, as well as on the abortion issue."[26]

The field's tendency to adopt "liberal" positions on sexual mores, gender relations, and reproductive politics plunged it into the heated public debate over family policy in the 1970s, fanned in large part by the growth of the media. There may have been vehement disagreement over "family values," but activists on both sides of the debate exploited new and old forms of communications technology to try to win the hearts and minds of Americans. Conservative Richard Viguerie pioneered computerized direct mailing as a method for grassroots political mobilization and fund-raising. Christian evangelists Pat Robertson and Jerry Falwell hosted their own popular television shows that hammered away at advocates of the ERA. Pro-ERA forces relied heavily on telegenic entertainers and celebrities such as Steinem, actress Marlo Thomas, and actor Alan Alda, all of whom enjoyed easy media access.

The TV comedy *Maude*—produced by Norman Lear, a prominent supporter of liberal causes—ran from 1972 to 1978. It starred Bea Arthur as an outspoken housewife who had been married four times, lived with her divorced daughter, and opted for an abortion when she became pregnant at the age of forty-seven. The episode in which Maude chooses to have an abortion drew a huge audience, as well as thousands of protest letters from outraged viewers. However, nothing captured the no-holds-barred approach to sensitive family issues better than Lear's raucous *All in the Family*, with the irascible Archie Bunker as the central character. Archie's conversations with his hippie son-in-law often degenerated into abusive shouting matches.

Few topics seemed to be off-limits for television. For instance, Masters and Johnson were cohosts on Mike Douglas's afternoon talk show for one week in 1975. The arrival of the nationwide version of *The Phil Donahue Show* in 1970 (later called simply *Donahue*) reinforced an emerging trend in broadcasting, as television tackled formerly taboo topics such as abortion, adultery, homosexuality, and abuse. Donahue (married to Marlo Thomas) viewed himself as a trailblazer, challenging what he called "the tremendous sexism" of daytime television. TV producers "thought women cared only about covered dishes and needle-point," he charged. By contrast, Donahue interviewed not only high-profile stars such as Dolly Parton, John Wayne, and Sammy Davis Jr. but also ordinary people willing to talk candidly about their personal problems and unconventional life choices on camera, such as one female guest who claimed to have had 2,686 sexual relationships with men. Donahue also pioneered audience involvement, taking telephone calls from viewers and bounding up and down the aisles to allow audience members to ask questions of the guests onstage. When critics accused him of having "freaks" on his program, Donahue—who remained on the air until 1996—responded by saying that "somebody's freaky is another person's personal problem."[27] Soon, other television hosts such as Sally Jesse Raphael, Geraldo Rivera, and Oprah Winfrey began to offer more sensational fare on their own shows. Daytime TV had come a long way since Paul Popenoe's appearances on Art Linkletter's *House Party*. Self-expression had become the new leitmotif of public life.

Politics copied the increasingly loud and edgy atmosphere of network television. Behind the growing adversarial nature of politics was the widespread perception that the stakes for marriage, families, and the status of women were never higher. Tempers flared when, during a 1973 public debate over the ERA, Betty Friedan declared that she would like to burn Phyllis Schlafly at the stake.[28]

The mounting media attention meant that few Americans were surprised when President Jimmy Carter announced in 1979 that marriage and the family were "under unprecedented pressure."[29] Numerous social scientists agreed that "stagflation" (stagnant unemployment and high inflation) caused by the economic downturn and spiraling oil prices placed severe burdens on families. Abortions, which had been legal nationwide since the 1973 U.S. Supreme Court ruling in *Roe v. Wade*, numbered 1.3 million in 1980 (or almost three in ten pregnancies). The incidence of teen suicide doubled in the 1970s. Record-high divorce rates (nearly 50 percent by 1990) were often attributed to the impact of no-fault divorce laws, starting with California's in 1970 (by 1985, all fifty states and the District of Columbia had such laws). No-fault divorce, which required no proof that a marriage had broken down, made it easier than ever to dissolve a marriage.[30] The rise in the number of households headed by women (20 percent in 1980) also troubled countless Americans, as did the news that in 1987 nearly 50 percent of poor families were headed by women.[31] This "feminization of poverty" overshadowed the real employment gains some women were making in the corporate, academic, medical, and legal worlds. While some Americans cheered the growth of the nation's social welfare programs, including Social Security, Medicare, food stamps, and workers' compensation, others worried that such programs accelerated rather than stopped the decline of the traditional family.

In the 1970s, alongside their familiar calls for emancipation from "the dead hand of traditional practice," marriage and family counselors appeared to be following David Mace's earlier advice to drop society's "disastrous laissez-faire policy" toward marriage and families and look toward government as an instrument of change.[32] When the newly elected Jimmy Carter announced in 1977 that he would honor his campaign pledge and convene a White House conference on the family, the AAMFC and NCFR rejoiced. Throughout the 1976 campaign, Carter had vowed that, if elected, he would consider the needs of the family in "every decision" he made. Such a promise suggested to professional groups such as the AAMFC that the state would become unprecedentedly involved in marriage and family matters. Carter's aim was to "identify public policies which strengthen and support families as well as those which harm or neglect family life."[33] As he told the National Conference of Catholic Charities, family "breakdown" could be countered by an expanded welfare state based on notions of "social justice." Carter genuinely believed that a White House conference on the family could devise concrete recommendations for solving the problems that afflicted American families in the 1970s. However, the president soon learned, to his chagrin, that he was opening up a political can of worms that would plague his bid for reelection in 1980.[34]

Creation of the White House Conference on Families (WHCF) was one of the most divisive acts of the Carter presidency and a landmark event in the annals of unintended consequences. The WHCF was a major factor in the rise of the "New Right," a political constituency whose emergence would mark a turning point in U.S. history and contribute significantly to Carter's defeat in 1980. The high point of the New Right was the 1979 founding of the Moral Majority, an organization dedicated to Christian conservative advocacy and headed by televangelist Jerry Falwell. The New Right was a formidable coalition of Mormons, fundamentalist Protestants, and conservative Roman Catholics who cast aside their historical religious differences and forged alliances over their common opposition to abortion, euthanasia, the ERA, pornography, state day care, and gay rights. Women played prominent leadership roles in the movement and served at the grassroots level as organizers and workers. *Roe v. Wade* and the ERA battle had already inspired the formation of the New Right, but Carter's WHCF enraged conservatives because it was seemingly "geared up to chang[e] the definition of the family."[35] A U.S. senator called the WHCF "Jimmy Carter's assault on the American Family."[36]

Opponents of Carter's WHCF often invoked abortion, gay rights, sex education, the ERA, or out-of-wedlock births as key issues, and they struck alliances with other conservatives who favored tax cuts and increased defense spending. Yet the overall theme of New Right, "pro-family" activists was that "the family does best without much outside interference."[37] Senator Orrin Hatch (R-Utah) warned that the WHCF was "organized at taxpayers' expense by the anti-family forces" of "professional 'experts' or self-styled 'child advocates.'"[38] A pro-family spokeswoman feared that the WHCF would be "heavily stacked with professionals and bureaucrats who had a vested interest in expanding the government's role in family matters."[39] Connaught (Connie) Marshner, a 1971 graduate of the University of South Carolina and the mother of four children, was a good example of the kind of women who became grassroots family activists in the 1970s. A conservative Christian, Marshner believed that families "consist of people related by heterosexual marriage, blood, and adoption." Families were not "religious cults" or "heterosexual or homosexual liaisons outside of marriage." Marshner was a firm opponent of "the therapeutic state invading the home."[40] In other words, conservatives attacked the WHCF not just because they thought it might normalize controversial social practices by stealth but also because it would authorize "professional 'experts,'" such as marriage and family counselors, to intervene in the private sphere of the family. To a large degree, opposition to the WHCF was a populist revolt against therapism. It was also the last such revolt.

The heated language of New Right figures about meddlesome "professional experts" was not just rhetoric. In the wake of Carter's announcement about the WHCF, representatives from numerous national nonprofit organizations met in March 1977 to form the Coalition for the White House Conference on Families. Initially numbering nineteen groups, the CWHCF grew to fifty-two by 1980, including the AAMFC, NCFR, and AASECT. Other organizations such as Parents without Partners, B'nai B'rith Women, Planned Parenthood—World Population, Zero Population Growth, and the National Gay Task Force joined the CWHCF, as did the National Conference of Catholic Charities (until discussion of abortion ended its participation). The CWHCF liked to describe itself as a group that straddled religious and political divides but was united in the belief that the definition of family had to be more inclusive and that "family life professionals" should be deeply involved in identifying the "special needs [of the family] that grow out of economic, cultural, structural, and lifestyles diversity." Claiming to encompass "a considerable portion of the nation's expertise concerning the family," the CWHCF recommended breaking with the traditional American attitude that "family policy is not for us" and copying countries such as Sweden, which had used government programs to, among other things, achieve "equality between the sexes."[41] As the CWHCF's chairman told HEW Secretary Joseph Califano, Carter's adviser on family matters, one of the "substantive issues" that concerned the group was "the varying ways in which diversity and pluralism of family styles will be understood and dealt with" at the conference.[42] Another CWHCF official told the conference's National Advisory Committee that it was "imperative" that it "enumerate diverse family forms and . . . make specific mention of but not limited to: extended families, single parent families, gay families and families without children."[43] The CWHCF enjoyed corporate support; it met in May 1978 at the Wingspread Conference in Racine, Wisconsin, sponsored by the Johnson Foundation and bankrolled by S. C. Johnson and Sons (makers of Johnson Wax). Unlike its adversaries on the political Right, the CWHCF was distressed when it learned in

1978 that Carter was rethinking the wisdom of holding the WHCF after all. To the CWHCF, Carter's brainchild was critical to achieving its aim of getting the federal government to take the initiative in enacting policies affecting the family.

The pivotal role played by the CWHCF in organizing the WHCF made it a target of growing conservative opposition on Capitol Hill. With the presidential election looming, Republicans attacked the CWHCF for "manipulating delegate selection" and accused it of a "liberal bias."[44] The New Right's success at electing WHCF delegates at state-level meetings puzzled, surprised, and enraged CWHCF members. In the face of the unexpectedly large turnout of Christian activists, one NCFR delegate to the Virginia conference lamented that "a year's work on my part . . . [was] all going down the tubes." She insisted that what happened in Virginia "wasn't the grass roots but just one hayfield," but in reality, she had just glimpsed one the most significant grassroots mobilizations in twentieth-century U.S. history.[45] Dean Honetschlager, a coordinator of the Minnesota state conference, told the press, "We frankly hadn't expected the abortion issue to be so big. That probably was naive of us. We had gotten little input from the national (conference) people on what to expect. We were reaching for diversity," he said, but apparently not the kind of diversity represented by the "pro-family, pro-life groups" that flooded the Minnesota meeting.[46]

Given the high emotions of the New Right movement and its adversaries on the political Left, it was not surprising that the conference itself was plagued by fits and starts. Originally, Carter had hoped that the WHCF would be a way to build bridges with Roman Catholics, who had never warmed up to him and his self-professed "born-again" Christian faith. Yet Catholics objected to the presence of a divorced mother of three as executive director and protested the pro-abortion views of some members of the WHCF's National Advisory Committee. Carter also bled support from the left wing of his own party—notably, among feminists such as Bella Abzug, whom he had fired in January 1978 from the President's Advisory Committee on Women after she was openly critical of the White House's stand on women's issues. Carter, sensing that the whole project was rapidly becoming a political hot potato, suggested delaying the WHCF until after the next election, but that merely sparked more indignation.

As 1980 unfolded, *Newsweek* called the WHCF showdown "the biggest political battle between liberals and conservatives" since the 1977 International Women's Year convention in Houston, Texas, which had pitted Schlafly's "pro-family rally" against pro-ERA spokeswomen Abzug, Steinem, Coretta Scott King, and First Lady Rosalyn Carter.[47] At the three regional conferences, liberal delegates pleaded for dialogue; in Los Angeles, actor Edward Asner called the conference a "forum for understanding and sharing," but conservatives, convinced that the WHCF had a hidden agenda, destroyed ballots and staged walkouts.

By the time all 115 members of the WHCF National Task Force assembled in Washington, D.C., in August 1980, few had any illusions that they would alter government policy toward the family one way or another. Recommendations tended to favor policies such as changes in the tax code, home care for the elderly, government-sponsored day care, amplified efforts to fight drug abuse, and less violence in the media. As historian Leo Ribuffo has written, "The WHCF recommendations became just another government report collecting dust on library shelves."[48] At that point, Carter simply wanted the WHCF to vanish down some memory hole, but his GOP opponent, Ronald Reagan, refused to cooperate. In September 1980 Reagan lambasted the WHCF's report and its recommendations, which, he maintained, were "unacceptable to the majority of American families and destructive of the family values they hold dear."[49] Reagan told the Republican National Convention that government was "strong enough to destroy families," but it could "never replace them."[50] Thus, by the time Americans trooped to the polling stations to vote for their next president on November 4, 1980, Carter's WHCF had turned into a political fiasco. Government intrusion in family matters was off the political agenda, at least for a while.

The fierce disagreements sparked by the WHCF revealed the grave differences of opinion over the nature, structure, and composition of the family. The fates of the ERA and the WHCF were sober reminders that many of the AAMFT's and NCFR's values were out of step with those of millions of Americans. A sizable and rapidly organizing segment of the population suspected that the state, in the form of the helping pro-

Judith Wallerstein.
(Courtesy of the National
Council on Family
Relations)

fessions, was determined to usurp parental authority and destroy marriages. To these Americans, the liberation movements of the 1960s had unleashed a host of social experiments that undermined the traditional family. Some social science appeared to back up these beliefs.

Psychologist and longtime NCFR member Judith Wallerstein argued that high divorce rates and the rising incidence of single-parent households punished children. When Wallerstein first began studying the effects of divorce on children in 1970, she tended to believe that they could navigate their way through life after their parents divorced but was astonished to find no research on children's reactions to marital breakup. What she discovered when she examined the experiences of 131 children from 60 well-educated, middle-class families surprised her even more: children of divorce tended to struggle socially, emotionally, and academically. As adults, these same children were often afraid of commitment and avoided marriage. In 1989 Wallerstein declared that "divorce was almost always more devastating for children than for their parents."[51] Wallerstein's findings were criticized by feminists, who thought she was trying to keep women in bad marriages. But Wallerstein insisted that she was not against divorce; she simply wanted to correct the notions of parents who thought that "divorce is no big deal because so many kids today have divorced parents."[52]

In her syndicated newspaper columns, policy analyst Maggie Gallagher praised Wallerstein's study and called no-fault divorce laws "pro-divorce bills." No-fault divorce laws caused "unnecessary" divorces, she asserted, which hurt children and helped "abolish" lifetime monogamy.[53] Marriage therapist David Popenoe, Paul Popenoe's son, argued that Wallerstein's findings about children of divorce were directly related to the phenomenon of a "fatherless America," a phrase describing the growing number of households in which there was no biological father. To Popenoe, children without fathers were more apt to become teenage mothers or juvenile delinquents. Popenoe's thesis about the shrinking number of men in married relationships dovetailed with the formation of the Christian men's group the Promise Keepers in 1990. The Promise Keepers called on American men to live with a Christ-centered view, which included taking charge of their families and reestablishing patriarchal authority. The Promise Keepers were a prime example of the attitude throughout the United States that the changes taking place in marriage and the family were anything but salutary and could be countered by individual actions at the grassroots level.

The ire directed at the CWHCF by conservative groups briefly hindered attempts by the NCFR and AAMFT to get government involved in making marriage and the family more egalitarian, but ironically, government involvement expanded in the 1990s and beyond in the form of programs designed to strengthen two-parent heterosexual families. States such as Minnesota and Florida offered discounts on marriage licences for couples who underwent premarital counseling. When Republicans regained control of both houses of Congress in 1994, welfare reform became closely linked to legislative attempts to stem the rise of single-parent households. "Marriage is the foundation of a successful society," Congress declared in 1996, the same year it passed the Defense of Marriage Act, which defined marriage as the union between one man and one woman. The spectacle of Republicans using the power of the federal government "to define and protect the institution of marriage" while overriding states' authority under the U.S. Constitution made some conservatives uneasy, but it anticipated similar pro-family initiatives during the presidency of George W. Bush. From 2002 to 2005 the White House allocated funds for pro-marriage public relations campaigns, marriage education classes, and research to study the effectiveness of premarital counseling. The 2005 Healthy Marriage Initiative earmarked $100 million a year from 2006 to 2010 to promote marriage.

Thanks to encouragement from the Bush presidency, conservative scholars and policy analysts advocated "responsible fatherhood" as a solution to poverty. Yet alongside their efforts to defend the heterosexual model of family health, governments relied on the terminology of therapism: "healthy marriages," government documents stated, were based on "ongoing [personal] growth," as well as "the use of effective communication skills and the use of successful conflict management skills." Despite their profound differences over what a "healthy marriage" might look like, conservatives, liberals, feminists, and other interested parties tended to agree that the psychological sciences were indispensable for the future of marriage and the family.[54] Therapism had co-opted the language that even conservative Americans used to communicate with each other and talk about their feelings.

Similarly, although evangelicals and other religious Americans might celebrate the heterosexual, two-parent, male-breadwinner family, they also developed a taste for how-to books on achieving marital bliss. The best-selling nonfiction book of 1974 was Marabel Morgan's *The Total Woman*, a user's guide for women to put the "sizzle" back in their marriages. Morgan, a devout Christian, encouraged women to submit to their husbands but also resorted to sexual explicitness in her books, which some Christian bookstores refused to carry. Other titles about marriage written by Christian women sold in the hundreds of thousands. The many Americans who rallied around the defense of "family values" in the 1970s and 1980s avidly read these books, which drew on features of Paul Popenoe's earlier versions of secularized marriage counseling. Just as Popenoe had taught women to settle for nothing less than emotional fulfillment in their marriages, so the popularization of expert-driven marriage counseling continued long after his AIFR went out of business.

Thus, despite the bitter battles over the WIICF, therapism seemed none the worse for wear. One therapist noted in 1980 that the zeitgeist was in the field's favor.[55] As the 1980s unfolded, therapism increasingly transcended political fault lines to become virtually a national value in itself. Meanwhile, demand kept rising for "relationship-oriented treatment." In 1980, 1.2 million couples sought help from therapists; by the early 1990s, that number had almost quadrupled.[56]

In a sign of the times, couples counseling made the breakthrough to network television. A 1988 episode of ABC's *thirtysomething*—appropriately titled "Therapy"—featured two of the main characters, Nancy and Elliot, spending time in a counselor's office in an effort to mend their failing marriage. Their complaints were typical of married partners: as a stay-at-home mother and wife, Nancy wanted more "space," and as a hardworking, full-time partner in an ad agency, Elliot wanted more sex. The plots of *thirtysomething* were based on the everyday lives of the seven characters—all middle-class, white, heterosexual Philadelphians in the late 1980s—including dating, raising children, building careers, and making home improvements. Professionals specifically praised the "Therapy" episode's depiction of counseling as "realistic" and the series in general for showing "how couples work," in the words of a Los Angeles clinical social worker. A San Diego therapist was not alone in encouraging his clients to watch the show. Some clients dismissed *thirtysomething* as "so Yuppie, so trite"—nothing but a bunch of advantaged young Americans talking incessantly about their feelings—but a Los Angeles psychiatrist insisted that "the show gives them a language" with which to express their emotions. Indeed, *thirtysomething* blended TV drama and nonjudgmental therapism in unprecedented ways. As one of its creators noted, "The reason therapists and people in therapy relate to our show is because we deal with ambivalence, we deal with inner conflicts. We don't have villains on our show; usually [it] is about somebody who is in conflict and is trying to resolve it, and that is what therapy is about."[57]

Another sign of therapism's expanding reach was African Americans' acceptance of therapy, beginning in the 1980s. Prior to the 1970s, African Americans had shown little interest in marriage or family counseling, preferring to consult their ministers, relatives, friends, or coworkers if they had marital problems. In 1965 there were only four nonwhite AAMC members, and until 1982, its national staff included no people of color. Not until the early years of the twenty-first century did the AAMFT elect its first nonwhite president.

Back in the 1950s and 1960s, white marriage experts had routinely failed to convince editors of black magazines to run articles about the benefits of marital and premarital counseling. Many African Americans viewed mainstream marriage counseling as detached from the challenges facing their families. In 1970 the African American president of NOW stated: "I don't think black women are going to have as much patience sitting around as many white women in the movement do, discussing identity and whether or not we can combine careers and marriages."[58] In part, African American wariness about therapy can be traced to the midcentury dominance of psychoanalysis, which "seemed foreign to blacks. They felt it was something devised for the white middle class."[59] When Assistant Secretary of Labor Daniel Moynihan released his controversial *The Negro Family: A Case for National Action* in 1965, he called for welfare policy reform to end the prevalence of female-headed African American households. His advocacy of male-dominated African American families to curb the spread of "broken homes" inspired some middle-class African Americans to endorse the notion that it was "the duty of every Negro woman, professional or otherwise, to help her husband assume his full height and stature as head of the family." But Moynihan's report also struck some black social scientists as patronizing and uninformed about the diversity of African American families. As one African American therapist later explained, African Americans had a "healthy cultural paranoia" about state-supported efforts to apply white models of marital relations to the lives of black men and women.[60]

Nonetheless, more and more low-income African Americans were exposed to marriage counseling in the 1970s, thanks to legislation such as California's Family Law Act of 1969, which required minors who applied for a marriage license to undergo premarital consultations if a judge deemed it advisable. Although this form of counseling was not identical to the voluntary services sought by white, middle-class Americans, it likely helped undermine African American resistance to professional treatment. In the 1980s and 1990s African American publications—including *Essence*, the first magazine targeting African American women—increasingly covered the topics of marriage and divorce. As a journalist for *Ebony* noted in 1978:

> A decade ago it was virtually unheard of for Black couples to seek out a marriage counselor for help with intimate problems. They settled for talk sessions with relatives, close friends, or perhaps a minister. In many cases the couple, unable to resolve their differences, grew farther and farther apart and eventually separated. Today, however, it is not unusual for Blacks to seek professional counseling when their marriages turn sour.[61]

In 1989 the *New York Times* reported that psychotherapy in general was gaining wider acceptance among middle-class African Americans, and the number of black therapists continued to climb (totaling about 4,000, by one estimate). According to an African American psychiatrist at Harvard University, with the passage of time, the "stigma of being crazy if you went to a psychotherapist" was fading among blacks.[62] In the 1990s cultural diversity workshops became common at meetings of family therapists, and researchers in the field paid more attention to blacks and other minorities.[63] A consensus among therapists—regardless of race—steadily emerged as the century came to a close: previous standards of marital normality needed to be questioned. Nancy Boyd-Franklin, an African American therapist and Rutgers University professor, told the AAMFT that therapists had to tailor their counseling to fit the uniqueness of minority families. Rather than ask clients, "Who are your parents?" Boyd-Franklin encouraged therapists to ask African Americans, "Who raised you?"[64] The notion that people in treatment should not conform to impersonal criteria for successful relationships meshed with the mounting belief that practitioners had to be more culturally sensitive about the lifestyles of minority families.

Black women in the 1970s may have been hesitant to discuss their feelings about balancing family and career, but by the early twenty-first century, this was no longer true. When President Barack Obama and his wife, Michelle, were interviewed in 2012 by *Ladies' Home Journal* for its signature "Can This Marriage Be Saved?" column, Mrs. Obama conceded that, early in their marriage, "there was a whole lot of work" to do as two working parents. "I had to change," she stated, "and start problem-solving. . . . I also had to admit that I needed space and I needed time. And the more time I could get to myself the less stress I felt. So it was a growth process for me individually and for us as couple, too."[65] Nothing could have been a bigger advertisement for the benefits of therapism for the African American marriage than the Obamas' confession that personal "growth" helped them deal with their marital "struggles."

The ascendancy of therapism coincided with the AAMFT's rising fortunes as an interest group: in June 1978 HEW rejected the American Family Therapy Association's opposition to the AAMFT's petition to be recognized as the national accrediting body in the field of marriage and family counseling. AFTA, founded in 1977 and led by psychiatrists, was "the new kid on the block," and it tried to elbow aside the AAMFT by testifying that family therapy included marriage counseling, but marriage counseling did not include family therapy. As it had done during the 1975–1976 showdown over CHAMPUS benefits, the AAMFT demonstrated that it could win battles on Capitol Hill, but its victory temporarily caused frosty relations between the two groups. In 1981 AAMFT president Donald S. Williamson, a family therapist with feet in both occupational camps, succeeded in defusing animosities. By 1982, when it decided to relocate its headquarters from California to Washington, D.C., the AAMFT was well on its way to becoming a "major trade organization," according to Nichols.[66]

As the AAMFT flexed its professional muscles, the field's shift toward therapy grew stronger during the 1980s. Williamson heralded a new "moral vision" and an "ethical stance toward human life and love" emerging out of the "family systems theory ethos." Second in stature only to Nichols during these heady times, Williamson had been ordained as a Methodist minister in Northern Ireland and, after immigrating to the United States, obtained a degree in pastoral psychology at Northwestern University in 1966. Heavily influenced by Carl Rogers, Williamson's approach to therapy focused on "intergenerational family theory," the goal of which was to help clients forge healthy peer relationships based on equality and devoid of fear. During his own childhood, Williamson had observed that both his mother and his father had been intimidated by their parents. Williamson thus praised "the women's movement" for its "focus on equality and collaboration" and its attention to the abuse of children, women, and the elderly in the family context.[67]

Williamson said good riddance to "the more punitive and divisive language" of the field's "pejorative diagnoses," as well as its reliance on "solitary hospitalization" as a mode of treatment. The "new value in psychotherapy" rejected the old paradigm based on "two kinds of people—the doctors and the patients." Williamson invoked Rogers's notion that "no objective position outside the [family] system is accessible to anyone." The days of "scapegoat[ing]" family members were over; family relations now featured "egalitarian relationships, especially in marriage," and, "thanks to the feminists, gender sensitivity" and "empathy." The "individual should have emotional space and free air to breathe," Williamson argued, although he failed to specify what, exactly, "unfree" air was. Some of what Williamson said harked back to the days of Emily Mudd, but there was no mistaking his conviction that marriage and the family stood on the verge of a major revolution.[68]

The case of Jean and Larry M. (pseudonyms), reported by two "non-sexist" therapists in 1977, demonstrated how the nature of therapy had both changed and remained the same since Miss X's visit to the MCP in 1968. Jean and Larry, a couple in their late twenties, sought marital therapy because they were "fighting all the time." Married for five years, they had a four-year-old daughter. Originally, Jean had felt "lucky" to find a "strong and competent" man who would provide security for her, but once they were married, she complained that they spent too little time together. For his part, Larry was uncomfortable that Jean was supporting the family financially while he completed his graduate education, and he compensated by spending more and more time on his studies. Jean retaliated by agreeing to sex only when he provided the intimacy she sought in other aspects of their relationship. Their therapists, mindful of feminism's attacks on the division of labor within matrimony, preferred to interpret their marital troubles in terms of the "power dynamics in the relationship" rather than subscribing to the Emily Mudd school of thought, which emphasized sexual differences. They focused on Jean's need for "individuation" and encouraged her to develop friendships at work, join "a women's group," and "keep a certain mutually agreed upon portion of her earnings as money she could spend on herself and not need to account for to her husband." This form of "economic leverage" was a big step toward "redistributing more equitably the overt power in the relationship." When Larry expressed "negativism" about the way the therapy was headed, the therapists recommended a "structured separation" that encouraged him to "abandon . . . his position of regression." For one week, Larry lived alone with their daughter while Jean "attended a workshop" and lived with a female ex-classmate. The separation seemed to do the trick: the power imbalance was rectified, and their "self-esteem" and "sexual relationship" improved. Whether therapy saved the marriage in the long term is unknown, but the lesson to the therapists was clear: trying "separation experiences," "open companionship," and "alternative marital life styles" led to "enhanced and conjoint growth." If it did not, they added, therapists had to "be prepared for the possibility that many of the couples" in therapy "will 'choose' to terminate their marriage. Such individuals can be helped effectively to achieve such a resolution." To the therapists, a marital relationship without an "equalized sharing of overt power" was no marriage at all.[69] The institution of marriage came second to the primary goal of "conjoint growth."

The expanding reach of therapism over the last decades of the twentieth century, fueled by developments in race and gender theory, was hailed by many in the mental health field, but it created unease among a handful of prominent social scientists. Two generations earlier, University of California–Berkeley sociologist Robert Nisbet had predicted in *Quest for Community* (1953) that the "clinical approach to happiness" would have a grave impact on the nation's institutions, notably, marriage and the family. According to Nisbet, "the obsessive craving of men for tranquility and belonging" put an enormous strain on marriage, already made "fragile" by sweeping economic and social changes, such as a rising standard of living. "Probably no other age in history has so completely identified (confused, some might say) marriage and romance as has our own," he grimly observed. The expectation that "cultivation of affection is the one remaining serious function of the family" was too much for the institution to bear.[70]

In *The Triumph of the Therapeutic* (1966), Philip Rieff, a University of Pennsylvania sociologist, lamented the rise of "psychological man," a "man of leisure, released by technology from the regimental discipline of work so as to secure his sense of well-being." According to Rieff, therapists taught "psychological man" to think that he was discontented and to seek out treatment in an effort to be happier.[71] University of Rochester history professor Christopher Lasch renewed the assault on professional culture in his best-selling *Culture of Narcissism* (1979), in which he echoed Rieff's loathing of everyday Americans' reliance on expert advice in an effort to achieve individual emotional health. Lasch agreed with Rieff that "the therapeutic outlook" of the twentieth century "trivializ[ed] politics" by encouraging people to seek inner emotional peace rather than participate in the everyday political process. Like Rieff, Lasch contended that a major turning point in history had been reached in the twentieth century with the emergence of "psychological man," who, "plagued by anxiety, depression, vague discontents, [and] a sense of inner emptiness . . . seeks neither individual self-aggrandizement nor spiritual transcendence but peace of mind." Abetting "psychological man" in his pursuit of "the modern equivalent of salvation, 'mental health,'" were therapists, "not priests or popular preachers of self-help or models of success like the captains of industry."[72] Lasch made it clear that he included marriage and family counselors in the category of the "helping professions" whose exertions, in his mind, served their own occupational interests more than the interests of the family. Counselors, he argued, "lodg[ed] therapeutic modes of thought more deeply than ever in the popular mind." Lasch continued his attacks on the "health industry's ministrations to the family" up to his death in 1994.[73]

Meanwhile, Robert Bellah, a sociologist at the University of California–Berkeley, joined the chorus of concern about therapeutic culture in *Habits of the Heart* (1985). Bellah and his coauthors—Richard Madsen, William M. Sullivan, Ann Swidler, and Steven M. Tipton—agreed with Lasch that "therapeutic modes of thought" had steadily seeped into the consciousness of countless Americans since World War II. The authors were trying to answer the question: "Is America possible?" Did the America originally described by Frenchman Alexis de Tocqueville in 1835 in *Democracy in America* have a future "as a society governed with the consent of its members, as a democratic republic . . . in the face of the realities of the late twentieth century?"[74] Bellah, described as a "communitarian," wrote that "individualism may have grown cancerous—that it may be destroying those social integuments that Tocqueville saw as moderating its more destructive potentialities, that it may be threatening the survival of freedom itself."[75] To Bellah and his coauthors, individualism was a belief in "the dignity, indeed the sacredness of the individual. Anything that would violate our right to think for ourselves, judge for ourselves, make our own decisions, live our lives as we see fit, is not only morally wrong, it is sacrilegious."[76] Yet this form of individualism had triumphed to such an extent in the twentieth century that it threatened private spheres such as love, marriage, and the family. Spearheading this type of individualism was the "therapeutic ideal"— that is, "an individual who is able to be the source of his own standards, to love himself before he asks for love from others, and to rely on his own judgment without deferring to others." One therapist quoted in *Habits of the Heart* said:

> Ultimately I think people want to know that they're O.K., and they're looking for somebody to tell them that, but . . . I think what's really needed is to have themselves say that I, Richard, am O.K. personally. What people really need is a self-validation, and once people can admit that they're O.K., even though I have shortcomings, everybody has shortcomings, but once they can admit that, all right I've got these, but I'm really O.K., somehow they get miraculously better.[77]

"Therapeutically self-actualizing persons" were thus freed from "the artificial constraints of social roles [and] the guilt-inducing demands of parents and other authorities."[78]

One measure of the inroads made by therapeutic individualism was the degree to which its ideals permeated popular language, with its own form of moral discourse and vocabulary. As one therapist commented about the meaning of life: "I just sort of accept the way the world is and then don't think about it a whole lot. I tend to operate on the assumption that what I want to do and what I feel is what I should do. What I think the universe wants from me is to take my values, whatever they might happen to be, and live up to them as much as I can. If I'm the best person I know how to be according to my lights, then something good will happen." Bellah and his coauthors argued that one of their core objectives in writing *Habits of the Heart* was to encourage "the all-too-inarticulate search" among Americans for "a moral language that will transcend their radical individualism."[79]

Bellah (who died in 2013), like Rieff, Nisbet, and Lasch before him, warned that the ascendancy of individualism, despite expectations, did not result in greater liberation; instead, it cast therapy as a model relationship that increasingly dominated the public and private worlds as the end of the century beckoned. Time and again, therapy has been used to cement teamwork in the workplace; in fact, it has progressively become part of the job itself. Workers get together in formal meetings or over meals while their employers ritualistically urge them to communicate their feelings. This form of expressive communication may reduce interpersonal friction and make some workers feel more emotionally secure on the job, but it is equally true that, thanks to the spread of therapeutic culture in the corporate domain, there is no opting out of the therapeutic model. How could there be when, following Carl Rogers, therapy was assumed to be democracy in action? The underlying assumption was that becoming a unique person through therapy helped society too. Thus, therapy's stress on personal autonomy actually fostered institutional conformity. It fit the bureaucratic world of work to a tee. "Much of our work is a form of therapy," wrote Bellah and his colleagues.[80]

One therapist who was deeply troubled by *Habits of the Heart*'s analysis of late-twentieth-century individualism was William J. Doherty, a professor of family social science at the University of Minnesota. Doherty was one of several individuals in the marital and family therapy field who engaged in some very public soul-searching about its direction at the dawn of the new millennium. Raised a Roman Catholic and destined for the priesthood at an early age, Doherty left the seminary, joined the Unitarian-Universalist faith, and decided to funnel his deep desire to help families into marriage and family therapy. After obtaining a Ph.D. in child development and family studies at the University of Connecticut in 1978, he joined the University of Minnesota's Department of Family Social Science in 1986. An NCFR past president and a prolific author, Doherty has most recently been involved in the Families and Democracy Project and the Citizen Health Care Project, a community organizing approach to working with families. This kind of com-

William J. Doherty.

munity work reflects his ongoing interest in the effects of mainstream culture on marriage and families.

From a professional standpoint, Doherty underwent two important changes during his lifetime. The first came in 1974 when he began work on his Ph.D. and embraced the "value-neutral approach of social science and therapy." Turning his back on his keen interest in moral issues—in part a legacy of his Catholic upbringing—Doherty "became a moral relativist," based on the following notion:

> Because different people in different social and cultural conditions value some behaviors more than others, there is no clear way to

decide what is right and what is wrong, and therefore people should be free to follow their own values unless their behavior infringes on someone else's rights. . . . I became a moral critic and sceptic [*sic*] who believed that the goal of social science and therapy were [*sic*] to be as value-free as possible, and that the chief threats to family science and family therapy were covert values that encouraged conformity to traditional social values. Having ascended Mount Olympus, I was largely unaware of what I was bringing to the moral table.[81]

In the spring of 1985, however, Doherty had his second professional and intellectual epiphany: he read *Habits of the Heart* and experienced "a wake-up call," his "first confrontation with how the skeptical, value free stance I had taken toward family science and family therapy was deeply flawed." Reading *Habits of the Heart* taught him that a value-neutral approach to family therapy was merely "swimming in the mainstream of American individualism," in particular, the consumerist attitude that a marriage was as disposable as a toaster or a pair of jeans. Doherty resolved that therapy had to move beyond a purely "self-oriented" stance and both engage the moral sensibilities of the therapist and "respect the autonomy and diversity" of clients.[82] Morality for Doherty was not simply a private matter; it was inevitably public because the decisions it involved touched other lives in more or less profound ways.

Thus, according to Doherty, therapists were dodging the complex moral responsibilities surrounding family issues when they took an individualized, value-neutral approach to counseling. Rather than shrugging off America's high divorce rate as merely an unintended consequence of well-intentioned efforts to repair marriage, Doherty accused his fellow therapists of actually undermining marital commitment. Incompetent therapists—that is, those who lacked training in working with couples—accounted for many marital failures, but so did "hyper-individualistic" therapists who essentially functioned as mouthpieces for individualism and consumerism. These therapists, Doherty contended, depicted marriage as "a venue for personal fulfillment stripped of ethical obligations." They effected a nonjudgmental stance that disguised a "consumerist cost-benefit analysis" based on questions such as, "What do you need to do for you?" and "What's in it for you to stay, what's in it for you not to stay?" Doherty recounted his shock when he heard experts talk about "starter marriages," as if matrimony were as temporary as purchasing a first house, or "leasing a marriage," as if it were no different from renting an automobile. No longer posing as a neutral therapist, Doherty admitted that he had become "an advocate for marriage." Clients "can call me off but they're going to have to look me in the eye and call me off."[83]

A third category of therapists who, in Doherty's opinion, undermined marriage were those who "pathologize." A therapist who applied medical labels to either individual clients or a relationship preached "a sense of fatalism and hopelessness" about avoiding divorce; for example, if a relationship were "sick," then anyone who chose to stay in it might be considered psychologically unwell.[84] The urge within the field to pathologize was gaining momentum as the 2013 publication date of the fifth edition of the American Psychiatric Association's *Diagnostic and Statistical Manual of Mental Disorders* loomed. Since the late 1990s, a group of researchers and therapists had been lobbying for inclusion of the "relational disorder" diagnosis in the new *DSM*. Relational disorders are defined as "persistent and painful patterns of feelings, behavior, and perceptions involving two or more partners in an important personal relationship." Typically, people suffering from relational disorders have problems with their primary support groups—notably, their families. In a relational disorder between two spouses, for example, even though neither person suffers from an individual disorder, the two could share one.[85] Or, as *Time* magazine put it in 2002, "I'm OK, you're OK, we're not OK."[86] When the *DSM*'s fifth edition finally appeared, relational disorder had not been adopted as a diagnosis, but the lobbying for its inclusion reflected a textbook therapist aim: the "pathologization" of human relationships, the most vital of personal behaviors.[87]

The movement to pathologize relational disorders bore out the concerns of James L. Framo, a professor of psychology and family studies at San Diego's United States International University. Back in the 1950s, Framo had been a pioneer in family therapy, challenging the conventional wisdom that bringing feuding spouses or children into the same treatment room was a recipe for disaster. Believing that, most often, "Johnnie's problem is his parents' disturbed marriage," Framo was a vocal advocate of merging marriage and family counseling.[88] He recalled, "There used to be a time when only wives called for appoint-ments for marital therapy. Now it's often the man who calls in a panic, requesting marital therapy because his wife is leaving him or has had an affair." Yet this seeming progress, Framo argued, was counterbal-anced by the presence of therapists who are "zealots, who have consid-erable influence, make men the enemy, do not permit dissent, blame and shame men (who are perceived as bad), and in the process of setting feminist agendas to correct wrongs done to women create new wrongs." These therapists, he alleged, were "caught up in the culture of victim-hood." Whole groups in the field, such as AFTA, were more interested in social activism and political correctness than rigorous family therapy. "Gender, diversity, race, class, and culture are certainly worthy causes, but are they why AFTA was formed?" he asked.[89]

Perhaps Framo's greatest worry about the field's direction had to do with the issue of reimbursement for services. In what might be called a requiem for psychotherapy, he observed that "most matters in human affairs come down to money," and for marriage and family therapy, that meant its future under managed care. The old "fee for service" model was disappearing as health maintenance organizations (HMOs) increas-ingly dominated the field. Typically, psychotherapy was lengthy and ex-pensive, so HMOs—driven chiefly by profit motives—steadily exerted their influence over diagnosis and treatment. According to Framo, the consequences could transform the very nature of treatment: "Will the *therapeutic* relationship and empathy disappear as healing elements in psychotherapy? Our society is oriented toward speed: we have instant oatmeal, microwave cooking, fast food, fast forward on the VCR, and hurried phone sex. So why not quick therapy?" Managed care compa-nies preferred to pay for the treatment of psychiatric disorders as de-fined by the *DSM*, so if therapists wanted third-party reimbursement, they were under pressure to adopt diagnoses such as relational disorder. To Framo, the "whole process is demeaning, ridiculous, and dishon-est."[90]

Thus, the hard reality of managed care was altering the nature of marriage and family counseling as it evolved in the early twenty-first century. Some counselors worried that managed care was "marginaliz-ing" the profession within the larger mental and physical health care fields by compelling it to accept the biomedical model of mental disorders that dominates the diagnostic, conceptual, and clinical approaches of the health care system. By switching from counseling to therapy, the AAMFT accepted that its purpose was to treat diagnosed nervous and mental disorders. Yet, by seeking inclusion as a "core" mental health profession, marriage and family therapists encountered two sobering facts: third-party reimbursement for services did not automatically follow, and their long-standing "multidisciplinary" background was fading fast, cutting the field off from exciting developments in psychology, social work, nursing, and the like. Some therapists even longed for a return to Emily Mudd's heyday, when the field's multidisciplinary nature empowered it to "expand the perspectives of the traditional mental health disciplines."[91]

If inclusion in the mental health care field came with a stiff price, on other fronts, marriage and family therapy was faring no better. The deluge of therapist advice available through new, cutting-edge communications technologies invited a kind of therapist fatigue among journalists. In 2010 one exasperated reporter pleaded, "Enough with all the marriage therapy!" The incessant references to the hard work that went into a successful marriage led her to suggest that marital problems might lie not with spouses but with the therapist's belief that marriage is "an endless improvement project."[92] A *New York Times* reporter wondered whether all the scrutiny devoted to marriage might actually undermine the institution.[93] A *Huffington Post* writer listed six reasons marriage counseling was "BS." "If you want to save your marriage, for the love of God, don't go to marriage counseling," she advised.[94] In 2012 a *New York Times* headline read: "Does Couples Therapy Work?" The writer's answer was no, unless therapists stopped being "emphatic, sensitive, calm, accepting" and resolved to "get in there, mix it up with the client, be a ninja," as one clinical social worker put it. In other words, in the early twenty-first century, the field was acknowledging that its "traditional, passive uh-huh, uh-huh" type of therapist did not suit the needs of couples in counseling.[95]

Amid all this controversy, even Oprah Winfrey, the wildly popular TV host, became the target of media scrutiny. No on-air personality did more in the late twentieth century to advance the notion of therapism than Winfrey, whose show, which aired nationally from 1986 to 2011, was the highest-ranked talk show in U.S. history. *The Oprah Winfrey Show* took up where *Donahue* left off. As one observer noted, "When Donahue interviews a hooker who services twenty men a night, he wants to know how much money she makes, [but] Oprah wants to know if she's sore." In the words of historian Eva Moskowitz, Winfrey "fundamentally reconstituted public debate, making stories of addiction, denial, and recovery the story of America."[96] Oprah disclosed that she was a victim of childhood sexual abuse, and her battles with her weight became legendary among her millions of avid fans. Over the years, she invited a succession of therapists to appear on her show, with the aim of spreading the message that the only sin left in America was keeping a personal secret. Yet by the early twenty-first century, Oprah's so-called experts had fallen on hard times. Many revealed that their own lives had been spinning out of control while they were dispensing expert advice about how to lose weight, make money, or keep their love alive. It turns out that Sharyn Wolf, a self-proclaimed marriage counselor who appeared eight times on *Oprah*, was in fact married and divorced four times (twice to the same man). After telling Oprah's audience that she was in "a long, happy marriage," she revealed that she and her husband had had sex only three times in thirteen years. "I lied to Oprah," Wolf confessed.[97]

If Doherty is right that consumerism is a major cause of therapism, then the fortunes of the latter have never looked so robust. Despite Doherty's "whistle-blowing," social scientists' attacks on therapeutic culture, the media's doubts about the effectiveness of therapy, therapists' lies on national television, and the field's serious differences of opinion, the destiny of the therapeutic sensibility seems secure in the near future. The moral discourse of therapism permeates everyday language to such an extent that Americans find it increasingly difficult to express themselves in terms different from the radical and utilitarian individualism decried in *Habits of the Heart*. Evangelical Christians appear to be as positive about the doctrine of self-fulfillment as their secular counterparts. Televangelist Joel Osteen, called "the new face of Christianity" by the *Manchester Guardian*, teaches Christian Americans how to "live at your full potential."[98] In fact, some of the highest divorce rates in the country are in the most churchgoing states. Covenant marriage, in which couples sign a prenuptial agreement making it harder to divorce, has had some success among couples who opt for it, but few have signed up. In Arkansas, for example, only 0.5 percent of all marriages between 2001 and 2004 were covenant marriages.[99] By the new millennium, the nation's old emphasis on "character" over "personality" had been routed by its addiction to casinos, malls, box stores, online shopping, video games, pornography, and easy credit. In the early years of the twenty-first century, "merchandise was the opiate of the masses," according to historian David Courtwright.[100] Thus, when Osteen and evangelical psychologist James Dobson tell their Christian followers to practice a bit of self-control and discipline in their family lives, they are preaching to an unconverted audience distracted by myriad market temptations. The concepts of "starter marriages" and "leasing a marriage" may appall Doherty, but they make a lot more sense to Americans than solemn pledges such as "til death do us part."[101]

There is no denying that some Americans find that their marriage experiments are in tune with the zeitgeist and that the "me marriage" is right for them. Nonetheless, there is overwhelming evidence that countless Americans are unhappy about the overall state of marriage. Even cheerleaders for the "democratization of marriage" are no longer sure that the advantages outweigh the disadvantages. As Stephanie Coontz uneasily admits, marriage's "optional" nature in the new millennium makes it more "brittle" than ever before. Coontz believes that, thanks to therapism's principles of openness, equality, and personal freedom, marriage "has become more joyful, more loving, and more satisfying for many couples," but she recognizes that these trends come with a cost that defies measurement. In reflecting on her own heterosexual marriage, she writes, "As a modern woman I live with an undercurrent of anxiety" that is missing in the diaries of women from earlier eras. "I know that if my husband and I stop negotiating, if too much time passes without any joy, or if a conflict drags on too long, neither of us *has* to stay with the other." Yet there is no way to roll back the "marriage revolution" that has been unfolding over the last century, Coontz asserts. Maybe so, but the price of this upheaval has been personal turmoil and social breakdown that would have astounded our ancestors. Thanks to marriage and family therapy, "the new values of love and self-fulfillment" have redefined intimacy and, in so doing, have cut a yawning swath through the hearts and minds of America's families.[102]

$\mathcal{N}otes$

ABBREVIATIONS

AHC   Paul Popenoe papers, American Heritage Center, University of Wyoming, Laramie

EHM   Emily Hartshorne Mudd Papers, Arthur and Elizabeth Schlesinger Library on the History of Women in America, Radcliffe Institute for Advanced Study, Harvard University, Cambridge, MA

KI   Kinsey Institute, Indiana University, Bloomington

KILC   Kinsey Institute Library and Collections, Indiana University, Bloomington

MFL   *Marriage and Family Living*

NLM   National Library of Medicine, Bethesda, MD

RLD   Robert Latou Dickinson Papers, Francis A. Countway Library of Medicine, Harvard University Medical Library, Boston, MA

RWW   Raymond W. Waggoner Papers, Bentley Historical Library, University of Michigan, Ann Arbor

SWHA   National Council on Family Relations Records, Social Welfare History Archives, Elmer L. Andersen Library, University of Minnesota, Minneapolis

INTRODUCTION

1. "'Love Story' Is Over: Al Gore and Wife, Tipper, Splitting after Forty-Year Marriage," http://articles.nydailynews.com/2010-06-02/gossip/27065990_1_al-gore-tipper-gore-gore-aide.

2. William J. Doherty, "Al and Tipper: We Hardly Knew Ye," *Psychology Today*, June 3, 2010, http://www.psychologytoday.com/blog/marriage-and-parenting-in-todays-culture/201006/al-and-tipper-we-hardly-knew-ye.

3. "Al and Tipper Gore Split: Separating after Forty Years of Marriage," http://www.huffingtonpost.com/2010/06/01/al-gore-tipper-gore-separ_n_596199.html.

4. "Breaking up Isn't so Very Hard to Do for Graying Generation," http://www.globalaging.org/elderrights/us/2010/breaking.htm.

5. Jeffrey Zaslow, "Til 40 Years Do Us Part," *Wall Street Journal*, June 3, 2010, http://online.wsj.com/article/SB10001424052748703561604575282850694192336.html.

6. Tara Parker-Pope, "The Happy Marriage Is the 'Me' Marriage," *New York*

Times, December 31, 2010,. http://www.nytimes.com/2011/01/02/weekin review/02parkerpope.html.

7. I use the generic term "marriage and family counselors" to describe professionals working in this field, even though there has been considerable debate over whether they are counselors or therapists.

8. William C. Nichols Jr., *The AAMFT: Fifty Years of Marital and Family Therapy* (Washington, DC: American Association for Marriage and Family Therapy, 1992), 14.

9. David Mace and Vera Mace, foreword to Emily H. Mudd, *The American Association of Marriage Counselors: The First 25 Years (1942–1967)* (Dallas: American Association of Marriage Counselors, 1967), 3.

10. Ronald W. Dworkin, "The Rise of the Caring Industry," *Policy Review* 161 (June 1, 2010), http://www.hoover.org/publications/policy-review/article/5339.

11. Rebecca Davis, *More Perfect Unions: The Search for Marital Bliss* (Cambridge, MA: Harvard University Press, 2010), 3, 253.

12. Eva S. Moskowitz, *In Therapy We Trust: America's Obsession with Self-Fulfillment* (Baltimore: Johns Hopkins University Press, 2001), 1. Robert Bellah and his coauthors define the "therapeutic attitude" as one that "denies all forms of obligations and commitment in relationships, replacing them only with the ideal of full, open, honest communication among self-actualized individuals." Robert N. Bellah, Richard Madsen, William M. Sullivan, Ann Swidler, and Steven M. Tipton, *Habits of the Heart: Individualism and Commitment in American Life* (Berkeley: University of California Press, 1985), p. 101.

13. James L. Nolan Jr., *The Therapeutic State: Justifying Government at Century's End* (New York: New York University Press, 1998), 7, 9.

14. Moskowitz, *In Therapy We Trust*, 97.

15. Nolan, *Therapeutic State*, 3–4.

16. Historian Stephanie Coontz has advanced the thesis of love conquering marriage most vociferously, yet she never defines what she means by "love." Does she mean intimacy, sexual compatibility, mutual affection and respect, or old-fashioned Victorian "sentimentality"? At times she appears to be arguing that what distinguished twentieth-century marriage was that Americans were freer than ever to choose their mates, but is that the same as choosing to marry for love? In any case, the high divorce rate of the last half century hardly proves that marrying for love, whatever that means, has been good for the institution. See Stephanie Coontz, *Marriage, a History: From Obedience to Intimacy, or How Love Conquered Marriage* (New York: Viking, 2005).

17. Nolan, *Therapeutic State*, 292.

18. Kristin Celello, *Making Marriage Work: A History of Marriage and Divorce in the Twentieth-Century United States* (Chapel Hill: University of North Carolina Press, 2009), 39.

19. Bellah et al., *Habits of the Heart*, 123–124.

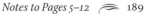

20. Raoul de Roussey de Sales, "Love in America," *Atlantic Monthly*, May 1938, http://www.theatlantic.com/past/docs/issues/38may/desales.htm.

21. According to marriage counseling pioneers Emily Mudd and Reuben Hill, Americans were "the most marrying people in the world." See Emily H. Mudd, Abraham Stone, Maurice J. Karpf, and Janet Folwer Nelson, eds., *Marriage Counseling: A Casebook* (New York: Association Press, 1958), 475.

22. Bellah et al., *Habits of the Heart*, 113.

23. Quoted in Davis, *More Perfect Unions*, 160.

24. Bellah et al., *Habits of the Heart*, 20, 306.

25. Alan Petigny, *The Permissive Society: America, 1941–1965* (New York: Cambridge University Press, 2009), 132.

26. Nolan, *Therapeutic State*, 2.

27. Bellah et al., *Habits of the Heart*, 127.

28. James L. Framo, "A Personal Retrospective of the Family Therapy Field: Then and Now," *Journal of Marital and Family Therapy* 22 (1996): 289.

29. Marvin B. Sussman, "Editor's Comments," *MFL* 30 (1968): 189. Sussman was quoting Catherine Chilman, from the office of Research and Demonstrations of the Social and Rehabilitation Service, Department of Health, Education, and Welfare.

30. H. Curtis Wood to Medora Bass, February 29, 1968, box 3, Medora Steedman Bass Collection, American Heritage Center, University of Wyoming, Laramie.

31. Ernest R. Groves, "The Marriage Panacea," *Social Forces* 12 (1934): 409.

32. Quoted in Christopher Lasch, *Haven in a Heartless World: The Family Besieged* (New York: Basic Books, 1977), 108.

33. Petigny, *Permissive Society*.

34. Coontz, *Marriage*, 233.

35. Robert A. Harper, "Failure in Marriage Counseling," *MFL* 17 (1955): 362.

36. Eva Moskowitz, "'It's Good to Blow Your Top': Women's Magazines and a Discourse of Discontent, 1945–1965," *Journal of Women's History* 8 (1996): 78, 84.

37. Steve Bruce, *Religion in the Modern World: From Cathedrals to Cults* (New York: Oxford University Press, 1996), 144–145.

38. William Masters to Emily Mudd, October 19, 1961, box 9, folder 429, EHM.

39. Ira D. Glick, Helen M. Berman, John F. Clarkin, and Douglas S. Rait, *Marital and Family Therapy* (Arlington, VA: American Psychiatric Publishing, 2000), 6.

40. Alan S. Gurman and Peter Fraenkel, "The History of Couple Therapy: A Millennial Review," *Family Process* 41 (2002): 203.

41. J. Cohen, J. Marecek, and J. Gillham, "Is Three a Crowd?" *American Journal of Orthopsychiatry* 76 (2006): 251–259.

42. Framo, "Personal Retrospective," 305.

43. Elizabeth Weil, "Does Couples Therapy Work?" *New York Times*, March

2, 2012, http://www.nytimes.com/2012/03/04/fashion/couples-therapists-con
front-the-stresses-of-their-field.html?pagewanted=all.

44. Martin King Whyte, ed., *Marriage in America: A Communitarian Perspective*
(Lanham, MD: Rowman and Littlefield, 2000), 1.

45. William J. Doherty, "How Therapists Harm Marriages and What We Can
Do about It," *Journal of Couple and Relationship Therapy* 1 (2002): 2.

46. Coontz, *Marriage*, 306.

47. Andrew J. Cherlin, *The Marriage-Go-Round: The State of Marriage and the
Family in America Today* (New York: Alfred A. Knopf, 2009).

CHAPTER ONE. A NUCLEUS OF PERSONS

1. Emily H. Mudd, interview by James W. Reed, May 21–August 3, 1974,
Schlesinger-Rockefeller Oral History Project, transcript, Arthur and Elizabeth
Schlesinger Library on the History of Women in America, Harvard University,
p. 11. Hereafter cited as Mudd interview.

2. Hirsch Lazar Silverman, "Educational and Professional Training of the
Marital Counselor: Historical Introduction," n.d., box 18, folder 816, EHM. In
Silverman's words: "One is struck with the fact that a core of names keeps recurring in differing and related events [in the early history of marriage coun-
seling]. Further it is clear that a nucleus of persons were deeply interested in
fostering and steering the emergence of a new profession, being as they were
involved in all sorts of interlocking activities and pursuits related to marriage
counseling."

3. James Reed, *From Private Vice to Public Virtue: The Birth Control Movement and
American Society since 1830* (New York: Basic Books, 1978), 127. The organization's
original name, the Marriage Counsel of Philadelphia, stood until 1947, when it
was changed to the Marriage Council of Philadelphia.

4. Quoted in Luigi Mastroianni Jr., "Emily Hartshorne Mudd," *Proceedings of
the American Philosophical Society* 144 (2000): 103.

5. William C. Nichols Jr., *The AAMFT: Fifty Years of Marital and Family Therapy*
(Washington, DC: AAMFT, 1992), 17.

6. William Menninger, acceptance speech, Second Annual Philadelphia Marriage Council Award, November 7, 1963, Emily Mudd Correspondence, 1970–
1976 Folder, RWW; emphasis in original.

7. Thomas D. Hamm, *The Quakers in America* (New York: Columbia University
Press, 2003), 188.

8. Mudd interview, 2.

9. Ibid., 23.

10. Abraham Stone and Hannah Stone, *A Marriage Manual: Practical Guide Book
to Sex and Marriage* (New York: Simon and Schuster, 1935), vi.

11. Quoted in David M. Kennedy, *Birth Control in America* (New Haven, CT:
Yale University Press, 1970), 127, 131.

12. Linda Gordon, *Woman's Body, Woman's Right: A Social History of Birth Control in America* (New York: Viking, 1976), 373.

13. Mudd interview, 171; emphasis in original.

14. Ibid., 226.

15. Ibid., 21.

16. Ibid., 26.

17. Gunnar Myrdal, *An American Dilemma: The Negro Problem and American Democracy* (New York: Harper and Row, 1944), 1:179, cited in Donald T. Critchlow, *Intended Consequences: Birth Control, Abortion, and the Federal Government in Modern America* (New York: Oxford University Press, 1999), 35–36.

18. Mudd interview, 30, 31, 233.

19. Reed, *From Private Vice to Public Virtue*, 233.

20. The secondary literature on the history of U.S. eugenics is extensive. The main titles include Mark H. Haller, *Eugenics: Hereditarian Attitudes in American Thought* (New Brunswick, NJ: Rutgers University Press, 1963); Daniel J. Kevles, *In the Name of Eugenics: Genetics and the Uses of Human Heredity* (New York: Knopf, 1985); Philip R. Reilly, *The Surgical Solution: A History of Involuntary Sterilization in the United States* (Baltimore: Johns Hopkins University Press, 1991); Edward J. Larson, *Sex, Race, and Science: Eugenics in the Deep South* (Baltimore: Johns Hopkins University Press, 1995); Nancy L. Gallagher, *Breeding Better Vermonters: The Eugenics Project in the Green Mountain State* (Hanover, NH: University Press of New England, 1999); Wendy Kline, *Building a Better Race: Gender, Sexuality, and Eugenics from the Turn of the Century to the Baby Boom* (Berkeley: University of California Press, 2001); Christine Rosen, *Preaching Eugenics: Religious Leaders and the American Eugenics Movement* (New York: Oxford University Press, 2004); Joanna Schoen, *Choice and Coercion: Birth Control, Sterilization, and Abortion in Public Health and Welfare* (Chapel Hill: University of North Carolina Press, 2005); Alexandra Minna Stern, *Eugenic Nation: Faults and Frontiers of Better Breeding in Modern America* (Berkeley: University of California Press, 2005); Angela Franks, *Margaret Sanger's Eugenic Legacy: The Control of Female Fertility* (Jefferson, NC: McFarland, 2005); and Ian Dowbiggin, *The Sterilization Movement and Global Fertility in the Twentieth Century* (New York: Oxford University Press, 2008).

21. Editorial, *New York Times*, June 22, 1932, quoted in Kevles, *In the Name of Eugenics*, 165.

22. Kline, *Building a Better Race*, 123.

23. Gladys Gaylord, "Report of Committee on Eugenics and the Family," *MFL* 3 (1941): 37–39.

24. Annette F. Timm, *The Politics of Fertility in Twentieth-Century Berlin* (Cambridge: Cambridge University Press, 2010), 103.

25. Emily H. Mudd, "Clinical Service in Germany," *Birth Control Review* 17 (1933): 16–17.

26. Ibid.

27. Emily H. Mudd, "Marital Advice Bureaus—The Next Step," *Birth Control Review* 15 (1931): 175; Emily H. Mudd, "Is Preventive Work the Next Step?" *Birth Control Review* 16 (1932): 42–43.

28. Mudd interview, 51–54.

29. Reed, *From Private Vice to Public Virtue*, 121–122.

30. Mudd interview, 49.

31. Ibid., 71–72.

32. Ibid., 59–60.

33. "Characteristics of Clients at Marriage Council of Philadelphia, 1954–1955," box 14, folder 603, EHM.

34. Kenneth E. Appel, "Freud and Psychiatry," *Bulletin of the New York Academy of Medicine* 32 (1956): 858–877. For the triumph of psychoanalysis within U.S. psychiatry, see Edward Shorter, *A History of Psychiatry: From the Era of the Asylum to the Age of Prozac* (New York: Wiley, 1997), 170–181.

35. Emily H. Mudd, "What Has Been the Most Important Discovery or Innovation in the Field of Sexuality during the Past Thirty Years?" *Medical Aspects of Human Sexuality* 6 (1972): 58–61.

36. Mudd interview, 55.

37. Ian Dowbiggin, *The Quest for Mental Health: A Tale of Science, Medicine, Scandal, Sorrow, and Mass Society* (Cambridge: Cambridge University Press, 2011), 90.

38. Mudd, "Is Preventive Work the Next Step?" 43.

39. Emily Hartshorne Mudd and Elizabeth Kirk Rose, "Development of Marriage Counsel of Philadelphia as a Community Service, 1932–1940," *Living* 2 (1940): 40–41.

40. James L. Nolan Jr., *The Therapeutic State: Justifying Government at Century's End* (New York: New York University Press, 1998), 5–7.

41. Eva S. Moskowitz, *In Therapy We Trust: America's Obsession with Self-Fulfillment* (Baltimore: Johns Hopkins University Press, 2001), 81.

42. Ernest W. Burgess, "Marriage Counselling in a Changing Society," *MFL* 5 (1943): 9.

43. Robert G. Foster, "Servicing the Family through Counseling Agencies," *American Sociological Review* 2 (1937): 764.

44. Moskowitz, *In Therapy We Trust*, 98.

45. National Conference on Family Life, "Report of Subcommittee on Marriage and Family Counseling," May 6–8, 1948, box 127, folder 5, Paul Popenoe Papers, AHC.

46. David Mace, "The State Regulation of Marriage Counseling," June 5–6, 1964, box 53, AAMFC Folder, SWHA.

47. Mildred Tate to Robert Foster, September 30, 1953, box 15, Robert Foster Folder #8, SWHA.

48. Mudd interview, 137.

49. Ibid., 205.

50. Paul Popenoe, "Forty Years of the AIFR," *Family Life* 30 (1970): 1.

51. Rebecca Davis, *More Perfect Unions: The Search for Marital Bliss* (Cambridge, MA: Harvard University Press, 2010), 34.

52. Kline, *Building a Better Race*, 142.

53. "Radio Electronic," *Time*, November 19, 1956.

54. Stern, *Eugenic Nation*, 160, 166.

55. For Catholic resistance to involuntary sterilization laws, see Reilly, *Surgical Solution*, 118–122.

56. Stern, *Eugenic Nation*, 161.

57. Mudd interview, 75, 196.

58. Edna Noble White, "Experiments in Family Consultation Centers," *Social Forces* 12 (1934): 560.

59. Paul Popenoe to Joe Jerkins, February 26, 1959, box 27, Popenoe Papers, AHC.

60. Stern, *Eugenic Nation*, 194.

61. Paul Popenoe, "Are Homosexuals Necessary?" AIFR Publication 542, n.d., box 47, AIFR Folder, AVS Records, SWHA.

62. Stern, *Eugenic Nation*, 198.

63. Molly Ladd-Taylor, "Eugenics, Sterilisation and Modern Marriage in the USA: The Strange Career of Paul Popenoe," *Gender and History* 13 (2001): 310, 316, 322.

64. "Marriage Checkup: A Workshop for Couples, Led by Dr. Paul Popenoe," July 20, 1965, box 47, AIFR Folder, AVS, SWHA.

65. Kristin Celello, *Making Marriage Work: A History of Marriage and Divorce in the Twentieth-Century United States* (Chapel Hill: University of North Carolina Press, 2009), 33.

66. Ernest R. Groves, "Mental Hygiene in the College and the University," *Social Forces* 8 (1929): 39; see also Ernest R. Groves, "A Decade of Marriage Counseling," *Annals of the American Academy of Political and Social Science* 212 (1940): 72–80.

67. Anna O. Stephens, "Premarital Sex Relationships," in *Successful Marriage: A Modern Guide to Love, Sex, and Family Life*, ed. Morris Fishbein and Ernest W. Burgess (Garden City, NY: Doubleday, 1955), 42.

68. Celello, *Making Marriage Work*, 34–35.

69. Ernest W. Burgess, Harvey J. Locke, and Mary Margaret Thomes, *The Family: From Institution to Companionship*, 3rd ed. (New York: American Book Company, 1963).

70. Celello, *Making Marriage Work*, 38.

71. Burgess, Locke, and Thomes, *The Family*, vii, 3–5.

72. "Marriage Test," *Time*, February 7, 1938, 24.

73. Ernest W. Burgess, "Predictive Factors in the Success or Failure of Marriage," *Living* 1 (1939): 1–3.

74. Groves, "A Decade of Marriage Counseling," 73.

75. Mudd interview, 222.

76. Groves, "Mental Hygiene in College and University," 37, 38, 39, 42.

77. Moskowitz, *In Therapy We Trust*, 82, 85.

78. Rosen, *Preaching Eugenics*, 156.

79. Dr. Sidney E. Goldstein, "The Need of a White House Conference on the Family," *Living* 1 (1939): 13–14; a reprint of Goldstein's address at the first annual meeting of the NCFR in New York City, September 17, 1938. See also Sidney E. Goldstein, "Rabbi Sidney E. Goldstein Discusses Family Problems," *Jewish Telegraphic Agency*, October 21, 1932, http://archive.jta.org/article/1932/10/21/2795177/rabbi-sidney-e-goldstein-discusses-family-problems.

80. Maida Solomon to Frank Kiernan, May 4, 1931, LWD, box 5, folder 35, Lester W. Dearborn Folder, MSSH Papers, Schlesinger Library.

81. Estelle B. Freedman, "'Uncontrolled Desires': The Response to the Sexual Psychopath, 1920–1960," *Journal of American History* 74 (1987): 103.

82. Davis, *More Perfect Unions*, 51–52.

83. Lester W. Dearborn, "Personal and Marriage Counseling in Boston," *Journal of Home Economics* 36 (1944): 557–559.

84. Celello, *Making Marriage Work*, 122.

85. "Scholars on Sex," *Time*, July 16, 1934.

86. "'Cafeteria-Style' Educator Helps the Teary Bride of a Few Weeks," *Boston Globe*, May 1, 1955, 71.

CHAPTER TWO. THE KINSEY CONNECTION

1. Ellen Herman, *The Romance of American Psychology: Political Culture in the Age of Experts* (Berkeley: University of California Press, 1995), 13.

2. *Life*, January 7, 1957, 68, cited in E. Brooks Holifield, *A History of Pastoral Care in America: From Salvation to Self-Realization* (Nashville, TN: Abingdon, 1983), 261.

3. Daniel Lerner and Richard Howard Stafford Crossman, *Sykewar: Psychological Warfare against Germany from D-Day to VE-Day* (New York: George W. Stewart, 1948).

4. Gerald N. Grob, "World War II and American Psychiatry," *Psychohistory Review* 19 (1990): 56–57.

5. Kyle Crichton, "Repairing War-Cracked Minds," *Collier's*, September 23, 1944, 22–23, cited in Alan Petigny, *The Permissive Society: America, 1941–1965* (New York: Cambridge University Press, 2009), 18.

6. Quoted in "Everybody's Mental Health," *Time*, December 10, 1956.

7. Holifield, *History of Pastoral Care*, 262.

8. Emily Mudd, "Summary Report," box 14, folder 620, EHM.

9. Evelyn Millis Duvall, "Growing Edges in Family Life Education," *MFL* 6 (1944): 21.

10. Ernest W. Burgess, "Postwar Problems of the Family," *MFL* 6 (1944): 50.

11. Quoted in Max Hastings, *All Hell Let Loose: The World at War, 1939–1945* (London: Harper Press, 2011), 328.

12. Estelle B. Freedman, "'Uncontrolled Desires': The Response to the Sexual Psychopath, 1920–1960," *Journal of American History* 74 (1987): 103.

13. Kristin Celello, *Making Marriage Work: A History of Marriage and Divorce in the Twentieth-Century United States* (Chapel Hill: University of North Carolina Press, 2009), 47, 58.

14. Historian Eva Moskowitz has argued that the AAMC's founding was the culmination of "an intense phase of professional development" dating back to earlier decades. Eva S. Moskowitz, *In Therapy We Trust: America's Obsession with Self-Fulfillment* (Baltimore: Johns Hopkins University Press, 2001), 98.

15. Robert Latou Dickinson, "Memorandum Concerning the Conference on Socio-Sexual Relations of Men and Women, 1940–1943," box 1, folder 90, RLD.

16. Emily Mudd, *The American Association of Marriage Counselors: The First 25 Years, 1942–1967* (Dallas: AAMC, 1968), 8.

17. Abraham Stone, "The Doctor Examines Marital Ills," speech at the New York County Lawyers' Association," cited in Emily Mudd, "Dr. Abraham Stone," *MFL* 22 (1960): 174.

18. Sophia Kleegman to Dickinson, November 13, 1950, box 1, folder 78, RLD.

19. Robert Laidlaw to Emily Mudd, May 10, 1977, box 4, folder 167, EHM. See also "The American Association of Marriage Counseling," in *Marriage Counseling: A Casebook*, ed. Emily H. Mudd, Abraham Stone, Maruice J. Karpf, and Janet Fowler Nelson (New York: Association Press, 1958), 484.

20. Robert Latou Dickinson, "Medical Analysis of a Thousand Marriages," *JAMA* 97 (1931): 529–535.

21. Emily H. Mudd, interview by James W. Reed, May 21–August 3, 1974, Schlesinger-Rockefeller Oral History Project, transcript, Arthur and Elizabeth Schlesinger Library on the History of Women in America, Harvard University, p. 153. Hereafter cited as Mudd interview.

22. Robert Laidlaw, "Robert L. Dickinson as Marriage Counselor and Educator for Family Living," October 24, 1951, box 1, folder 83, RLD.

23. James H. Jones, *Alfred C. Kinsey: A Public/Private Life* (New York: W. W. Norton, 1997), 291, 503–508.

24. Ian Dowbiggin, *The Sterilization Movement and Global Fertility in the Twentieth Century* (New York: Oxford University Press, 2008), 56.

25. Ibid., 9.

26. Rebecca M. Kluchin, *Fit to Be Tied: Sterilization and Reproductive Rights in America, 1950–1980* (New Brunswick, NJ: Rutgers University Press, 2011), 35.

27. Mudd interview, 72.

28. Dowbiggin, *Sterilization Movement*, 52.

29. Matthew Connelly, *Fatal Misconception: The Struggle to Control World Population* (Cambridge, MA: Harvard University Press, 2008), 179, 189, 277, 285, 289, 306, 307, 353, 355.

30. Mudd interview, 226.

31. Robert Laidlaw, "Medical and Cultural Implications of the Kinsey Re-

ports," lecture to University of Pennsylvania medical students, October 7, 1953, box 16, folder 749, EHM.

32. Joanne Meyerowitz, *How Sex Changed: A History of Transsexuality in the United States* (Cambridge, MA: Harvard University Press, 2002), 249.

33. Quoted in Miriam G. Reumann, *American Sexual Character: Sex, Gender, and National Identity in the Kinsey Reports* (Berkeley: University of California Press, 2005), 188.

34. For an exception, see Regina Markell Morantz, "The Scientist as Sex Crusader: Alfred C. Kinsey and American Culture," *American Quarterly* 29 (1977): 563–589.

35. Paul Gebhard to Robert Laidlaw, November 7, 1956, Laidlaw Folder, KILC.

36. Carlfred B. Broderick and Sandra S. Schrader, "The History of Professional Marriage and Family Therapy," in *Handbook of Family Therapy*, ed. Alan Gurman and David P. Kniskern (New York: Brunner/Mazel, 1981), 10.

37. Judson Landis, "An Evaluation of Marriage Education," *MFL* 10 (1948): 82.

38. Beth L. Bailey, "Scientific Truth . . . and Love: The Marriage Education Movement in the United States, " *Journal of Social History* 20 (1987): 720.

39. "The Grandmother of Sex Education," *Vassar Alumni Quarterly* 97 (2000), http://vq.vassar.edu/issue/winter_2000/article/grandmother_of_sex_ed.

40. Jones, *Alfred C. Kinsey*, 340.

41. Ibid., 324, 336.

42. Alfred Kinsey to Emily Mudd, September 27, 1944, box 16, folder 730, EHM.

43. Alfred Kinsey to Emily Mudd, May 15, 1944, box 16, folder 729, EHM.

44. Mudd interview, 176–177.

45. Alfred Kinsey to Claire E. Folsome, July 26, 1944, Emily H. Mudd Folder, KILC.

46. Alfred Kinsey to Emily Mudd, May 16, 1944, Emily Mudd Folder, KILC; emphasis added. Kinsey's associate Wardell Pomeroy admitted that "Kinsey had perceived how useful his studies would be to the burgeoning specialty of marriage counseling." Wardell Baxter Pomeroy, *Dr. Kinsey and the Institute for Sex Research* (New Haven, CT: Yale University Press, 1972), 142.

47. Frances Dow, minutes of Alfred Kinsey's "Sex Offenders" talk, AAMC meeting, December 28, 1949, AAMC Folder, KILC.

48. Emily Mudd to Alfred Kinsey, February 3, 1947, Emily Mudd Folder, KILC.

49. Jonathan Gathorne-Hardy, *Sex the Measure of All Things: A Life of Alfred C. Kinsey* (Bloomington: Indiana University Press, 2004), 381.

50. Mudd interview, 161.

51. Emily Mudd to Alfred Kinsey, February 3, 1947, box 16, folder 734, EHM.

52. Robert Laidlaw to "Dear Member," December 26, 1948, box 1, folder 1, RLD.

53. Mudd interview, 169.

54. Abraham Stone, review of Kinsey's *Sexual Behavior in the Human Male*, *MFL* 10 (1948): 97.

55. Alfred Kinsey to Emily Mudd, November 23, 1951, box 16, folder 739, EHM.

56. Emily Mudd to Alfred Kinsey, March 23, 1953, box 16, folder 741, EHM.

57. See Emily Mudd, "Summary Report, United States Public Health Service Projects MH-57C, MH-57C2, MH-57C3, MH-57C5, 1947–57," box 14, folder 617, EHM. See also Kenneth Appel to Robert Felix, July 14, 1955, and "A Research Program to Investigate the Impact of Frigidity and Impotence upon Sexual Behavior and Attitudes of Marriage Partners," October 17, 1955, box 14, folder 620, EHM.

58. Jones, *Alfred C. Kinsey*, 712, 723.

59. Billy Graham, "The Bible and Dr. Kinsey," delivered on *The Hour of Decision* radio program, September 13, 1953; R. Marie Griffith, "The Religious Encounters of Alfred C. Kinsey," *Journal of American History* 95 (2008): 364, 367.

60. As historian James Reed has argued, "Kinsey's subjects were not representative of American women. His sample was disproportionately drawn from urban, well-educated Protestant groups. These women averaged only 1.09 live births. . . . Kinsey's sample was biased toward infertility in comparison with women of similar socioeconomic status." James Reed, *From Private Vice to Public Virtue: The Birth Control Movement and American Society since 1830* (New York: Basic Books, 1978), 125. In a January 6, 1954, letter to Kinsey, Mudd referred to "the over-loading of our sample with college students" (box 16, folder 744, EHM).

61. Paul Popenoe to "Mr. Seale," May 30, 1957, box 27, Paul Popenoe Papers, AHC.

62. "Sex and the Church," *Time*, June 7, 1948, http://www.pbs.org/wgbh /amex/kinsey/sfeature/sf_response_male.html.

63. Jones, *Alfred C. Kinsey*, 575.

64. Emily H. Mudd, "Sexual Problems in Marriage Counseling," n.d. [likely 1956], box 16, folder 746, EHM.

65. Abraham Stone, "How the Report Affects Marriage Counseling," in *Sex Habits of American Men: A Symposium on the Kinsey Report*, ed. Albert Deutsch (New York: Prentice-Hall, 1948), 162.

66. Robert Laidlaw, "Medical and Cultural Implications of the Kinsey Reports," University of Pennsylvania lecture, October 7, 1953, box 16, folder 749, EHM.

67. Emily Mudd and Bill Davidson, "How Dr. Kinsey's Report on Women May Help Your Marriage," *Collier's*, September 18, 1953, http://www.pbs.org /wgbh/amex/kinsey/sfeature/sf_response_female.html.

68. Emily Mudd, lecture on the "Implications of the Kinsey Report on Women for Marriage and Sexual Adjustment," October 14, 1953, box 16, folder 750, EHM.

69. Stone, "How the Report Affects Marriage Counseling," 164–165, 172.

70. Jones, *Alfred C. Kinsey*, 486.

71. Ibid., 386.

72. Mudd interview, 176–177.

73. Morantz, "The Scientist as Sex Crusader," 585.

CHAPTER THREE. MEDICAL MISSION TO MOSCOW

1. Norbert Muhlen, "Submission to Moscow," *New Leader* 29 (October 12, 1944): 11. See also Hugh Wilford, "Playing the CIA Tine? The *New Leader* and the Cultural Cold War," *Diplomatic History* 27 (2003): 15–34.

2. Nikolai Krementsov, "In the Shadow of the Bomb: U.S.-Soviet Biomedical Relations in the Early Cold War, 1944–1948," *Journal of Cold War Studies* 9 (2007): 44. Krementsov's analysis of Soviet-U.S. exchanges of biomedical information in the early Cold War provides an invaluable and incisive glimpse into how the Soviets used "science as a propaganda tool" (67). He also argues provocatively that "science played a much more direct and important role in the actual formulation of certain Cold War policies" than historians have imagined (43).

3. John F. Hutchinson, "Dancing with Commissars: Sigerist and Soviet Medicine," in *Making Medical History: The Life and Times of Henry E. Sigerist*, ed. Elizabeth Fee and Theodore M. Brown (Baltimore: Johns Hopkins University Press, 1997), 239.

4. Kate Weigand, *Red Feminism: American Communism and the Making of Women's Liberation* (Baltimore: Johns Hopkins University Press, 2001), 9, 10.

5. Joseph E. Davies, *Mission to Moscow* (New York: Simon and Schuster, 1941). In 1943 Davies's book was made into a major motion picture of the same name. See Ronald Radosh and Allis Radosh, "A Great Historic Mistake: The Making of *Mission to Moscow*," *Film History* 16 (2004): 358–377. For the scientists' 1944 visit, see A. Baird Hastings and Michael B. Shimkin, "Medical Research Mission to the Soviet Union," *Science* 103 (1946): 605–608, and Nikolai Krementsov, *The Cure: A Story of Cancer and Politics from the Annals of the Cold War* (Chicago: University of Chicago Press, 2002), 62–63. The Mudds' 1946 "Medical Mission to Moscow" must be distinguished from a 1961 visit of the same name. See LeRoy R. Swift, "Medical Mission to Moscow," *Journal of the National Medical Association* 53 (July 1961): 346–351.

6. The FBI suspected that Robert Leslie of the ASMS was a Soviet spy but eventually concluded that although he was a member of the CPUSA and a member of the executive board of the communist publication *New Masses*, he was not guilty of espionage. J. P. Coyne to D. M. Ladd, November 28, 1947, "FBI Office Memorandum Re: Dr. Robert Lincoln Leslie," box 1, folder 2, American-Soviet Medical Society Records, 1942–1987, NLM.

7. The only account of the ASMS is Walter Lear's "Hot War Creation, Cold War Casualty," in Fee and Brown, *Making Medical History*, 259–287. Although Lear concedes that, by 1947, the Kremlin had decided to scale back contact with foreign scientists, he blames the demise of the ASMS on "the cold war offensive against the USSR and everything tainted or alleged to be tainted by communism" (279).

8. For Emily Mudd's version of events surrounding the Medical Mission to Moscow, see Emily H. Mudd, interview by James W. Reed, May 21–August 3, 1974, Schlesinger-Rockefeller Oral History Project, transcript, Arthur and Elizabeth Schlesinger Library on the History of Women in America, Harvard University, pp. 140–150. Hereafter cited as Mudd interview. I wish to thank the Schlesinger Library for permission to quote from this document and Reed for his thoughts on Mudd and the history of the birth control movement.

9. Henry E. Sigerist, *Socialized Medicine in the Soviet Union* (New York: W. W. Norton, 1937), 308.

10. This was certainly Sigerist's view. He wrote: "The Russian Revolution liberated women, according them equal rights with men in all spheres of economic, state, cultural, social, and political life. If the Revolution had achieved nothing else, this alone would be enough to make it an event of great historical significance." Sigerist, *Socialized Medicine in the Soviet Union*, 238.

11. Mudd interview, 22, 146.

12. Krementsov, "In the Shadow of the Bomb," 44.

13. Another high point for the NCASF came in 1944 when, at its dinner marking the twenty-sixth anniversary of the Soviet Red Army, Generals Marshall, MacArthur, Eisenhower, Pershing, and Clark sent their congratulations. The celebration included a rally at Madison Square Garden, with a speech by Vice President Henry A. Wallace. Joanne Melish, "American Soviet Friendship," in *Encyclopedia of the American Left*, ed. Mari Jo Buhle, Paul Buhle, and Dan Georgakas (New York: Garland Publishing, 1990), 29–32.

14. When critics pointed out these trends, friendship societies typically accused them of being unpatriotic admirers of Nazism. Louis Nemzer, "The Soviet Friendship Societies," *Public Opinion Quarterly* 13 (1949): 278, 279, 284; Melish, "American Soviet Friendship," 31. The propensity to defend the Soviet Union indiscriminately could lead to embarrassing situations when the topic was experimental science. For example, in 1949 the NCASF castigated U.S. geneticist Hermann J. Muller for attacking the theories of Soviet biologists Ivan Michurin and Trofim Lysenko. The NCASF tacitly endorsed the official Soviet viewpoint that Muller, in opposing the theory of the inheritance of acquired characteristics to explain evolution, was, by default, a backer of Nazi racial doctrines. "American-Soviet Facts: The Controversy over Soviet Genetic Theories," *NCASF News-Letter*, January 7, 1949, box 14, folder 11, Abraham Stone Papers, Francis A. Countway Library of Medicine, Harvard School of Medicine. See also Nikolai Krementsov, *Stalinist Science* (Princeton, NJ: Princeton University Press, 1997), especially 158–183.

15. See Guide to the National Council of Soviet-American Friendship Records, Tamiment Library and Robert F. Wagner Labor Archives, New York, NY, http://dlib.nyu.edu/findingaids/html/tamwag/ncasf.html.

16. Jacalyn Duffin, "The Guru and the Godfather: Henry Sigerist, Hugh MacLean, and the Politics of Health Care Reform in 1940s Canada," *Canadian*

Bulletin of Medical History 9 (1992): 191–218; Jacalyn Duffin and Leslie A. Falk, "Sigerist in Saskatchewan: The Quest for Balance in Social and Technical Medicine," *Bulletin of the History of Medicine* 70 (1996): 658–683. See also Janet Farrar Worthington, "Flawed Apostle," *Hopkins Medical News* (Winter 1999), http://www.hopkinsmedicine.org/hmn/W99/annals.html.

17. Henry Sigerist, "Editorial on American-Soviet Relations," *American Review of Soviet Medicine*, January 1948, box 5, Editorial on American-Soviet Relations Folder, NLM. The Anglo-Soviet Medical Committee was founded a year before the ASMS.

18. Sigerist was a member of the American-Russian Institute's board of directors.

19. Krementsov, *Stalinist Science*, 116; Lear, "Hot War Creation, Cold War Casualty," 270.

20. In fact, President Harry Truman extended his personal "greetings to the [second] annual meeting of the American-Soviet Medical Society and my good wishes for a successful session. May the good offices of the medical profession help to bring about the betterment of humanity and assist in the building of a broader understanding as a foundation for a lasting peace." Harry Truman to the American-Soviet Medical Society, December 14, 1945, box 4, folder 177, EHM.

21. Fishbein quoted in Howard Rushmore, "Red 'Front' in Drive to Socialize U.S. Medicine," *New York Journal-American*, August 12, 1945. Fishbein was not the only authority who had a low opinion of the Soviet scientific literature that the ASMS wanted to publish. Jonathan Rhoads, of the University of Pennsylvania's Department of Surgical Research, stated that a paper by one Soviet scientist would be considered "second rate" if it had been written by a U.S. researcher. Jonathan Rhoads to Stuart Mudd, June 4, 1945, box 7, Stuart Mudd Papers, University Archives and Records Center, University of Pennsylvania School of Medicine. The problem only grew worse for the ASMS when, in 1947, the Soviet government threatened its scientists with severe punishment if they disclosed advances in science, medicine, technology, or economics. See Robert S. Morison to Stuart Mudd, June 16, 1947, Stuart Mudd Papers.

22. "Medical Exchange with Russia Ends," *New York Times*, November 19, 1948, 19.

23. See Alfred Newton Richards Papers, 1910–1966, University Archives and Records Center, University of Pennsylvania.

24. Emily Mudd to George Brodbeck, June 11, 1946, box 4, folder 177, EHM.

25. Rose Maurer was married to Columbia University sociologist John Somerville. They lived in the USSR from 1935 to 1937. See "John Somerville, 1905–1994," *Proceedings and Addresses of the American Philosophical Association* 67 (1994): 52–53. In the 1960s and 1970s Rose Maurer Somerville was an editorial assistant for the NCFR's journal.

26. Emily Mudd was not the only advocate of marriage counseling in the

ASMS. Abraham Stone was ASMS secretary for its entire existence. He and his wife, Hannah, authored *Marriage Manual: A Practical Guide to Sex and Marriage* (1935), one of the first books on the topic. The Stones were close friends with the Mudds: Emily once called Hannah "the Madonna" of the Margaret Sanger Birth Control Clinical Research Bureau, which Stone headed until her death in 1941. Given their common causes and mutual respect, there is good reason to conclude that the Stones endorsed the Mudds' motives for undertaking their mission to Moscow. The Stones too saw the trip as a means of importing Soviet policies and theories about marriage and the family. See "Hannah Stone: The Madonna of the Clinic," *Margaret Sanger Papers Project* 9 (Winter 1994–1995), http://www.nyu.edu/projects/sanger/secure/newsletter/articles/hannah_stone .html.

27. Stuart Mudd and Emily H. Mudd, "Recent Observations on Programs for Medicine and National Health in the USSR," *Proceedings of the American Philosophical Society* 91 (1947): 181–188; "Programs for Medicine and National Health in the USSR," *Science* 105 (1947): 269–273, 306–309; Stuart Mudd and Emily Mudd, "Medical Mission to Moscow," *General Magazine and Historical Chronicle* 49 (1947): 205–218.

28. Krementsov, "In the Shadow of the Bomb," 60.

29. Maurer was skeptical about Stalin's commitment to women's rights and questioned why the nation's leadership did not appoint women to represent the Soviet Union at international gatherings, including the United Nations Committee on the Status of Women. Maurer to Emily Mudd, August 4, 1946, box 4, folder 177, EHM.

30. Mudd and Mudd, "Medical Mission to Moscow," 205–218.

31. Mudd interview, 145–146.

32. Paul Starr, *The Social Transformation of American Medicine* (New York: Basic Books, 1982), 283. See also Ronald L. Numbers, "The Third Party: Health Insurance in America," in *The Therapeutic Revolution: Essays in the Social History of American Medicine*, ed. Morris J. Vogel and Charles E. Rosenberg (Philadelphia: University of Pennsylvania Press, 1979), 184. For Sigerist's involvement in the debate over "socialized medicine," see Elizabeth Fee, "The Pleasures and Perils of Prophetic Advocacy: Socialized Medicine and the Politics of American Medical Reform," in Fee and Brown, *Making Medical History*, 197–228.

33. Weigand, *Red Feminism*, 46.

34. Elizabeth Rose, *A Mother's Job: The History of Day Care, 1890–1960* (New York: Oxford University Press, 1999), 153–154, 171.

35. Leo P. Ribuffo, "Family Policy Past as Prologue: Jimmy Carter, the White House Conference on Families, and the Mobilization of the New Christian Right," *Review of Policy Research* 23 (2006): 316.

36. William Rorabaugh, Donald T. Critchlow, and Paula Baker, *America's Promise: A Concise History of the United States*, vol. 2 (Lanham, MD: Rowman and Littlefield, 2004), 593.

37. Rose, *Mother's Job*, 155, 156.

38. Ibid., 162.

39. Ibid., 166, 167.

40. William M. Tuttle Jr., "Rosie the Riveter and Her Latchkey Children: What Americans Can Learn about Child Day Care from the Second World War," in *A History of Child Welfare*, ed. Eve P. Smith and Lisa A. Merkel (New Brunswick, NJ: Transaction, 1995), 99.

41. Rose, *Mother's Job*, 182, 186–187.

42. Weigand, *Red Feminism*, 46–67.

43. Amy Swerdlow, "The Congress of American Women: Left-Feminist Peace Politics in the Cold War," in *U.S. History as Women's History: New Feminist Essays*, ed. Linda K. Kerber, Alice Kessler-Harris, and Kathryn Kish Sklar (Chapel Hill: University of North Carolina Press, 1995), 296–312. For the close contact between the CAW and the NCASF, see U.S. Congress, House Committee on Un-American Activities, "Report on the Congress of American Women," House Report 1953, 81st Cong., 2nd sess., October 23, 1949, p. 26. Hereafter cited as HUAC, "Report."

44. Congress of American Women, "Resolution on the Family," box 5, CAW Folder, NLM.

45. Dorothy Dunbar Bromley, "Visitor Found Russian People Want No War but Would Fight," *New York Herald-Tribune*, November 17, 1946.

46. HUAC, "Report," 105–107.

47. Mudd and Mudd, "Medical Mission to Moscow," 205–218.

48. Emily Mudd and Stuart Mudd, "Outline for Proposed Articles: Recent Observations of Men, Women, and Children in the USSR," box 4, folder 185, EHM.

49. Mudd interview, 146.

50. Orianna Atkinson, *Women's Home Companion*, November 1946, 144; Ludwell Denny, *Washington Daily News*, April 28, 1947, 27; Ferdinand Kuhn Jr., *Washington Post*, May 14, 1947, 1; and Harold Davis, *Washington Times-Herald*, May 2, 1947, 7, all quoted in HUAC, "Report," 19–20.

51. Hutchinson, "Dancing with Commissars," 252.

52. Henry E. Sigerist, *Medicine and Health in the Soviet Union* (New York: Citadel Press, 1947), 96, cited in Emily H. Mudd, "The Family in the Soviet Union," *MFL* 10 (1948): 7.

53. Thanks to the intervention of Viacheslav Molotov, Stalin's former commissar for foreign affairs, Parin was discharged in October 1953 from the notorious Vladimir Prison, where he had been serving a twenty-five-year sentence under maximum security. Krementsov, *The Cure*, 201–202.

54. Lear, "Hot War Creation, Cold War Casualty," 277.

55. *Baldwin Hourglass*, January 23, 1947, box 4, folder 187, EHM.

56. Emily Mudd to Mrs. Frederick W. Mueller, May 19, 1947, box 4, folder 190, EHM.

57. Stuart Mudd to Alfred Newton Richards, December 5, 1947, box 4, folder 192, EHM.

58. Stuart Mudd to Elizabeth Frazier, December 8, 1947, box 4, folder 192, EHM.

59. Emily Mudd to the NCASF, December 9, 1947, box 4, folder 192, EHM. For Mudd's version of events involving the attack on the MCP, see Mudd interview, 132–136. See also Philip Jenkins, *The Cold War at Home: The Red Scare in Pennsylvania, 1945–1960* (Chapel Hill: University of North Carolina Press, 1999).

60. The FBI claimed that Leslie's luggage contained a typewritten memo stating that he and the Mudds were "all good comrades and fellow Marxists," but I have found no evidence that they were either Marxists or communists, beyond their membership in the NCASF. FBI Report, October 22, 1946, box 1, folder 1, NLM.

61. Mudd interview, 146.

62. Weigand, *Red Feminism*, 22.

63. Krementsov, "In the Shadow of the Bomb," 62.

64. Alan Petigny, *The Permissive Society: America, 1941–1965* (New York: Cambridge University Press, 2009), 133.

65. Mudd interview, 180.

CHAPTER FOUR. SAVING PEOPLE, NOT MARRIAGES

1. Judson T. Landis, "The Teaching of Marriage and Family Courses in Colleges," *MFL* 21 (1959): 39.

2. Carlfred B. Broderick and Sandra S. Schrader, "The History of Professional Marriage and Family Therapy," in *Handbook of Family Therapy*, ed. Alan Gurman and David P. Kniskern (New York: Brunner/Mazel, 1981), 13.

3. Emily H. Mudd, *The American Association of Marriage Counselors: The First 25 Years, 1942–1967* (Dallas: AAMC, 1968), 8.

4. National Conference on Family Life, "Report of Subcommittee on Marriage and Family Counseling: The Marriage and Family Counselor—A Resource to the Family," May 6–8, 1948, box 127, folder 5, AHC.

5. Emily H. Mudd, interview by James W. Reed, May 21–August 3, 1974, Schlesinger-Rockefeller Oral History Project, transcript, Arthur and Elizabeth Schlesinger Library on the History of Women in America, Harvard University, p. 77. Hereafter cited as Mudd interview.

6. Robert Harper to Alfred Kinsey, April 10, 1953, Robert A. Harper Folder, KILC.

7. Jack R. Ewalt, "Goals of the Joint Commission on Mental Illness and Health," *American Journal of Public Health* 47 (January 1957): 19.

8. Gerald N. Grob, *The Mad among Us: A History of the Care of America's Mentally Ill* (Cambridge, MA: Harvard University Press, 1994), 245–246.

9. Mudd interview, 82–83.

10. Kenneth E. Appel, "Problems with Which People Want Help in Sex and Marriage," in *Man and Wife*, ed. Emily H. Mudd and Aaron Krich (New York:

W. W. Norton, 1957), quoted in Emily H. Mudd, Abraham Stone, Maurice J. Kaprf, and Janet Folwer Nelson, eds., *Marriage Counseling: A Casebook* (New York: Association Press, 1958), 469–470.

11. Mudd interview, 130.

12. Ellen Herman, *The Romance of American Psychology: Political Culture in the Age of Experts* (Berkeley: University of California Press, 1995), 261.

13. Harold Baron to Gladys Groves, July 20, 1953, box 15, folder 7, SWHA.

14. David Mace, "The Many Costs of a Campus Marriage," *McCall's*, January 1962, 126, 128.

15. Henry Bowman, "A Critical Evaluation of Marriage and Family Education," *MFL* 15 (1953): 306.

16. Ernest R. Groves, "A Decade of Marriage Counseling," *Annals of the American Academy of Political and Social Science* 212 (1940): 73, 74–75.

17. David Mace, "The State Regulation of Marriage Counseling," box 53, AAMFT Folder, SWHA.

18. "Social Unions Seen as Aid to Families," *New York Times*, August 29, 1951.

19. Robert N. Bellah, Richard Madsen, William M. Sullivan, Ann Swidler, and Steven M. Tipton, *Habits of the Heart: Individualism and Commitment in American Life* (Berkeley: University of California Press, 1985), 281.

20. Eva S. Moskowitz, *In Therapy We Trust: America's Obsession with Self-Fulfillment* (Baltimore: Johns Hopkins University Press, 2001), 157.

21. Ibid., 258–259.

22. "Art Linkletter, TV Host, Dies at 97," *New York Times*, May 26, 2010, http://www.nytimes.com/2010/05/27/arts/27linkletter.html?pagewanted=all.

23. Ruth Jewson to Aaron Rutledge, June 15, 1960, box 13, Aaron Rutledge Folder, SWHA.

24. Walter R. Stokes and David R. Mace, "Premarital Sexual Behavior," *MFL* 15 (1953): 239.

25. Robert Harper to Robert Foster, May 1, 1951, box 15, Robert Foster Folder #1, SWHA; Harper to Foster, April 19, 1953, box 15, Robert Foster Folder #6, SWHA.

26. Dorothy Dyer to Robert Foster, September 5, 1953, box 15, Robert Foster Folder #7, SWHA.

27. Robert Foster to Judson Landis, February 18, 1952, box 15, folder 3, SWHA.

28. Mudd interview, 275–276.

29. Robert Harper to Alfred Kinsey, April 10, 1953, Robert A. Harper Folder, KI.

30. Anna O. Stephens, "Premarital Sex Relationships," in *Successful Marriage: A Modern Guide to Love, Sex, and Family Life*, ed. Morris Fishbein and Ernest W. Burgess (Garden City, NY: Doubleday, 1955), 49, 50.

31. Robert Latou Dickinson to Alfred Kinsey, August 7, 1947, box 1, folder 77, RLD.

32. Aaron L. Rutledge, "Introduction," *Pastoral Psychology* 12 (1961): 34.

33. Stokes and Mace, "Premarital Sexual Behavior," 235, 237–238.

34. Dorothy Dyer to Robert Foster, March 6, 1953, box 15, Robert Foster Folder #5; Reverend Bernard Schiller to Robert Foster, June 19, 1953, box 15, Robert Foster Folder #7; John E. Riley to Gladys Groves, October 1, 1953, box 15, Robert Foster Folder #8, all in SWHA.

35. Dorothy Dyer to Robert Foster, July 2, 1953, box 15, Robert Foster Folder #7, SWHA.

36. Robert Foster to Judson Landis, March 5, 1952, box 15, Robert Foster Folder #3, SWHA.

37. Dorothy Dyer to Robert Foster, September 5, 1953, box 15, Robert Foster Folder #7, SWHA.

38. Quoted in Earle M. Marsh, "Obstetrical Opportunities for Marriage Counseling," *MFL* 15 (1953): 150.

39. Kristin Celello, *Making Marriage Work: A History of Marriage and Divorce in the Twentieth-Century United States* (Chapel Hill: University of North Carolina Press, 2009), 71.

40. Stephanie Coontz, *Marriage, a History: From Obedience to Intimacy, or How Love Conquered Marriage* (New York: Viking, 2005), 235.

41. William J. Goode, "Education for Divorce," *MFL* 9 (1947): 35–36.

42. Christine R. Barber, "The Women's Movement and Marital Therapy" (M.A. thesis, Bryn Mawr, 1975), 29, box 1, folder 5, EHM. Barber's thesis was based on interviews with Emily Mudd. See also Emily H. Mudd, *The Practice of Marriage Counseling* (New York: Association Press, 1951), chaps. 1, 9, 10.

43. Robert Harper, "Failure in Marriage Counseling," *MFL* 17 (1955): 362.

44. Judson T. Landis, "The Challenge of Marriage and Family Life Education," *MFL* 19 (1957): 251.

45. Atlee L. Stroup, Paul Glasser, Walter R. Stokes, Marie W. Kargman, and Aaron L. Rutledge, "The Orientation and Focus of Marriage Counseling," *MFL* 21 (1959): 25.

46. Aaron L. Rutledge, "Should the Marriage Counselor Ever Recommend Divorce?" *MFL* 25 (1963): 319–325. As sociologist Kingsley Davis noted in 1955, "The literature on marriage counseling suggests a conservative attitude toward divorce, but a more professional, or disinterested, attitude is emerging. It is recognized that the goal of making marriages work does not preclude the possibility that divorce itself may be desirable." Kingsley Davis, "Divorce," in Fishbein and Burgess, *Successful Marriage*, 472.

47. Judd Marmor, "Psychological Trends in American Family Relationships," *MFL* 13 (1951): 145–147; Robert Harper, "Democratic Family Living," *MFL* 15 (1953): 195. For this aspect of therapism, see Bellah et al., *Habits of the Heart*, 126.

48. Landis, "Challenge of Marriage and Family Life Education," 249.

49. Alan Petigny, *The Permissive Society: America, 1941–1965* (New York: Cambridge University Press, 2009), 139.

50. William C. Nichols Jr., *The AAMFT: Fifty Years of Marital and Family Therapy* (Washington, DC: AAMFT, 1992), 8, 10.

51. Robert Foster to Gladys Groves, December 22, 1949, box 15, Robert Foster Folder #1, SWHA; Robert Foster to Helen Hiltner, January 2, 1953, box 15, Robert Foster Folder #5, SWHA.

52. Emily Mudd, "The Contemporary Status of Marriage Counseling," *Annals of the American Academy of Political and Social Science* 272 (1950): 105–106.

53. Emily Mudd, "Psychiatry and Marital Problems," *Eugenics Quarterly* 2 (1955): 111.

54. Leon J. Saul, Robert W. Laidlaw, Janet F. Nelson, Ralph Ormsby, Abraham Stone, Sidney Eisenberg, Kenneth E. Appel, and Emily H. Mudd, "Can One Partner Be Successfully Counseled without the Other?" *MFL* 15 (1953): 63, 64.

55. Alan S. Gurman and Peter Fraenkel, "The History of Couple Therapy: A Millennial Review," *Family Process* 41 (2002): 205.

56. Nichols, *AAMFT*, 16.

57. Albert Ellis, "A Critical Evaluation of Marriage Counseling," *MFL* 18 (1956): 70–71.

58. Nichols, *AAMFT*, 5.

59. Ibid., 22.

60. Herman, *Romance of American Psychology*, 266.

61. Carl Rogers, *On Becoming a Person* (Boston: Houghton Mifflin, 1961), 91, cited in Petigny, *Permissive Society*, 46.

62. Carl R. Rogers, *Becoming Partners: Marriage and Its Alternatives* (New York: Dell Publishing, 1972), 206.

63. Cited in Herman, *Romance of American Psychology*, 268.

64. Carl R. Rogers, "Wartime Issues in Family Counseling," *MFL* 6 (1944): 68–69, 84.

65. Bellah et al., *Habits of the Heart*, 126–127.

66. Carl R. Rogers, "A Personal Formulation of Client-Centered Therapy," *MFL* 14 (1952): 355.

67. Mudd interview, 205.

68. Stokes and Mace, "Premarital Sexual Behavior," 243.

69. Albert Ellis, "Marriage Counseling with Couples Indicating Sexual Incompatibility," *MFL* 15 (1953): 53–59; "Letters to the Editor," *MFL* 15 (1953): 250, 253.

70. Ellis, "Critical Evaluation of Marriage Counseling," 65–71.

71. Orlo Strunk Jr., "A Prolegomenon to a History of Pastoral Counseling," in *Clinical Handbook of Pastoral Counseling*, ed. Robert J. Wicks, Richard D. Parsons, and Donald Capps (New York: Integration Books, 1985), 21.

72. William J. Rorabaugh, Donald T. Critchlow, and Paula Baker, *America's Promise: A Concise History of the United States*, vol. 2 (Lanham, MD: Rowman and Littlefield, 2004), 595.

73. Rebecca Davis, *More Perfect Unions: The Search for Marital Bliss* (Cambridge, MA: Harvard University Press, 2010), 137.

74. Gerald Gurin, Joseph Veroff, and Sheila Field, *Americans View Their Mental Health: A Nationwide Interview Survey* (New York: Basic Books, 1960), 306–309.

See also E. Brooks Holifield, *A History of Pastoral Care in America: From Salvation to Self-Realization* (Nashville, TN: Abingdon, 1983), 274.

75. Charles A. Van Wagner, "The AAPC: The Beginning Years, 1963–1965," *Journal of Pastoral Care* 37 (1983): 165.

76. Susan E. Myers-Shirk, "'To Be Fully Human': U.S. Protestant Psychotherapeutic Culture and the Subversion of the Domestic Ideal, 1945–1965," *Journal of Women's History* 12 (2000): 114. See also William H. Whyte Jr., *The Organization Man* (New York: Simon and Schuster, 1956), 379–380.

77. Holifield, *History of Pastoral Care*, 266. See also Steve Bruce, *Religion in the Modern World: From Cathedrals to Cults* (New York: Oxford University Press, 1996), 144–145, cited in Petigny, *Permissive Society*, 36–37.

78. Ewalt, "Goals of the Joint Commission on Mental Illness and Health," 22.

79. Groves, "A Decade of Marriage Counseling," 77.

80. Leland Foster Wood, "The Training of Ministers for Marriage and Family Counseling," *MFL* 12 (1950): 47.

81. Aaron L. Rutledge, "Marriage Counseling Today and Tomorrow," *MFL* 19 (1957): 386.

82. Quoted in Holifield, *History of Pastoral Care*, 274.

83. See "Application for Advanced Training for Seminary Teachers of Pastoral Care Grant, 1964–1969," box 14, folder 621, EHM.

84. Hilda M. Goodwin, "Marriage Counseling and the Minister," *Journal of Religion and Health* 3 (1964): 180.

85. Rabbi Jerome Weistrop to Emily Mudd, November 15, 1975, box 14, folder 625, EHM.

86. Goodwin, "Marriage Counseling and the Minister," 182.

87. Myers-Shirk, "To Be Fully Human," 112–136.

88. Holifield, *History of Pastoral Care*, 259.

89. Myers-Shirk, "To Be Fully Human," 117.

90. Goodwin, "Marriage Counseling and the Minister," 181.

91. Quoted in Petigny, *Permissive Society*, 78–79.

92. John R. Cavanagh, *Fundamental Pastoral Counseling: Technic and Psychology* (Milwaukee: Bruce Publishing Company, 1962), 60.

93. David R. Mace, "Marriage Guidance in England," *MFL* 7 (1945): 1–2, 5.

94. "David Mace, 83, Dies: Specialist on Marriage," *New York Times*, December 12, 1990, http://www.nytimes.com/1990/12/12/obituaries/david-mace-83-dies-specialist-on-marriage.html.

95. Nichols, *AAMFT*, 21.

96. David R. Mace to Ruth Jewson, December 28, 1960, box 16, David Mace Folder (1960–1961), SWHA.

CHAPTER FIVE. FROM COUNSELING TO THERAPY

1. Eva S. Moskowitz, *In Therapy We Trust: America's Obsession with Self-Fulfillment* (Baltimore: Johns Hopkins University Press, 2001), 192–193. See also Ger-

208 Notes to Pages 119–124

ald N. Grob, *The Mad among Us: A History of the Care of America's Mentally Ill* (Cambridge, MA: Harvard University Press, 1994), 252–256.

2. Emily H. Mudd, interview by James W. Reed, May 21–August 3, 1974, Schlesinger-Rockefeller Oral History Project, transcript, Arthur and Elizabeth Schlesinger Library on the History of Women in America, Harvard University, p. 215. Hereafter cited as Mudd interview.

3. AAMC, "The State Regulation of Marriage Counselors," report of conference held in New York City, June 5–6, 1964, box 53, AAMFT Folder, SWHA.

4. David Mace and Vera Mace, *Marriage Enrichment Retreats: Story of a Quaker Project* (Philadelphia: Friends General Conference, n.d.), http://www.gutenberg .org/files/29899/29899-h/29899-h.htm.

5. "History of Better Marriages," http://www.bettermarriages.org/?history ofacme.

6. Jeffrey M. Burns, *Disturbing the Peace: A History of the Christian Family Movement, 1949–1974* (Notre Dame, IN: University of Notre Dame Press, 1999), 207.

7. Dennis J. Geany, "Christian Family Movement, 1960," *America*, May 7, 1960, http://www.americamagazine.org/content/article.cfm?article_id=13063.

8. David R. Mace and Vera C. Mace, "Marriage Enrichment: Wave of the Future?" *Family Coordinator* 24 (1975): 133, 134, 135.

9. Ellen Herman, *The Romance of American Psychology: Political Culture in the Age of Experts* (Berkeley: University of California Press, 1995), 294.

10. Allan M. Brandt, *The Cigarette Century: The Rise, Fall, and Deadly Persistence of the Product That Defined America* (New York: Basic Books, 2009), 211–239.

11. "Barbara Seaman, 72, Dies: Cited Risks of the Pill," *New York Times*, March 1, 2008, http://www.nytimes.com/2008/03/01/nyregion/01seaman.html. See also Andrea Tone, *Devices and Desires: A History of Contraceptives in America* (New York: Hill and Wang, 2001), 245, 246.

12. Paul Starr, *The Social Transformation of American Medicine* (New York: Basic Books, 1982), 379.

13. Peter G. Filene, *In the Arms of Others: A Cultural History of the Right-to-Die in America* (Chicago: Ivan R. Dee, 1998), 68.

14. Edward Shorter, *Bedside Manners: The Troubled History of Doctors and Patients* (New York: Viking, 1985), 211–240.

15. Herman, *Romance of American Psychology*, 297–298.

16. Betty Friedan, *The Feminine Mystique*, 10th anniversary ed. (New York: W. W. Norton, 1974), 15, 313, 334–335.

17. Daniel Horowitz, "Rethinking Betty Friedan and *The Feminine Mystique*: Labor Union Radicalism and Feminism in Cold War America," *American Quarterly* 48 (1996): 1–42. See also Judith Hennessee, *Betty Friedan: Her Life* (New York: Random House, 1999); Daniel Horowitz, *Betty Friedan and the Making of "The Feminine Mystique": The American Left, the Cold War, and Modern Feminism* (Amherst: University of Massachusetts Press, 1998).

18. Friedan, *Feminine Mystique*, 104.

19. Ibid., 15.

20. Ibid., 63.

21. Eva Moskowitz, "'It's Good to Blow Your Top': Women's Magazines and a Discourse of Discontent, 1945–1965," *Journal of Women's History* 8 (1996): 67–98.

22. Alan Petigny has argued convincingly that the standard historiographic characterization of the 1950s "as a time when the stay-at-home wife was the cultural ideal and gender roles stood firm" does not fit the facts. Alan Petigny, *The Permissive Society: America, 1941–1965* (New York: Cambridge University Press, 2009), 134.

23. Stephanie Coontz, "Why Gender Equality Stalled," *New York Times*, February 16, 2013, http://www.nytimes.com/2013/02/17/opinion/sunday/why -gender-equality-stalled.html?ref=opinion.

24. For a sampling of these letters to *McCall's*, see Moskowitz, "It's Good to Blow Your Top," 88.

25. Friedan, *Feminine Mystique*, 311.

26. Herman, *Romance of American Psychology*, 292, 299, 300, 311.

27. Emily H. Mudd, "Women's Conflicting Values," *MFL* 8 (1946): 58–61.

28. Emily H. Mudd, "Women's Conflicting Values in Relation to Marriage Adjustment," in *Successful Marriage: A Modern Guide to Love, Sex, and Family Life*, ed. Morris Fishbein and Ernest W. Burgess (Garden City, NY: Doubleday, 1955), 488.

29. Rose Maurer, "Recent Trends in the Soviet Family," *American Sociological Review* 9 (1944): 242–249.

30. Mudd, "Women's Conflicting Values in Relation to Marriage Adjustment," 490.

31. Friedan, *Feminine Mystique*, 261.

32. Elizabeth Fraterrigo, Playboy *and the Making of the Good Life in Modern America* (New York: Oxford University Press, 2009), 176–177.

33. Friedan, *Feminine Mystique*, 328–329.

34. Emily H. Mudd, "Historical Background of Ethical Considerations in Sex Research and Sex Therapy," paper presented at the Conference on Ethical Issues in Sex Therapy and Sex Research, 1976, p. 7, box 4, folder 166, EHM.

35. Neville R. Vines, "Confidential: Memorandum," December 1, 1975, box 14, folder 609, EHM.

36. Emily Hartshorne Mudd, "Sexual Problems in Marriage Counseling," n.d., box 16, folder 746, EHM.

37. Quoted in Raymond Waggoner, "The Responsibility of the Physician as a Marriage Counselor," box 9, Marriage Counseling Folder, 1970, RWW.

38. Tom W. Smith, "The Polls: A Report—The Sexual Revolution?" *Public Opinion Quarterly* 54 (1990): 415–435.

39. Thomas Maier, *Masters of Sex: The Life and Times of William Masters and Virginia Johnson, the Couple Who Taught America How to Love* (New York: Basic Books, 2009), 174–175.

40. Petigny, *Permissive Society*, 32, 133.

41. Fraterrigo, Playboy *and the Making of the Good Life*, 21.

42. Ibid., 55, 56–57.

43. Ibid., 106–112.

44. Janice M. Irvine, *Talk about Sex: The Battles over Sex Education in the United States* (Los Angeles: University of California Press, 2002), 23.

45. For Calderone's correspondence with Ruth Jewson, see box 15, Mary Calderone Folder, SWHA.

46. Irvine, *Talk about Sex*, 27–28.

47. Mary S. Calderone, statement before the Senate Government Operations Subcommittee on Foreign Aid Expenditures, August 31, 1965, box 40, AHC.

48. Mary Calderone to Raymond Waggoner, July 17, 1972, box 10, folder 445, EHM.

49. Maier, *Masters of Sex*, 172.

50. Hugh Hefner, who became good friends with Masters and Johnson, believed she added credibility to their work by conveying the message that their findings were more than just "a male's point of view." Maier, *Masters of Sex*, 205.

51. David Allyn, *Make Love, Not War: The Sexual Revolution: An Unfettered History* (Boston: Little, Brown, 2000), 169.

52. Maier, *Masters of Sex*, 206.

53. Ibid., 261.

54. William Masters and Virginia Johnson, "Sex after Sixty-Five," *Saturday Evening Post* 249 (March 1977): 48–52.

55. Maier, *Masters of Sex*, 301.

56. Janice M. Irvine, *Disorders of Desire: Sex and Gender in Modern American Sexology* (Philadelphia: Temple University Press, 1990), 201.

57. "Rx for Marital Sex Ills," *Boston Globe*, April 27, 1970.

58. "Repairing the Conjugal Bed," *Time*, May 25, 1970.

59. "*Playboy* Interview: Masters and Johnson," *Playboy*, May 1968, 202. See also Vern L. Bullough, *Science in the Bedroom: A History of Sex Research* (New York: Basic Books, 1994), 204.

60. Edward Shorter, *A History of Psychiatry: From the Era of the Asylum to the Age of Prozac* (New York: Wiley, 1997), 300–302.

61. Natalie Shainess, "Statement Prepared for the Subcommittee on Postal Operations Hearings at the House of Representatives, Tuesday, Nov. 17, 1970," box 12, APA Ethics Committee Folder, RWW.

62. Barbara Yuncker, "The New Sex Report," *New York Post*, May 9, 1970; A. J. Vogel, "Are Masters and Johnson Really Infallible?" *Hospital Physician*, November 1970, 105–112.

63. William Masters and Virginia Johnson, "Current and Future Trends in Sex and Sexuality," October 10, 1974, box 9, folder 450, EHM.

64. Maier, *Masters of Sex*, 215.

65. William C. Nichols Jr., *The AAMFT: Fifty Years of Marital and Family Therapy* (Washington, DC: AAMFT, 1992), 21.

66. Maier, *Masters of Sex*, 190–191.

67. William Masters to Emily Mudd, October 19, 1961, box 9, folder 429, EHM.

68. According to Broderick and Schrader, the AAMC rejected Masters's and Johnson's applications for membership. Its committee on membership refused to make an exception for the two sexologists, who had no training as relational counselors. Later, Masters and Johnson refused to make any presentations to the group and never responded to belated invitations to resubmit their applications. Carlfred B. Broderick and Sandra S. Schrader, "The History of Professional Marriage and Family Therapy," in *Handbook of Family Therapy*, ed. Alan Gurman and David P. Kniskern (New York: Brunner/Mazel, 1981), 31.

69. Frederick G. Humphrey to Raymond Waggoner, February 26, 1974, box 10, folder 449, EHM.

70. Mudd interview, 181–187.

71. Robert Kolodny to Raymond Waggoner, February 21, 1974, box 7, RBRF Correspondence 1974 Folder, RWW.

72. Broderick and Schrader, "History of Professional Marriage and Family Therapy," 16.

73. Alan S. Gurman and Peter Fraenkel, "The History of Couple Therapy: A Millennial Review," *Family Process* 41 (2002): 208–209.

74. Nathan W. Ackerman, "Family Psychotherapy Today," *Family Process* 9 (1970): 124.

75. Michael E. Staub, *Madness Is Civilization: When the Diagnosis Was Social, 1948–1980* (Chicago: University of Chicago Press, 2011), 45.

76. Broderick and Schrader, "History of Professional Marriage and Family Therapy," 19.

77. James L. Framo, "A Personal Retrospective of the Family Therapy Field: Then and Now," *Journal of Marital and Family Therapy* 22 (1996): 293–294.

78. Ibid., 291.

79. "Lyman C. Wynne," *Lancet* 369 (March 10, 2007): 820.

80. Staub, *Madness Is Civilization*, 51, 53. See also "Family Schizophrenia," *Time*, October 27, 1961.

81. Peter Fraenkel, "Systems Approaches to Couple Therapy," in *Clinical Handbook of Marriage and Couples Interventions*, ed. W. K. Halford and H. J. Markman (New York: John Wiley and Sons, 1997), 380.

82. Nichols, *AAMFT*, 136.

83. Lorna L. Hecker and Joseph L. Wetchler, eds., *An Introduction to Marriage and Family Therapy* (Binghamton, NY: Haworth Press, 2003), 57–58.

84. Gurman and Fraenkel, "History of Couple Therapy," 214.

85. Guest stars included comedians Robert Klein, Rich Little, Joan Rivers,

Phyllis Diller, and Vicki Lawrence. Advice columnist Ann Landers was also a guest.

86. Moskowitz, *In Therapy We Trust*, 230, 232.

87. Elizabeth Weil, "Does Couples Therapy Work?" *New York Times*, March 2, 2012, http://www.nytimes.com/2012/03/04/fashion/couples-therapists-con front-the-stresses-of-their-field.html?pagewanted=all.

88. Framo, "Personal Retrospective," 305.

89. Michael P. Nichols and Richard C. Schwartz, *Family Therapy: Concepts and Methods* (Boston: Allyn and Bacon, 1998), 122.

90. Gurman and Fraenkel, "History of Couple Therapy," 220.

91. Broderick and Schrader, "History of Professional Marriage and Family Therapy," 15.

92. Ibid., 31.

93. Nichols, *AAMFT*, 86.

94. William Nichols, "A Family Therapist for Life: Observations and Options," address to the American Psychological Association, August 4, 2011, Washington, D.C., pp. 3–4, 5, courtesy of the author.

95. Personal communication from William C. Nichols, December 1, 2012.

96. Nichols, *AAMFT*, 83.

97. Donald S. Williamson, *The Intimacy Paradox: Personal Authority in the Family System* (New York: Guilford Press, 1991), 214.

98. William C. Nichols, "The Field of Marriage Counseling: A Brief Overview," *Family Coordinator* 22 (1973): 12.

99. Ernest R. Groves, "A Decade of Marriage Counseling," *Annals of the American Academy of Political and Social Science* 212 (1940): 79.

100. Bill Davidson, "Quack Marriage Counselors: A Growing National Scandal," *Saturday Evening Post*, January 5–12, 1963, 17–25; Peggy Streit, "Marriage Counselors—Helpers and Hurters," *New York Times Magazine*, November 3, 1963, 26, 107–108.

101. Davidson, "Quack Marriage Counselors," 20–21.

102. Irvine, *Disorders of Desire*, 283.

103. "Dr. Helen Singer Kaplan, 66, Dies: Pioneer in Sex Therapy Field," *New York Times*, August 19, 1995, http://www.nytimes.com/1995/08/19/obituaries/dr -helen-kaplan-66-dies-pioneer-in-sex-therapy-field.html.

104. Irvine, *Disorders of Desire*, 100.

105. William H. Masters, "Phony Sex Clinics—Medicine's Newest Nightmare," *Today's Health*, November 1974, 23; "The State of Sexual Therapy," *St. Louis Post-Dispatch*, July 23, 1974, 2D.

106. Irvine, *Disorders of Desire*, 72.

107. "Sexology on the Defensive, *Time*, June 13, 1983; Philip M. Boffey, "Sexology Struggling to Establish Itself amid Wide Hostility," *New York Times*, May 31, 1983, C1, C3.

108. Rebecca Davis, *More Perfect Unions: The Search for Marital Bliss* (Cambridge, MA: Harvard University Press, 2010), 190, 223.

109. Nichols, *AAMFT*, 28.

110. Ibid., 32–33.

111. Ibid., 51.

112. American Association of Marriage and Family Counselors, "Marriage Counselors Sue Department of Defense over Benefit Cuts," April 28, 1975, box 53, AAMFC Folder, SWHA.

113. American Association of Marriage and Family Counselors, "Marriage Counselors Win Injunction against CHAMPUS," June 10, 1975, box 53, AAMFC Folder, SWHA; Nichols, *AAMFT*, 62–64.

114. Williamson, *Intimacy Paradox*, 213–215.

115. Nichols, *AAMFT*, 65–69.

CHAPTER SIX. A NEW VALUE IN PSYCHOTHERAPY

1. Laurence C. Maud, "Case Summary: 4136B," February 29, 1968, box 14, folder 629, EHM.

2. James Davison Hunter, *Culture Wars: The Struggle to Define America* (New York: Basic Books, 1992).

3. James H. Jones, *Alfred C. Kinsey: A Public/Private Life* (New York: W. W. Norton, 1997), 484.

4. William Nichols, personal communication, January 5, 2013.

5. Eric Nagourney, "Wardell B. Pomeroy, 87: Aided Kinsey's Studies on Sex," *New York Times*, September 12, 2001, http://www.nytimes.com/2001/09/12/us /wardell-b-pomeroy-87-aided-kinsey-s-studies-on-sex.html?src=pm; Paul H. Gebhard, "In Memoriam: Wardell B. Pomeroy," *Archives of Sexual Behavior* 31 (2002): 155–156.

6. William C. Nichols Jr., *The AAMFT: Fifty Years of Marital and Family Therapy* (Washington, DC: AAMFT, 1992), 38.

7. "Marge" to Emily Mudd, July 11, 1972, box 6, folder 293, EHM.

8. Jones, *Alfred C. Kinsey*, 481 482.

9. Nagourney, "Wardell B. Pomeroy."

10. Nichols, *AAMFT*, 43.

11. "Marge" to Emily Mudd, July 11, 1972.

12. William Nichols, personal communication, December 11, 2012.

13. Jim Rue, "Memo: To All Members of AAMFC," September 21, 1973, box 6, folder 293, EHM.

14. Donald J. Troy, "National Alliance for Family Life," *Journal of Family Counseling* 2 (1974): 3–5. For the AAMFC reaction to Rue's activities, see Board of Directors, AAMFC, "Memo: To AAMFC Members," May 29, 1973, box 6, folder 293, EHM.

15. Ruth H. Jewson and James Walters, *The National Council on Family Relations: A Fifty-Year History, 1938–1987* (St. Paul, MN: National Council on Family Relations, 1988), 57.

16. William C. Nichols Jr., "The Field of Marriage Counseling: A Brief Overview," *Family Coordinator* 22 (1973): 3, 11, 12.

17. Craig A. Everett, Robert Ernest Lee, and William C. Nichols, eds., *When Marriages Fail: Systemic Family Therapy Interventions and Issues* (Binghamton, NY: Haworth Press, 2006), 5.

18. David G. Rice and Joy K. Rice, "Non-Sexist 'Marital' Therapy," *Journal of Marriage and Family Counseling* 3 (1977): 4.

19. Sylvia Gingras-Baker, "Sex Role Stereotyping and Marriage Counseling," *Journal of Marriage and Family Counseling* 2 (1976): 364.

20. Rebecca Davis, *More Perfect Unions: The Search for Marital Bliss* (Cambridge, MA: Harvard University Press, 2010), 190.

21. Rachel T. Hare-Mustin, "The Problem of Gender in Family Therapy Theory," *Family Process* 26 (1987): 15–27.

22. Donald T. Critchlow, *Phyllis Schlafly and Grassroots Conservatism: A Woman's Crusade* (Princeton, NJ: Princeton University Press, 2005).

23. David T. Courtwright, *No Right Turn: Conservative Politics in a Liberal America* (Cambridge, MA: Harvard University Press, 2010), 124.

24. Donald T. Critchlow, *The Conservative Ascendancy: How the GOP Right Made Political History* (Cambridge, MA: Harvard University Press, 2007), 161.

25. William Nichols to Dean Hoffman, January 10, 1977, box 12, William C. Nichols Folder, SWHA.

26. William Nichols to Wallace C. Fulton, July 8, 1977, box 12, William C. Nichols Folder, SWHA.

27. Eva S. Moskowitz, *In Therapy We Trust: America's Obsession with Self-Fulfillment* (Baltimore: Johns Hopkins University Press, 2001), 260–261.

28. Courtwright, *No Right Turn*, 126; Critchlow, *Phyllis Schlafly*, 226–227.

29. Jimmy Carter, "White House Conference on Families Remarks at a White House Reception," July 20, 1979, *The American Presidency Project*, http://www.presidency.ucsb.edu/ws/index.php?pid=32629.

30. Davis, *More Perfect Unions*, 177, 187.

31. James T. Patterson, *America in the Twentieth Century: A History* (Fort Worth, TX: Harcourt, Brace, 1994), 485–486.

32. Jewson and Walters, *National Council on Family Relations*, 46.

33. Jimmy Carter, "White House Conference on Families Memorandum from the President," October 15, 1979, *The American Presidency Project*, http://www.presidency.ucsb.edu/ws/index.php?pid=31537.

34. Leo P. Ribuffo, "Family Policy Past as Prologue: Jimmy Carter, the White House Conference on Families, and the Mobilization of the New Christian Right," *Review of Policy Research* 23 (2006): 311–337.

35. Ibid., 325.

36. Gordon Humphry (R-N.H.), "Dear Concerned Neighbor," n.d., box 3, New Right Folder, SWHA.

37. "Family Slate Elected," *Las Vegas Review Journal*, February 28, 1980.

38. Orrin Hatch, "Dear Friend," n.d., box 3, New Right Folder, SWHA.

39. "Virginia Conference on Family Life Erupts in Emotion," *Washington Post*, November 15, 1979, C1.

40. Kenneth J. Heineman, *God Is a Conservative: Religion, Politics, and Morality in Contemporary America* (New York: New York University Press, 1998), 111.

41. Robert M. Rice, memo to Members of the Coalition for the White House Conference on Families, December 19, 1977, box 23, WHCF 1980 Folder #17, SWHA.

42. Robert Rice to Joseph Califano, June 29, 1978, box 23, WHCF 1980 Folder #17, SWHA.

43. Virginia Martin to the National Advisory Committee, September 7, 1979, box 23, WHCF Folder #18, SWHA.

44. W. Keith Daugherty, "Memo: 1980 White House Conference on Families" to Republican Senators and Representatives, April 14, 1980, box 3, New Right Folder, SWHA. Daugherty, general director of the Family Service Association of America, claimed that Republican allegations about the CWHCF were "distorted and divisive."

45. "Virginia Conference on Family Life."

46. "Antiabortion Forces Dominate State Meetings on Family," *Minneapolis Tribune*, January 25, 1980, A1.

47. Hunter, *Culture Wars*, 179–180.

48. Ribuffo, "Family Policy Past as Prologue," 329.

49. "Ronald Reagan Announces the Formation of the Family Policy Advisory Board," *Right Woman* 4 (August/September 1980).

50. Ribuffo, "Family Policy Past as Prologue," 329.

51. Judith Wallerstein and Sandra Blakeslee, *Second Chances: Men, Women, and Children a Decade after Divorce* (New York: Ticknor and Fields, 1989), 297.

52. Sandra Blakeslee, "Major Study Assesses the Children of Divorce," *New York Times*, April 10, 1984, http://www.nytimes.com/1984/04/10/science/major -study-assesses-the-children-of-divorce-by-sandra-blakeslee.html?page wanted=all; Sandra Blakeslee, "Divorce Has Consequences," *Slate*, July 13, 2012, http://www.slate.com/articles/double_x/doublex/2012/07/judith_wallerstein _and_divorce_how_one_woman_changed_the_way_we_think_about_breakups _.2.html.

53. Maggie Gallagher, "Veto This Bill for New York's Families, Dave," *New York Post*, July 8, 2010, http://www.nypost.com/p/news/opinion/opedcolum nists/veto_this_bill_for_ny_families_dave_pERLjK9e1xuF1kP8YGeIlK. See also Maggie Gallagher, *The Abolition of Marriage: How We Destroy Lasting Love* (Washington, DC: Regnery, 1996).

54. Davis, *More Perfect Unions*, 241–251.

55. David H. Olson et al., "Marital and Family Therapy: A Decade Review," *Journal of Marriage and Family* 42 (1980): 973.

56. Davis, *More Perfect Unions*, 231; Kristin Celello, *Making Marriage Work: A*

History of Marriage and Divorce in the Twentieth-Century United States (Chapel Hill: University of North Carolina Press, 2009), 157.

57. Patricia Hersch, *"thirtysomething* Therapy," *Los Angeles Times*, December 6, 1988.

58. Valerie Jo Bradley, "Black Woman Heads Drive to Liberate Women," *Jet*, June 4, 1970, 48–49.

59. Lena Williams, "Psychotherapy Gaining Favor among Blacks," *New York Times*, November 22, 1989, A1, C7.

60. Davis, *More Perfect Unions*, 223–224; Celello, *Making Marriage Work*, 116.

61. Lynn Norment, "How to Save a Failing Marriage," *Ebony*, February 1978, 105, cited in Celello, *Making Marriage Work*, 156.

62. Williams, "Psychotherapy Gaining Favor among Blacks," A1.

63. Monica McGoldrick and Kenneth V. Hardy, eds., *Re-Visioning Family Therapy: Race, Culture, and Gender in Clinical Practice* (New York: Guilford Press, 2008), 21.

64. Davis, *More Perfect Unions*, 229–230.

65. "Barack and Michelle Obama: The Full Interview," *Ladies' Home Journal*, http://www.lhj.com/style/covers/barack-and-michelle-obama-the-full-inter view/?page=4.

66. Nichols, *AAMFT*, 64, 88–92; Donald S. Williamson, *The Intimacy Paradox: Personal Authority in the Family System* (New York: Guilford Press, 1991), 214–218.

67. David M. Lawson, "Donald S. Williamson: Intergenerational Family Theorist and Therapist," *Family Journal* 2 (1994): 167–174.

68. Williamson, *Intimacy Paradox*, 219–220.

69. Rice and Rice, "Non-Sexist 'Marital' Therapy," 5, 8, 9.

70. Robert A. Nisbet, *The Quest for Community* (New York: Oxford University Press, 1953), 63, 66, 73.

71. Philip Rieff, *The Triumph of the Therapeutic: Uses of Faith after Freud* (New York: Harper and Row, 1966), 236, 242.

72. Christopher Lasch, *The Culture of Narcissism: American Life in an Age of Diminishing Expectations* (New York: W. W. Norton, 1979), 13–14.

73. Christopher Lasch, *Haven in a Heartless World: The Family Besieged* (New York: Basic Books, 1977), 109–110.

74. Robert N. Bellah, "Individualism and Commitment in American Life," February 20, 1986, http://www.robertbellah.com/lectures_4.htm.

75. Robert N. Bellah, Richard Madsen, William M. Sullivan, Ann Swidler, and Steven M. Tipton, *Habits of the Heart: Individualism and Commitment in American Life* (Berkeley: University of California Press, 1985), vii.

76. Ibid., 142.

77. Ibid., 99.

78. Ibid., 101.

79. Ibid., 14, 21.

80. Ibid., 100–101, 121–128.

81. William J. Doherty, "Continuities and Diversities: A Professional Autobiography," *Marriage and Family Review* 3–4 (2001): 12.

82. Ibid., 12–13.

83. William J. Doherty, "How Therapists Harm Marriages and What We Can Do about It," *Journal of Couple and Relationship Therapy* 1 (2002): 1–17.

84. Ibid., 11.

85. Ian Dowbiggin, "Follow the Money: Why Relationships May Soon Be Psychiatric Diseases," *Huffington Post*, April 6, 2012, http://www.huffingtonpost .com/ian-dowbiggin/relationships-may-soon-be-diseases_b_1408948.html.

86. "I'm OK, You're OK, We're Not OK," *Time*, September 16, 2002, http:// www.time.com/time/magazine/article/0,9171,1003247,00.html.

87. James L. Nolan Jr., *The Therapeutic State: Justifying Government at Century's End* (New York: New York University Press, 1998), 9.

88. "James L. Framo, 79: Pioneer in Family and Marital Therapy," *Los Angeles Times*, September 6, 2001, http://articles.latimes.com/2001/sep/06/local/me-42825.

89. James L. Framo, "A Personal Retrospective of the Family Therapy Field: Then and Now," *Journal of Marital and Family Therapy* 22 (1996): 305, 308.

90. Ibid., 306–307.

91. Cleveland G. Shields, Lyman C. Wynne, Susan H. McDaniel, and Barbara A. Gawinski, "The Marginalization of Family Therapy: A Historical and Continuing Problem," *Journal of Marital and Family Therapy* 20 (1994): 117, 122–123, 125. See also Kenneth V. Hardy, "Marginalization or Development? A Response to Shields, Wynne, McDaniel, and Gawinski," *Journal of Marital and Family Therapy* 20 (1994): 139–143.

92. Jessica Grose, "Can This Marriage Be Fun?" *Slate*, April 29, 2010, http:// www.slate.com/articles/double_x/doublex/2010/04/can_this_marriage_be_fun .html.

93. Elizabeth Weil, "Married (Happily) with Issues," *New York Times*, December 6, 2009. http://www.nytimes.com/2009/12/06/magazine/06marriage-t .html?pagewanted=all&_r=0.

94. Laura Doyle, "6 Reasons Marriage Counseling Is BS," *Huffington Post*, October 13, 2012, http://www.huffingtonpost.com/laura-doyle/marriage-coun seling_b_1933187.html.

95. Elizabeth Weil, "Does Couples Therapy Work?" *New York Times*, March 2, 2012, http://www.nytimes.com/2012/03/04/fashion/couples-therapists-con front-the-stresses-of-their-field.html?pagewanted=all.

96. Moskowitz, *In Therapy We Trust*, 262–277.

97. "Oprah's So-Called Experts," *Maclean's*, March 14, 2011, 55–56; Sharyn Wolf, "My Response to 'I Lied to Oprah,'" *Huffington Post*, March 29, 2011, http://www.huffingtonpost.com/sharyn-wolf/my-response-to-i-lied-to-_1_b _840778.html.

98. Daniel Kalder, "Joel Osteen: The New Face of Christianity," *Manchester*

Guardian, March 7, 2012, http://www.guardian.co.uk/world/2010/mar/07/joel -osteen-america-pastor.

99. Davis, *More Perfect Unions*, 240.

100. Courtwright, *No Right Turn*, 261.

101. Doherty, "How Therapists Harm Marriages," 6, 7.

102. Stephanie Coontz, *Marriage, a History: From Obedience to Intimacy, or How Love Conquered Marriage* (New York: Viking, 2005), 301, 306, 312–313; emphasis in original.

Selected Bibliography

ARCHIVAL COLLECTIONS

American-Soviet Medical Society Papers. National Library of Medicine, Bethesda, MD.

Bass, Medora Steedman. Collection. American Heritage Center, University of Wyoming, Laramie.

The Kinsey Institute Library and Special Collections, Indiana University, Bloomington.

Massachusetts Society for Social Health. Records, 1915–1965. Arthur and Elizabeth Schlesinger Library on the History of Women in America, Harvard University, Cambridge, MA.

Mudd, Emily Hartshorne. Interview by James W. Reed, May 21–August 3, 1974. Schlesinger-Rockefeller Oral History Project. Transcript, Arthur and Elizabeth Schlesinger Library on the History of Women in America, Harvard University, Cambridge, MA.

Mudd, Emily Hartshorne. Papers. Arthur and Elizabeth Schlesinger Library on the History of Women in America, Radcliffe Institute for Advanced Study, Harvard University, Cambridge, MA.

Mudd, Stuart. Papers. University Archives and Records Center, University of Pennsylvania School of Medicine, Philadelphia.

National Council on Family Relations. Records. Social Welfare History Archives, Elmer L. Andersen Library, University of Minnesota, Minneapolis.

Popenoe, Paul Bowman. Papers, 1874–1991. American Heritage Center, University of Wyoming, Laramie.

Stone, Abraham. Papers. Francis A. Countway Library of Medicine, Harvard School of Medicine, Cambridge, MA.

BOOKS AND ARTICLES

Abbott, Elizabeth. *A History of Marriage.* Toronto: Penguin Canada, 2010.

Allyn, David. *Make Love, Not War: The Sexual Revolution: An Unfettered History.* Boston: Little, Brown, 2000.

Appel, Kenneth E., et al. "Training in Psychotherapy: The Use of Marriage Counseling in a University Teaching Clinic." *American Journal of Psychiatry* 117 (1961): 709–712.

Bailey, Beth L. "Scientific Truth . . . and Love: The Marriage Education Movement in the United States." *Journal of Social History* 20 (1987): 711–732.

Bellah, Robert N., Richard Madsen, William M. Sullivan, Ann Swidler, and Steven M. Tipton. *Habits of the Heart: Individualism and Commitment in American Life*. Berkeley: University of California Press, 1985.

Bendroth, Margaret L. *Growing up Protestant: Parents, Children, and Mainline Churches*. New Brunswick, NJ: Rutgers University Press, 2002.

Brothers, Barbara Jo, ed. *Couples Therapy in Managed Care: Facing the Crisis*. Binghamton, NY: Haworth Press, 1999.

Brown, Kristi, ed. *Family Counseling: An Annotated Bibliography*. Cambridge, MA: Oelgeschlager, Gunn, and Hain, 1981.

Bullough, Vern L. "American Physicians and Sex Research and Expertise, 1900–1990." *Journal of the History of Medicine and Allied Sciences* 52 (1997): 236–257.

———. *Science in the Bedroom: A History of Sex Research*. New York: Basic Books, 1994.

Burgess, Ernest W., Harvey J. Locke, and Mary Margaret Thomes. *The Family: From Institution to Companionship*. 3rd ed. New York: American Book Company, 1963.

Burnham, John C. "The Progressive Era Revolution in American Attitudes toward Sex." *Journal of American History* 59 (1973): 885–908.

Burns, Jeffrey C. *Disturbing the Peace: A History of the Christian Family Movement, 1949–1974*. Notre Dame, IN: University of Notre Dame Press, 1999.

Caldwell, Benjamin E., and Scott R. Woolley. "Marriage and Family Therapists' Endorsement of Myths about Marriage." *American Journal of Family Therapy* 36 (2008): 367–387.

Cavanagh, John R. *Fundamental Pastoral Counseling: Technic and Psychology*. Milwaukee: Bruce Publishing Company, 1962.

Celello, Kristin. *Making Marriage Work: A History of Marriage and Divorce in the Twentieth-Century United States*. Chapel Hill: University of North Carolina Press, 2009.

Chalfant, H. Paul, et al. "The Clergy as a Resource for Those Encountering Psychological Distress." *Review of Religious Research* 31 (1990): 305–313.

Cherlin, Andrew J. *The Marriage-Go-Round: The State of Marriage and the Family in America Today*. New York: Alfred A. Knopf, 2009.

Chesler, Ellen. *Woman of Valor: Margaret Sanger and the Birth Control Movement in America*. New York: Simon and Schuster, 1992.

Chriss, James J., ed. *Counseling and the Therapeutic State*. New York: Aldine de Gruyter, 1999.

Christensen, Harold T., and Robert E. Philbrick. "Family Size as a Factor in the Marital Adjustments of College Couples." *American Sociological Review* 17 (1952): 306–312.

Christensen, Lisa L., et al. "Marriage and Family Therapists Evaluate Managed Mental Health Care: A Qualitative Inquiry." *Journal of Marital and Family Therapy* 27 (2001): 509–514.

———. "The Practice of Marriage and Family Therapists with Managed Care Clients." *Contemporary Family Therapy* 23 (2001): 169–180.

Clemens, Alphonse H. *Marriage and the Family: An Integrated Approach for Catholics*. New York: Prentice-Hall, 1957.

Connelly, Matthew. *Fatal Misconception: The Struggle to Control World Population*. Cambridge, MA: Harvard University Press, 2008.

Coontz, Stephanie. *Marriage, a History: From Obedience to Intimacy, or How Love Conquered Marriage*. New York: Viking, 2005.

Corliss, Richard. "Behavior: The Marriage Savers." *Time*, January 19, 2004. http://www.time.com/time/magazine/article/0,9171,993151-2,00.html.

Cott, Nancy. *Public Vows: A History of Marriage and the Nation*. Cambridge, MA: Harvard University Press, 2000.

Courtwright, David T. *No Right Turn: Conservative Politics in a Liberal America*. Cambridge. MA: Harvard University Press, 2010.

Critchlow, Donald T. *Intended Consequences: Birth Control, Abortion, and the Federal Government in Modern America*. New York: Oxford University Press, 1999.

———. *Phyllis Schlafly and Grassroots Conservatism: A Woman's Crusade*. Princeton, NJ: Princeton University Press, 2005.

Curtis, Jack, and Mary Brian Mahan. "A Pilot Study in the Prediction of Success in Catholic Marriages." *MFL* 18 (1956): 145–150.

Datillio, Frank M., and Louis Bevilacqua, eds. *Comparative Treatments for Relationship Dysfunction*. New York: Springer, 2000.

Davis, Rebecca. *More Perfect Unions: The Search for Marital Bliss*. Cambridge, MA: Harvard University Press, 2010.

Davis, Tom. *Sacred Work: Planned Parenthood and Its Clergy Alliances*. New Brunswick, NJ: Rutgers University Press, 2005.

Deutsch, Albert, ed. *Sex Habits of American Men: A Symposium on the Kinsey Report*. New York: Prentice-Hall, 1948.

Doherty, William J. *Soul Searching: Why Psychotherapy Must Promote Moral Responsibility*. New York: Basic Books, 1996.

Doherty, William J., and Deborah Simmons. "Clinical Practice Patterns of Marriage and Family Therapists: A National Survey of Therapists and Their Clients." *Journal of Marital and Family Therapy* 22 (1996): 9–25.

Dowbiggin, Ian. *A Merciful End: The Euthanasia Movement in Modern America*. New York: Oxford University Press, 2003.

———. *The Quest for Mental Health: A Tale of Science, Medicine, Scandal, Sorrow, and Mass Society*. Cambridge: Cambridge University Press, 2011.

———. *The Sterilization Movement and Global Fertility in the Twentieth Century*. New York: Oxford University Press, 2008.

Duvall, Evelyn, and Sylvanus Duvall. *Saving Your Marriage*. New York: Public Affairs Committee, 1954.

Duvall, Evelyn R., and Reuben Hill. *Being Married*. New York: Association Press, 1960.

———. *When You Marry*. New York: Association Press, 1953.

Duvall, Sylvanus M. "The Minister as Marriage Counselor." *MFL* 9 (1947): 63–65.

Dworkin, Ronald W. "Psychotherapy and the Pursuit of Happiness." *New Atlantis* 35 (Spring, 2012): 69–83.

———. "The Rise of the Caring Industry." *Policy Review* 161 (June 1, 2010). http://www.hoover.org/publications/policy-review/article/5339.

Ellis, Albert. "A Critical Evaluation of Marriage Counseling." *MFL* 18 (1956): 65–71.

Everett, Craig A., Robert Ernest Lee, and William C. Nichols, eds. *When Marriages Fail: Systemic Family Therapy Interventions and Issues*. Binghamton, NY: Haworth Press, 2006.

Fee, Elizabeth, and Theodore M. Brown, eds. *Making Medical History: The Life and Times of Henry E. Sigerist*. Baltimore: Johns Hopkins University Press, 1997.

Fishbein, Morris, and Ernest W. Burgess, eds. *Successful Marriage: A Modern Guide to Love, Sex, and Family Life*. Garden City, NY: Doubleday, 1955.

Flippen, J. Brooks. *Jimmy Carter, the Politics of the Family, and the Rise of the Religious Right*. Athens: University of Georgia Press, 2011.

Fosdick, Harry Emerson. "The Minister and Psychotherapy." *Pastoral Psychology* 11 (1960): 11–13.

Framo, James L. "A Personal Retrospective of the Family Therapy Field: Then and Now." *Journal of Marital and Family Therapy* 22 (1996): 289–316.

Franks, Angela. *Margaret Sanger's Eugenic Legacy: The Control of Female Fertility*. Jefferson, NC: McFarland, 2005.

Fraterrigo, Elizabeth. Playboy *and the Making of the Good Life in Modern America*. New York: Oxford University Press, 2009.

Freedman, Estelle B. "'Uncontrolled Desires': The Response to the Sexual Psychopath, 1920–1960." *Journal of American History* 74 (1987): 83–106.

Gallagher, Nancy L. *Breeding Better Vermonters: The Eugenics Project in the Green Mountain State*. Hanover, NH: University Press of New England, 1999.

Gathorne-Hardy, Jonathan. *Sex the Measure of All Things: A Life of Alfred C. Kinsey*. Bloomington: Indiana University Press, 2004.

Geddes, Donald, ed. *An Analysis of the Kinsey Reports on Sexual Behavior in the Human Male and Female*. New York: Dutton, 1954.

Gerodetti, Natalia. "Eugenic Family Policies and Social Democrats: 'Positive' Eugenics and Marriage Advice Bureaus." *Journal of Historical Sociology* 19 (2006): 217–244.

Gillespie, C. Kevin. *Psychology and American Catholicism: From Confession to Therapy?* New York: Crossroad Publishing, 2001.

Gladding, Samuel T. *Family Therapy: History, Theory, and Practice*. Upper Saddle River, NJ: Merrill Prentice Hall, 2002.

Glick, Ira D., Helen M. Berman, John F. Clarkin, and Douglas S. Rait. *Marital and Family Therapy*. Arlington, VA: American Psychiatric Publishing, 2000.

Goldstein, Sidney E. "Rabbi Sidney E. Goldstein Discusses Family Problems." *Jewish Telegraphic Agency*, October 21, 1932. http://archive.jta.org/article/1932/10/21/2795177/rabbi-sidney-e-goldstein-discusses-family-problems.

Goode, William J. "Education for Divorce." *MFL* 9 (1947): 35–36.

Goodwin, Hilda M. "Marriage Counseling and the Minister." *Journal of Religion and Health* 3 (1964): 176–183.

Goodwin, Hilda M., and Elaine Dorfman. "Ministers Evaluate Their Training in Marriage Counseling." *Journal of Religion and Health* 4 (1965): 414–420.

Gordon, Linda. *The Moral Property of Women: A History of Birth Control Politics in America*. Urbana: University of Illinois Press, 2002.

Griffith, R. Marie. "The Religious Encounters of Alfred C. Kinsey." *Journal of American History* 95 (2008): 349–377.

Groves, Ernest R. "A Decade of Marriage Counseling." *Annals of the American Academy of Political and Social Science* 212 (1940): 72–80.

———. *The Family and Its Social Functions*. Philadelphia: J. B. Lippincott, 1940.

———. *The Marriage Crisis*. New York: Longmans, Green, 1928.

———. "The Marriage Panacea." *Social Forces* 12 (1934): 406–412.

———. "Mental Hygiene in the College and the University." *Social Forces* 8 (1929): 37–50.

———. *Sex Fulfillment in Marriage*. New York: Emerson Books, 1942.

Gurman, Alan S., and Peter Fraenkel. "The History of Couple Therapy: A Millennial Review." *Family Process* 41 (2002): 199–260.

Haller, Mark H. *Eugenics: Hereditarian Attitudes in American Thought*. New Brunswick, NJ: Rutgers University Press, 1963.

Hamm, Thomas D. *The Quakers in America*. New York: Columbia University Press, 2003.

Harper, Robert A. "Failure in Marriage Counseling." *MFL* 17 (1955): 359–362.

Hartog, Hendrik. *Man and Wife in America: A History*. Cambridge, MA: Harvard University Press, 2000.

Hecker, Lorna L., and Joseph L. Wetchler, eds. *An Introduction to Marriage and Family Therapy*. Binghamton, NY: Haworth Press, 2003.

Heineman, Kenneth J. *God Is a Conservative: Religion, Politics, and Morality in Contemporary America*. New York: New York University Press, 1998.

Herman, Ellen. *The Romance of American Psychology: Political Culture in the Age of Experts*. Berkeley: University of California Press, 1995.

Holifield, E. Brooks. *A History of Pastoral Care in America: From Salvation to Self-Realization*. Nashville, TN: Abingdon, 1983.

Horowitz, Daniel. *Betty Friedan and the Making of "The Feminine Mystique": The American Left, the Cold War, and Modern Feminism*. Amherst: University of Massachusetts Press, 1998.

———. "Rethinking Betty Friedan and *The Feminine Mystique*: Labor Union Radicalism and Feminism in Cold War America." *American Quarterly* 48 (1996): 1–42.

Hunter, James Davison. *Culture Wars: The Struggle to Define America*. New York: Basic Books, 1992.

Irvine, Janice M. *Disorders of Desire: Sex and Gender in Modern American Sexology*. Philadelphia: Temple University Press, 1990.

———. *Talk about Sex: The Battles over Sex Education in the United States*. Los Angeles: University of California Press, 2002.

Jenkins, Philip. *The Cold War at Home: The Red Scare in Pennsylvania, 1945–1960*. Chapel Hill: University of North Carolina Press, 1999.

Jones, James H. *Alfred C. Kinsey: A Public/Private Life*. New York: W. W. Norton, 1997.

Karpf, Maurice J. "Some Guiding Principles in Marriage Counseling." *MFL* 13 (1951): 49–51, 55.

Kevles, Daniel J. *In the Name of Eugenics: Genetics and the Uses of Human Heredity*. New York: Knopf, 1985.

Kline, Wendy. *Building a Better Race: Gender, Sexuality, and Eugenics from the Turn of the Century to the Baby Boom*. Berkeley: University of California Press, 2001.

Kluchin, Rebecca M. *Fit to Be Tied: Sterilization and Reproductive Rights in America, 1950–1980*. New Brunswick, NJ: Rutgers University Press, 2011.

Kopp, Marie E. "Development of Marriage Consultation Centers as a New Field of Social Medicine." *American Journal of Obstetrics and Gynecology* 26 (1933): 122–134.

———. "Marriage Counseling in European Countries: Its Present Status and Trends." *Journal of Heredity* 29 (1938): 153–160.

Kupfer, David J., et al., eds. *A Research Agenda for DSM-V*. Arlington, VA: American Psychiatric Association, 2002.

Ladd-Taylor, Molly. "Eugenics, Sterilisation and Modern Marriage in the USA: The Strange Career of Paul Popenoe." *Gender and History* 13 (2001): 298–327.

Laidlaw, Robert W. "A Clinical Approach to Homosexuality." *MFL* 14 (1952): 44–46.

Landis, Judson T. "The Challenge of Marriage and Family Life Education." *MFL* 19 (1957): 247–252.

———. "The Teaching of Marriage and Family Courses in Colleges." *MFL* 21 (1959): 36–40.

Larson, Edward J. *Sex, Race, and Science: Eugenics in the Deep South*. Baltimore: Johns Hopkins University Press, 1995.

Lasch, Christopher. *The Culture of Narcissism: American Life in an Age of Diminishing Expectations*. New York: W. W. Norton, 1979.

———. *Haven in a Heartless World: The Family Besieged*. New York: Basic Books, 1977.

Lasch-Quinn, Elizabeth. *Race Experts: How Racial Etiquette, Sensitivity Training, and New Age Therapy Hijacked the Civil Rights Revolution*. New York: W. W. Norton, 2001.

Lawson, David M. "Donald S. Williamson: Intergenerational Family Theorist and Therapist." *Family Journal* 2 (1994): 167–174.

Levey, Jane F. "Imagining the Family in Postwar Popular Culture: The Case of *The Egg and I* and *Cheaper by the Dozen*." *Journal of Women's History* 13 (2001): 125–150.

Levine, Lena. *The Modern Book of Marriage*. New York: Bartholomew House, 1957.

Mace, David R. "What Is a Marriage Counselor?" *MFL* 16 (1954): 135.

Mace, David R., and Vera Mace. "Marriage Enrichment: Wave of the Future?" *Family Coordinator* 24 (1975): 131–135.

———. *The Soviet Family*. New York: Doubleday, 1963.

Maier, Thomas. *Masters of Sex: The Life and Times of William Masters and Virginia Johnson, the Couple Who Taught America How to Love*. New York: Basic Books, 2009.

Manus, Gerald I. "Marriage Counseling: A Technique in Search of a Theory." *Journal of Marriage and Family* 28 (1966): 449–453.

Marmor, Judd. "Psychological Trends in American Family Relationships." *MFL* 13 (1951): 145–147.

May, Elaine Tyler. *Homeward Bound: American Families in the Cold War Era*. Rev. ed. New York: Basic Books, 2008.

McGreevy, John T. *Catholicism and American Freedom: A History*. New York: W. W. Norton, 2003.

McMillan, Emile L. "Problem Build-up: A Description of Couples in Marriage Counseling." *Family Coordinator* 18 (1969): 260–267.

Meyerowitz, Joanne, ed. *Not June Cleaver: Women and Gender in Postwar America, 1945–1960*. Philadelphia: Temple University Press, 1994.

Mezydlo, Leonard, et al. "The Clergy as Marriage Counselors: A Service Revisited." *Journal of Religion and Health* 12 (1973): 278–288.

Mintz, Steven, and Susan Kellogg. *Domestic Revolutions: A Social History of American Family Life*. New York: Free Press, 1988.

Moran, Jeffrey P. *Teaching Sex: The Shaping of Adolescence in the 20th Century*. Cambridge, MA: Harvard University Press, 2000.

Morantz, Regina Markell. "The Scientist as Sex Crusader: Alfred C. Kinsey and American Culture." *American Quarterly* 29 (1977): 563–589.

Moskowitz, Eva S. *In Therapy We Trust: America's Obsession with Self-Fulfillment*. Baltimore: Johns Hopkins University Press, 2001.

———. "'It's Good to Blow Your Top': Women's Magazines and a Discourse of Discontent, 1945–1965." *Journal of Women's History* 8 (1996): 67–98.

Mudd, Emily H. "Emily Mudd Talks on Women's Place in Postwar Russia." *Vassar Chronicle* 4 (1947): 3.

———. "Knowns and Unknowns in Marriage Counseling Research." *MFL* 19 (1957): 75–81.

————. "Marriage and Family Counseling." *MFL* 8 (1946): 69–70.

————. *The Practice of Marriage Counseling*. New York: Association Press, 1951.

Mudd, Emily H., et al. "Population, Health, and Family." *Annals of the New York Academy of Sciences* 216 (1973): 145–151.

Mudd, Emily H., and Elizabeth Kirk Rose. "Development of Marriage Counsel of Philadelphia as a Community Service, 1932–1940." *Living* 2 (1940): 40–41.

Mudd, Emily H., Abraham Stone, Maurice J. Karpf, and Janet Folwer Nelson, eds. *Marriage Counseling: A Casebook*. New York: Association Press, 1958.

Myrdal, Gunnar. *Population: A Problem for Democracy*. Cambridge, MA: Harvard University Press, 1940.

Neuhaus, Jessamyn. "The Importance of Being Orgasmic: Sexuality, Gender, and Marital Sex Manuals in the United States, 1920–1963." *Journal of the History of Sexuality* 9 (2000): 447–473.

Nichols, William C., Jr. *The AAMFT: Fifty Years of Marital and Family Therapy*. Washington, DC: AAMFT, 1992.

————. "The Field of Marriage Counseling: A Brief Overview." *Family Coordinator* 22 (1973): 3–13.

————. "The Marriage Relationship." *Family Coordinator* 27 (1978): 185–191.

Nichols, William C., Jr., and Craig A. Everett. *Systemic Family Therapy: An Integrative Approach*. New York: Guilford Press, 1986.

Nisbet, Robert A. *Prejudices: A Philosophical Dictionary*. Cambridge, MA: Harvard University Press, 1983.

————. *The Quest for Community*. New York: Oxford University Press, 1953.

Nolan, James L., Jr. *The Therapeutic State: Justifying Government at Century's End*. New York: New York University Press, 1998.

Olson, David H. "Marital and Family Therapy: Integrative Review and Critique." *Journal of Marriage and Family* 32 (1970): 501–538.

Olson, David H., et al. "Marital and Family Therapy: A Decade Review." *Journal of Marriage and Family* 42 (1980): 973–993.

Peterson, Karen S. "Heading to a Marriage Counselor?" *USA Today*, June 29, 1999. http://lists101.his.com/pipermail/smartmarriages/1999-June/002215 .html.

————. "Troublesome Friendship or Relational Disorder?" *USA Today*, September 8, 2002. http://www.usatoday.com/news/health/2002-09-08-relation ship_x.htm.

Petigny, Alan. *The Permissive Society: America, 1941–1965*. New York: Cambridge University Press, 2009.

Pomeroy, Wardell Baxter. *Dr. Kinsey and the Institute for Sex Research*. New Haven, CT: Yale University Press, 1972.

Reed, James. *From Private Vice to Public Virtue: The Birth Control Movement and American Society since 1830*. New York: Basic Books, 1978.

Reilly, Philip R. *The Surgical Solution: A History of Involuntary Sterilization in the United States*. Baltimore: Johns Hopkins University Press, 1991.

Ribuffo, Leo P. "Family Policy Past as Prologue: Jimmy Carter, the White House Conference on Families, and the Mobilization of the New Christian Right." *Review of Policy Research* 23 (2006): 311–337.

Rieff, Philip. *The Triumph of the Therapeutic: Uses of Faith after Freud*. New York: Harper and Row, 1966.

Rose, Elizabeth. *A Mother's Job: The History of Day Care, 1890–1960*. New York: Oxford University Press, 1999.

Rosen, Christine. *Preaching Eugenics: Religious Leaders and the American Eugenics Movement*. New York: Oxford University Press, 2004.

Roskoff, Lori. *Love on the Rocks: Men, Women, and Alcohol in Post–World War II America*. Chapel Hill: University of North Carolina Press, 2002.

Rutledge, Aaron L. "Marriage Counseling Today and Tomorrow." *MFL* 19 (1957): 386–392.

———. "Should the Marriage Counselor Ever Recommend Divorce?" *MFL* 25 (1963): 319–325.

Sager, C. J. "The Development of Marriage Therapy: An Historical Review." *American Journal of Orthopsychiatry* 36 (1966): 458–467.

Saul, Leon J., Robert W. Laidlaw, Janet F. Nelson, Ralph Ormsby, Abraham Stone, Sidney Eisenberg, Kenneth E. Appel, and Emily H. Mudd. "Can One Partner Be Successfully Counseled without the Other?" *MFL* 15 (1953): 59–64.

Schoen, Joanna. *Choice and Coercion: Birth Control, Sterilization, and Abortion in Public Health and Welfare*. Chapel Hill: University of North Carolina Press, 2005.

Schumacher, Sallie S. "The Reproductive Biology Research Foundation Treatment Approach to Sexual Inadequacy." *Professional Psychology* 2 (Fall 1971): 363–365.

Seligman, Martin E. P. "The Effectiveness of Psychotherapy: The *Consumer Reports* Study." *American Psychologist* 50 (1995): 965–974.

Selinske, Joanne. "A History of the National Council on Family Relations, 1938–1975." Master's thesis, Purdue University, 1976.

Shields, Cleveland G., Lyman C. Wynne, Susan H. McDaniel, and Barbara A. Gawinski. "The Marginalization of Family Therapy: A Historical and Continuing Problem." *Journal of Marital and Family Therapy* 20 (1994): 117–138.

Shumway, David R. *Modern Love: Romance, Intimacy, and the Marriage Crisis*. New York: New York University Press, 2003.

Simmons, Christina. *Making Marriage Modern: Women's Sexuality from the Progressive Era to World War II*. New York: Oxford University Press, 2009.

———. "'Modern Marriage' for African Americans, 1920–1940." *Canadian Review of American Studies* 30 (2000): 273–301.

Smith, Rebecca M., et al. "Marriage and Family Enrichment: A New Professional Area." *Family Coordinator* 28 (1979): 87–93.

Starr, Paul. *The Social Transformation of American Medicine*. New York: Basic Books, 1982.

Staub, Michael E. *Madness Is Civilization: When the Diagnosis Was Social, 1948–1980*. Chicago: University of Chicago Press, 2011.

Stern, Alexandra Minna. *Eugenic Nation: Faults and Frontiers of Better Breeding in Modern America*. Berkeley: University of California Press, 2005.

———. "A Quiet Revolution: The Birth of the Genetic Counselor at Sarah Lawrence College, 1969." *Journal of Genetic Counseling* 18 (2009): 1–11.

Stokes, Walter R., et al. "The Married Virgin." *MFL* 13 (1951): 29–34.

Stokes, Walter R., and David R. Mace. "Premarital Sexual Behavior." *MFL* 15 (1953): 234–249.

Stone, Abraham. "Planned Parenthood around the World." *MFL* 15 (1953): 98–101.

Stroup, Atlee L., Paul Glasser, Walter R. Stokes, Marie W. Kargman, and Aaron L. Rutledge. "The Orientation and Focus of Marriage Counseling." *MFL* 21 (1959): 20–28.

Tentler, Leslie Woodcock. *Catholics and Contraception: An American History*. Ithaca, NY: Cornell University Press, 2004.

Timm, Annette F. "The Legacy of Bevölkerungspolitik: Venereal Disease Control and Marriage Counseling in Post–WW II Berlin." *Canadian Journal of History* 33 (1998): 173–214.

———. *The Politics of Fertility in Twentieth-Century Berlin*. Cambridge: Cambridge University Press, 2010.

Troy, Donald J. "National Alliance for Family Life." *Journal of Family Counseling* 2 (1974): 3–5.

Van Wagner, Charles A. "The AAPC: The Beginning Years, 1963–1965." *Journal of Pastoral Care* 37 (1983): 163–179.

Wauck, Le Roy A. "The Clergy as Marriage Counselors." *Journal of Religion and Health* 5 (1966): 252–259.

Weaver, Andrew J., et al. "Marriage and Family Therapists and the Clergy: A Need for Clinical Collaboration, Training, and Research." *Journal of Marital and Family Therapy* 23 (1997): 13–25.

Weigand, Kate. *Red Feminism: American Communism and the Making of Women's Liberation*. Baltimore: Johns Hopkins University Press, 2001.

White, Edna Noble. "Experiments in Family Consultation Centers." *Social Forces* 12 (1934): 557–562.

Whyte, Martin King, ed. *Marriage in America: A Communitarian Perspective*. Lanham, MD: Rowman and Littlefield, 2000.

Wicks, Robert J., et al., eds. *Clinical Handbook of Pastoral Counseling*. New York: Paulist Press, 1984.

Williamson, Donald S. *The Intimacy Paradox: Personal Authority in the Family System*. New York: Guilford Press, 1991.

Index